(photo © Clickos / DT)

The 465 bus will take you from crowded Kingston-upon-Thames into the heart of the **Surrey countryside**. A view over the Weald from Box Hill.

Walk from the bus at **Bradwell** to the 7th-century chapel of St-Peter-in-the-Wall by the Blackwater Estuary in a remote corner of Essex.

(photo © Chillingworths / DT)

Classic Marlow: the town is one of several riverside communities that are worth a stop when following our route from High Wycombe to Reading.

(photo © Peter Elvidge / DT)

(photo © June Webber)

Homage to fishermen: sculpture at **Holes Bay** on our journey from Poole to Wimborne Minster in Dorset.

Vintage seaside, though the Grand Pier at **Weston-super-Mare** is a new take on an old theme. After a fire in 2008, the end-of-pier buildings were completely rebuilt.

(photo © Acceleratorhams / DT)

(photo © hidden europe)

Riding the Atlantic Highway on the 319 bus at Fairy Cross, **north Devon**. A community initiative in the village supported the erection of two striking bus shelters.

(photo © hidden europe)

Life on St Mary's in the **Isles of Scilly** is dominated more by boats than buses. But we make time for a ride on the St Mary's community bus.

South and Southwest England

(photo © Martin Kemp / DT)

Open heathland and wild ponies evoke the spirit of an untamed landscape in the **New Forest** National Park. It is on our route from Southampton to Lymington.

The **Isle of Wight** is ideal for exploring by bus. Carisbrooke Castle lies just a short walk from our West Wight journey.

(photo © Chris Moncrieff / DT)

Caernarfon Castle (Castell Caernarfon) is one of a number of castles in Gwynedd that together constitute a UNESCO World Heritage Site.

The **Brecon Beacons** (Bannau Brycheiniog) are home to increasing numbers of red kites. The birds are a common sight nowadays from buses travelling between Brecon and Merthyr.

Wales and the Marches

Cardiff (Caerdydd), **capital of Wales**. The city's showpiece buldings include the Pierhead (left), the Senedd (right), and Canolfan Mileniwm Cymru (background).

Blaenavon (Blaenafon). Isolated terraces of houses on the hills around the Lwyd Valley recall the **mining heritage** of industrial south Wales.

Arriva at the ready, with passengers boarding the 740 bus that runs across the border from **Ludlow** to Knighton. Journey 21 is the only international route in this book!

Aberaeron on the shores of Cardigan Bay is the perfect stopping-off point on the journey south from Aberystwyth to the Pembrokeshire Coast National Park.

(photo © Davidmartyn / DT)

Worcester, end point of our bus journey from Birmingham.

The Radcliffe Camera in Oxford, the destination of our route **across the Cotswolds** from Cheltenham.

(photo © Paul Cowan / DT)

Cotswolds
and the Midlands

Our Cheltenham to Oxford journey skirts the edge of **Burford**, a small Cotswold town in the Windrush Valley that well deserves a visit.

(photo © Tonybrindley / DT)

Birmingham, a city of commerce and industry, is the starting point for our run out to Worcester.

At the heart of England's smallest county: the butter cross in **Oakham**, the county town of Rutland. Our journey from Corby ends in Oakham.

Worth the ride: the Chapter House at **Lichfield Cathedral**. The journey from Stafford ends at Lichfield.

Slow travel Fenland-style. Punts awaiting punters in the **heart of Cambridge**. The university city is showcased in Journey 34, but also features in Journeys 32 and 33.

East Anglia and the Fens

Tribute to an adventurous traveller, Captain George Vancouver, in **King's Lynn** – starting point of our bus ride to the centre of Norfolk.

The sedate community of **Southwold** on the coast of Suffolk is a good place to relax at the end of the bus journey from Great Yarmouth.

Explore the **coasts of Norfolk and Suffolk** by bus and stop off for fresh fish along the way.

FISH FOR SALE

SH COMPANY

Look, no hands! The **guided busway** in Cambridgeshire makes sure that buses avoid commuter traffic.

A hint of **old Fenland ways**: our bus journey from Chatteris to Cambridge explores rural Cambridgeshire.

(photo © Brendan Fox)

(photo © Frederick Sneddon / DT)

(photo © Andrew Emptage / DT)

Peak District solitude at **Mam Tor** above Castleton, end point of the bus route from Sheffield.

Fast-flowing rivers powered the mills that feature in our bus journey from Derby into the **Peak District**. Lumsdale (above) is a great walk from this route.

Pennines
and North of England

Bolton Abbey is the perfect place to stop off when following our Pride of the Dales bus route from Ilkley to Grassington in the **Yorkshire Dales National Park**.

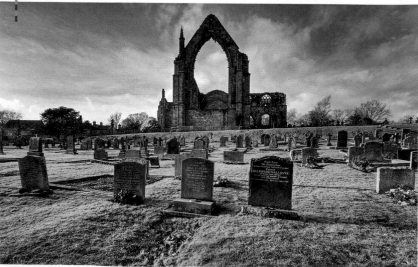

43

A creative river crossing: the **Transporter Bridge** at Middlesbrough. The Teesside town is the starting point for the bus route to Newcastle upon Tyne.

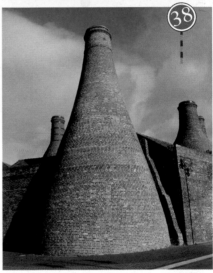

38

This fine bottle oven is part of the **Gladstone Pottery Museum**. You can stop off here when following our urban exploration bus route through the Potteries.

The cultural landscape of **Swaledale**, with its distinctive barns and limestone walls, is revealed on the summer bus service from Lancaster to Richmond.

41

(50)

Surveying the **Isle of Harris** (Na Hearadh in Gaelic). Our bus journey through this Hebridean island takes us to the very end of civilisation.

Crofting traditions are still strong on South Uist (Uibhist a Deas in Gaelic). The penultimate journey in this book takes in several islands in the **Outer Hebrides**.

(49)

Scotland

(44)

It is a stiff climb from the end of Journey 44 up to the Salisbury Crags, but it's worth the effort for the **view of Edinburgh**. The Dugald Stewart Monument is in the foreground.

Arran, so very easy to reach by ferry from the Scottish mainland, boasts a rich mix of **landscapes and history**.

Kilchurn Castle on Loch Awe lies close to our bus journey that spans the Scottish Highlands, linking Dundee with Oban.

The **Paps of Jura** (Sgurr na Cìche in Gaelic) dominate the Jura landscape. Our bus journey to Inverlussa follows the island's only road. The journey ends, like so many of the adventures in this book, with tea and cake.

Bus-Pass Britain Rides Again
The 50 Journeys

Orkney Islands

KEY
— London and the Home Counties
— South and Southwest England
— Wales and the Marches
— Cotswolds and the Midlands
— East Anglia and the Fens
— Pennines and North of England
— Scotland

LONDON

Cockfosters
5
Romfor
3
4
1
Paddington
Stratford
2
Clapham
7
Bromley
Streatham
6
Downe

Outer Hebrides
Thurso
John o'Groats
Stornoway
50
Skye
49
Fraserburgh
Moray Firth
Inverness
Mallaig
Loch Ness
Spey
Don
Aberdeen
Ben Nevis
Dee
GRAMPIAN MTS.
Pitlochry
Montrose
Mull
47
Tay
Dundee
Oban
Perth
46
SCOTLAND
Forth
48
Glasgow
Edinburgh
45
Clyde
Berwick-upon-Tweed
Ayr
Tweed
Campbeltown
Arran
44
CHEVIOT HILLS
The Cheviot
Dumfries
42
Tyne
Newcastle upon Tyne
Stranraer
Carlisle
Durham
43
NORTH SEA
Keswick
Middlesbrough
Isle of Man
41
Richmond
Scarborough
Swale
40
Lancaster
York
Kingston upon Hull
IRISH SEA
Leeds
Manchester
39
Sheffield
Liverpool
37
Skegness
Bangor
Buxton
38
36
Lincoln
Crome
Snowdon
Wrexham
Derby
Trent
King's Lynn
31
Norwich
25
Stafford
29
Peterborough
35
Newtown
Wolverhampton
ENGLAND
32
Ipswich
Aberystwyth
WALES
Birmingham
27
33
Cambridge
26
21
Coventry
34
Cardigan
Wye
28
Northampton
22
Worcester
Leicester
Luton
11
24
23
Gloucester
Oxford
Swansea
30
12
London
10
Broads
17
COTSWOLD HILLS
Swindon
Thames
Canterbury
Cardiff
Bristol
Reading
8
Dorking
Dove
Barnstaple
Taunton
Salisbury
SOUTH
9
19
Southampton
16
DOWNS
Brighton
18
DARTMOOR
Exeter
13
Poole
14
Isle of Wight
Eastbourne
Plymouth
15
Portland Bill
ENGLISH CHANNEL
20
Isles of Scilly
Penzance

Bradt

0   100km
0   60 miles

Foreword

O n a chilly morning in 2008, Janice Booth (who is a contributor to this volume) and I waited at the bus stop at Land's End clutching our bus passes. It was 1 April (no kidding!), the day that marked the launch of the concessionary bus-pass scheme for England. Other parts of the UK had long enjoyed such schemes. We had virgin bus passes in our hands.

'First ones I've seen!' said the bus driver cheerily as we climbed aboard. Janice and I took a week to travel from Land's End to Lowestoft Ness, respectively the westernmost and easternmost points of the English mainland. That journey, made by local buses, forged our love of bus travel and led to this book's predecessor, *Bus-Pass Britain*, published by Bradt Travel Guides in 2011.

The popularity of that volume showed that we are not alone in our enthusiasm. Bus passes have given mobility to an older generation, but of course the majority of users of British buses are well below pension age. *Bus-Pass Britain* tapped a vein of enthusiasm for bus travel among travellers of *all* ages. In this second book, we present 50 new journeys – written by ordinary members of the travelling public who have an extraordinary affection for their local bus routes.

We have changed the regional mix a little. Last time we had one route in Greater London; this time we have seven. Last time, all 50 routes were on the British mainland; this time we have half a dozen island adventures. We've included more routes in Wales and Scotland. Climb aboard and join us as we celebrate another 50 of the nation's favourite journeys. Just be warned – bus travel can become seriously addictive!

Hilary Bradt

Bus-Pass Britain Rides Again: More of the Nation's Favourite Bus Journeys
First published September 2013
Bradt Travel Guides Ltd
IDC House, The Vale, Chalfont St Peter, Bucks SL9 9RZ, England
www.bradtguides.com

Bus-Pass Britain project managers: Nicky Gardner and Susanne Kries
Book editors: Nicky Gardner and Susanne Kries
Book design: Shane O'Dwyer
Cover illustration: Neil Gower (www.neilgower.com)
Colour map: David McCutcheon FBCart.S (www.dvdmaps.co.uk)
Route sketch maps: hidden europe
Typesetting and layout: hidden europe (www.hiddeneurope.co.uk)
Print management: Jellyfish Print Solutions
Digital conversion: Firsty Group

ISBN-13: 978 1 84162 465 5 (print)
e-ISBN: 978 1 84162 799 1 (e-pub)
e-ISBN: 978 1 84162 673 4 (mobi)

British Library Cataloguing in Publication Data
A catalogue record for this book is available from the British Library

Some **photographs** have been sourced from photo agencies. Where this is
the case, the following abbreviations have been added next to the name of
the photographer: DT (Dreamstime.com), IS (iStockphoto.com).

Printed and bound in India by Replika Press Pvt. Ltd.

Welcome Aboard

The numbers in parentheses below refer to the numbers of specific journeys in this book.

We have always loved local buses. The bus that trundles from village to village is an **antidote to globalisation**, a chance to mark the importance of community in a frenetic world. We may be inclined to complain about the quality and frequency of our bus services, but these islands are blessed with one of the finest local bus networks anywhere in Europe.

At the heart of *Bus-Pass Britain Rides Again* are 50 journeys that cover the **length and breadth of Britain** (including six routes on offshore islands). The routes reveal the variety of Britain's landscapes: from the Isles of Scilly (20) to Tayside (47), from the Fens (32) to the Firth of Clyde (45, 56). We map urban Britain too, taking local buses through our cities and their edgelands – the unsung spaces where town and country blur.

A community of writers

The really special thing about this book is the way it came to be. It resulted from a **community-writing initiative** in which members of the public were invited to write about their favourite bus routes. The writers whose work features in this book responded to our invites on Twitter and in other media. The *Daily Express* gave the project some handsome coverage. So too did *Bus User* magazine. A particularly rich crop of potential contributors came through publicity in *hidden europe* magazine. Others heard of the venture from regional groups for writers around Britain.

The book is thus a celebration of journeys that have meaning for the people who describe them. And many routes reveal something of the mind and soul of the writer. Read on and you'll discover **50 different voices**, 50 compelling reasons why we should cherish our local bus services as valuable community assets.

FREEDOM TO ROAM

The concessionary bus passes introduced in England in 2008 (and earlier in Wales and Scotland) have energised an older generation, encouraging them to explore their home region and further afield. Yet you don't need to wait for retirement age to start exploring Britain by bus. In most parts of the country, good **regional passes** allow travellers of *any* age to benefit from the freedom to roam at will. We mention many such passes in this book.

Travellers once wedded to their cars are discovering that a ride on the village bus can be a very **congenial experience**. Indeed one sceptical participant in the project experienced a Damascene conversion when he eventually joined the crowd at his local bus shelter (see pages 270–2). The book is thus full of **intriguing characters**. We track down a bus driver who also has a regular radio show – very appropriately called *Request Stop* (20). And we recall Kate Barton who, one hundred years ago, became the first woman in Britain to become a bus driver (see page 144).

Taking a break from the bus journeys, we check out Britain's best bus stops – from Art Deco bus shelters in Brighton to a fabulously well-appointed bus shelter at Baltasound on the island of Unst in the Shetlands (read more on page 248).

We also explore Britain's most frequent bus routes. At peak times, over 100 buses an hour stream along the Wilmslow Road Bus Corridor into the centre of Manchester. And we discover Britain's least frequent bus route – one which operated on just three days in 2013 (discover the answer on page 85).

THE 50 JOURNEYS

This volume contains a **wonderful variety** of bus journeys. Some of the shortest (9, 17, 20 and 34) are done and dusted within half an hour. At the other extreme, we have routes that extend to over three hours, including journeys through the Scottish Highlands (47), Snowdonia (25) and the Yorkshire Dales National Park (41).

The variety captured in our 50 journeys is extraordinary. Britain's **rural landscapes** slip by beyond the bus window. There are journeys through serenely beautiful countryside (18, 21 and 40 are all good examples) and we have routes that lead into forlorn and empty wilderness. For a taste of the latter, we particularly recommend the three Hebridean itineraries that conclude the book (48, 49 and 50).

Yet packed into these 50 essays you'll find more than merely a feast of fine landscapes. Join us on forays through urban Britain, most conspicuously in the section on London, but also through **unsung cityscapes** from the Potteries (38) to Teesside (43).

Some of our writers capture with great delicacy that distinctive **end-of-the-road feeling**. It is no surprise perhaps to encounter that at a remote headland in north Devon (19), in an old mining village in the Cumbrian hills (42) or on a Scottish island (48 and 50). But we were greatly impressed to also encounter that sense of isolation within 45 miles of London on a journey that concludes by an Essex estuary (11).

So much for the world beyond the bus window. For some of our contributors, the bus journey is more than an invitation to adventure. It is a **gateway to the soul**. Journeys invite reflection and meditation. A route that is at one level a prosaic trundle along the shores of the Bristol Channel (17) turns out to be a meditation on childhood. Another run, this one through the English Midlands (28), reflects on the new, the old, the lost and the foretold. One writer ponders on the strangeness of returning to old haunts (14), while another reflects with passion and energy on chances taken (and chances missed) on the top deck (7).

The landscapes through which we travel are indeed varied. But so too are the soulscapes and mindscapes captured in *Bus-Pass Britain Rides Again*. So **climb aboard** and take a seat on the top deck as we set off to explore Britain by bus.

Nicky Gardner and Susanne Kries
Editors, *Bus-Pass Britain Rides Again*

HOW TO USE THIS BOOK

This book is as easy to use as hopping on your local bus. We have divided Great Britain into **eight regions**. Well do we know that the coverage is not absolutely even, but we are keen to showcase the variety of bus journeys across Britain – and equally anxious to show the many ways in which even the most prosaic journey can inspire a good writer. Some texts are ones that you can easily follow yourself, and they were written with that intention in mind. Others attempt something more ambitious: they reveal how journeys are the midwives of thought. A bus journey can be a portal to the soul, an invitation to reflection. Those essays are perhaps best read in the comfort of an armchair on a winter evening.

You will find an **index map** showing the location of each of our 50 routes on the last of the colour pages at the start of this book. All but the shortest routes (and that includes most of the London journeys) are accompanied by a **simple sketch map** – nothing fancy, but just enough detail for you to identify the main *en route* points mentioned in the text. We give a typical travel time in minutes between each point on that map. Bear in mind that on some routes these average travel times can vary considerably from one trip to another. In urban areas, timetables often allow for longer journey times at peak hours. In rural areas, occasional buses may make deviations off the main route to serve villages that might otherwise have no bus service at all.

In the **introductory notes** at the start of each route, we give an indication of service frequency, an important consideration if you are planning to stop off along the length of a journey. Some of our routes run several times each hour, others as little as only once each week. Careful planning always pays off. We also always cite the **Ordnance Survey** 1:50,000 Landranger maps relevant to each essay in the order in which they occur if you follow the route as we describe it. And we mention the likely travel time if you follow the entire journey.

Our **bus stop mini-features** are just like bus stops: places to linger and ponder while you wait to embark on your next journey. We hope they'll make you think or smile – or both! In the **postscripts section** at the end of the book, you'll find some good tips on journey planning.

Finally, we should add a note of caution. Bus timetables are famously volatile. They often vary from season to season. Bus numbers and routings also change. Cuts in public subsidies mean that frequencies on some routes are being trimmed for 2014, and some services cut altogether. Not, as far as we know, any of those featured in this book. But it always pays to check the current situation before setting out.

50 BUS JOURNEYS

London Paddington to Bow Church Clapham Junction to Shoreditch Highbury Corner to Leamouth Romford to Stratford Trafalgar Square to Cockfosters Bromley to Downe Streatham to Paddington Kingston-upon-Thames to Dorking Horsham to Burgess Hill Canterbury to Broadstairs Burnham-on-Crouch to Bradwell Waterside High Wycombe to Reading Southampton to Lymington Newport to Totland (Isle of Wight) Poole to Wimborne Minster Wimborne Minster to Shaftesbury Weston-super-Mare to Sand Bay Okehampton to Newton Abbot Barnstaple to Hartland St Mary's circular route (Isles of Scilly) Ludlow to Knighton Newtown to Cardiff Brynmawr to Newport Swansea to Pennard Cliffs Bangor to Aberystwyth Aberystwyth to Cardigan Corby to Oakham Birmingham to Worcester Stafford to Lichfield Cheltenham to Oxford King's Lynn to East Dereham Chatteris to Cambridge Cambridge to Peterborough Cambridge city service Great Yarmouth to Southwold Derby to Bakewell Sheffield to Castleton Newcastle-under-Lyme to Hanley Warrington to Altrincham Ilkley to Grassington Lancaster to Richmond Carlisle to Nenthead Middlesbrough to Newcastle upon Tyne Dumfries to Edinburgh Brodick to Blackwaterfood (Isle of Arran) Dunoon to Carrick Castle Dundee to Oban Feolin to Inverlussa (Isle of Jura) Berneray to Eriskay Tarbert to Hushinish (Isle of Harris)

LONDON

London's buses are the city's most conspicuous ambassadors. They embody the **spirit of London**. For many visitors to England, the capital's red buses are as intimately associated with London as Big Ben and beefeaters. Time-worn London buses have proved to be a valuable export commodity. London's classic **red double-deckers** have made their way around the world. There is even a well-aged London Routemaster on the loose in the southernmost city of the planet: Ushuaia in Tierra del Fuego, at the southernmost tip of South America.

Most Londoners might be surprised to learn that the omnibus trade in their city owes its origins as much to French as to English ingenuity. The mathematician Blaise Pascal had the idea of introducing shared *carrosses* running on set routes in Paris in the mid-17th century. It wasn't a success. Even the largest cities were very walkable in those days.

1829: LONDON'S FIRST BUS ROUTE

After the Industrial Revolution, cities expanded in an urbanising Europe. Horse-drawn buses plying fixed routes returned to Paris in 1819. **George Shillibeer**, a Londoner by birth, worked in the coach trade in Paris in the 1820s. Shillibeer saw how successful the omnibus was in Paris and copied the idea for London.

Along with the buses (of his own design) which Shillibeer imported from France, he brought the drivers and conductors too. London's first buses were thus staffed mainly by Frenchmen, giving Londoners the chance to brush up their conversational French while trundling from Paddington to the City.

Nowadays, the London omnibus is a place to catch snippets of many languages. Polish and Punjabi mingle on the top deck.

And that's still the place for a grandstand view of the capital. In the early 1890s, the then Prime Minister **William Gladstone** advised visitors from overseas that 'the way to see London is from the top of a bus – from the top of a bus, gentlemen.'

In Gladstone's day, the top deck was a cold and windy place. Horse-drawn double-deck buses had an enclosed lower level, but the seating upstairs was open to the elements. Times have changed, and modern buses are full of creature comforts. There are no longer French-speaking conductors – indeed no conductors at all. But cost-cutting hasn't dimmed the view from the top deck. And we kick off our exploration of Britain's best bus journeys with **seven capital excursions** through London and its suburbs.

In *Bus-Pass Britain*, we included just one London route. That was the number 15, a fabulous ride for sightseeing that takes in Trafalgar Square and St Paul's on its journey from Regent Street to the East End. But London is a city of many shades and here we present seven very **different perspectives** on the city. Our selection includes journeys that cover prime sights, but we also want to reflect the variety of cityscapes that host the life of the capital. Join us on the top deck as we set off to explore London by day and by night. ■

Schematic map of the London bus routes included in this book. The numbers on the map refer to the seven journeys described in the following pages.

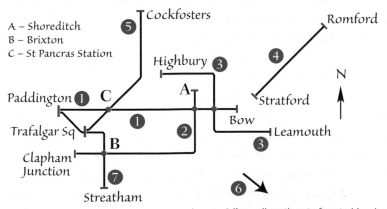

A – Shoreditch
B – Brixton
C – St Pancras Station

Cockfosters
Romford
Highbury
Paddington
Trafalgar Sq
Clapham Junction
Streatham
Stratford
Bow
Leamouth
N

Journey 6 lies well southeast of central London

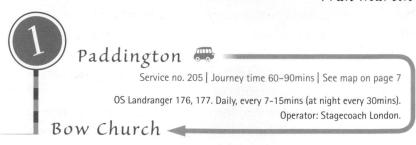

A DIVINE CAPITAL TASTER

Fran Martin

1

Paddington 🚌

Service no. 205 | Journey time 60–90mins | See map on page 7

OS Landranger 176, 177. Daily, every 7-15mins (at night every 30mins).
Operator: Stagecoach London.

Bow Church ◄

Let us start at the beginning. When **George Shillibeer** created London's first-ever omnibus service, he chose a route that ran east from Paddington towards the City. And the first part of London's 205 bus route, on its journey from Paddington to Bow, follows much the same itinerary.

The 205 is thus the lineal descendant of Shillibeer's pioneer service, which took to London's streets on 4 July 1829. Almost 200 years later, this is still **one of the capital's premier routes**. It serves a string of London's main-line railway stations which didn't exist in Shillibeer's day, and then concludes its journey at an East End church which has for over seven centuries echoed to the sound of the psalms.

There is a **touch of the Divine** about the 205. Few other London bus routes offer such an ecumenical mix of faiths and religions. Join me on the top deck for a seven-mile ride that catches the spirit of a city that makes space for mosques and synagogues alongside churches representing a dozen shades of Christianity.

The route kicks off in humble manner. That somehow suits a journey that is a veritable pilgrimage to various temples of prayer. Our journey starts at a bus stop that is tucked away behind Paddington Station.

Hardly are we on our way when we reach **Chapel Street**, which is oddly devoid of chapels. But, just off to our right, comes the first of many surprises presented by the 205. Here is a church dedicated to an early 18th-century Swedish queen. The Ulrika Eleanora Church in Harcourt Street still caters to the Swedish Lutheran diaspora.

Then it's all stops east through more secular terrain, though **Madame Tussauds** makes space for Pope John-Paul II and a clutch of other religious leaders. It is surely the only place where you'll find archbishops rubbing shoulders with the goddesses of the silver screen.

Just past Tussauds, the conspicuous church on the right is dedicated to **St Marylebone**. It has given its name to this part of London. Anglicans who worship at the church this year mark the bicentennial of the laying of the foundation stone. Today St Marylebone's makes its mark on more than just the spirit. It also offers a healing and counselling service.

Of vices and virtues

Now we are in **Euston Road** and, as we shuffle east in crowded traffic, the landscape of faith is becoming more textured. The path of true dissent is represented by Friends House to our right, the headquarters of the Quakers in Britain. Its excellent café is a good spot for a break (open 08.00–20.00 Mon–Fri, 08.30–15.30 Sat).

Euston Road drops very gently downhill towards London's most ornate railway station at St Pancras. Just before this amazing

FADING FAITH

Not all London churches have been as successful as St Marylebone's. Just east of Nash's lovely Park Crescent, our bus passes **Holy Trinity Church**. From a distance, its Grecian lines and lantern tower look very fine, but close-up the appeal fades. The building is long abandoned and in a troubled state of disrepair.

Gothic extravaganza there is a temple of another kind on the left. Yes, those who regularly use the British Library speak with almost religious devotion of this testament to the written word.

I like the strong colours of the library building, but **St Pancras station** just adjacent nudges the library into the architectural shadows. St Pancras is a temple devoted to trains. And it even comes with a lesson or two on faith, hope and charity. Climb up the grand staircase of the St Pancras Renaissance Hotel, part of the main station building, and you'll find the ceilings decorated with E W Godwin's tributes to various shades of virtue. Here we have a sermon, but one that is by no means crusty and conservative. It is light in touch, full of Oriental accents and whimsy.

Oriental accents of another kind feature in the next church on our ride. **King's Cross Methodist Church** is non-conformism with a twist. Sunday services are held in Cantonese and Mandarin, catering to the Chinese Methodist community.

The Methodist theme stays with us as we head east through twilight zones, the edgelands of the City that are punching their way back into fashion. We cut through Pentonville and soon we are slipping south down City Road, passing John Wesley's House and the **Museum of Methodism** (open 10.00–16.00 Mon–Sat, 12.00–13.45 Sun).

A PLURALITY OF FAITHS

Having been born and brought up as a Catholic, I have a soft spot for the next church on our pilgrimage. Most on the bus will miss **St Mary Moorfields** with its inconspicuous entrance on Eldon Street, but it is truly one of London's hidden gems. It is a very special haven of quiet and peace in the middle of London's bustling financial district.

The street names on this part of the 205 route recall lost meadows. Here is Wormwood Street and there is Camomile Street. 'Yes, hop off here for **Bevis Marks**,' says a man on the top deck. So I take his advice. No-one should miss this opportunity.

THREADS OF BELIEF

Route 205 serves **Finsbury Square,** a patch of green in the heart of London that might really claim to be the touchstone for English Methodism. **John and Charles Wesley** both preached here. This is a part of London that has always been receptive to new religious ideas. Finsbury Square has at various times been home to a rabbinical seminary and a Greek Orthodox church.

For here is one of England's most beautiful synagogues. Just like that Catholic church we saw earlier, the synagogue is tucked away and not easy to spot.

Back on the 205, the double-decker nudges its way along **Whitechapel High Street.** Bangladeshi has eclipsed Yiddish, synagogues have made way for mosques. We cruise past the dramatic East London Mosque into Stepney. You'll have to look hard in Stepney nowadays to find any trace of the Huguenots who settled here in the 17th century. Subsequent waves of migrants have covered the traces of those French Protestants. And many of those migrants have reached out to touch the hearts and souls of all Londoners. So it's not just Buddhists who make their way to the **London Buddhist Centre,** which is in Roman Road just a short walk north of Stepney Green.

Our journey ends at **Bow Church.** The parish church at Bow was built to serve Catholics in what was then a rural hamlet. Shifting its pieties post-Reformation to Anglicanism, the church now serves as a focal point of one of London's most multi-cultural communities.

This bus route, which ends in the shadow of the **Olympic Park,** captures post-Olympic England – a country which has an extraordinary variety of faiths and cultures. ∎

ABOUT THE AUTHOR | **FRAN MARTIN** lives and works in London. Her first love is walking, but she makes time too for anything to do with visual arts.

SHADES OF THE SUBURBS
LONDON'S SOCIAL MIX

Francesca Rushton &
Gregory Gardner

2 Clapham Junction

Service no. 35 | Journey time 50–80mins | See map on page 7

OS Landranger 176. Daily, every 10mins (at night every 20–30mins).
Operator: Abellio London.

Shoreditch

There are quicker routes from Clapham Junction to Shoreditch, and the 35 wins no prizes as a route for classic sightseeing in the capital. Yet this journey is a favourite of ours because it affords awesome insights into the lives of **real Londoners** as the residents of contrasting boroughs hop on and off. Aboard the 35 – which runs 24 hours a day, seven days a week – you'll see Clapham's yuppies, the bustle of Brixton and Camberwell, the suits of the City and the hipsters of Shoreditch.

The bus stops behind **Clapham Junction Station** are on the proverbial wrong side of the tracks. Inauspicious though the spot may be, it is the place to catch the spirit of the 35. A fractured view of tower blocks to the northwest, the rumble of trains from the bridge overhead, and scents of fast-food chicken from across the road are the sights, sounds and smells at the starting point of our journey on the 35. Grab yourself a seat near the front of the top deck and watch the social landscape change.

You'll soon be marvelling at the grand town houses and up-market eateries as you head east towards **Clapham Common**. Look right on a summer's weekend and the Common, the biggest park *en route*, will be buzzing with picnickers, footballers and dog walkers among others. The picnics might not be suited to winter but a small café close to the bandstand can warm you up with cups of tea and a decent bacon sandwich. Regardless of season, the bars, Irish pubs and chain restaurants around the Common's tube station are often full of young professionals enjoying their weekends.

Clapham's residents are typecast as rich, sporty and/or Australian, while the Clash's *The Guns of Brixton* typifies the associations of the 35's next significant stopping point. The stereotypes may be overblown – particularly given Brixton's recent gentrification – but make your own inferences as the 35 heads into **Brixton** along Acre Lane, the scene of social unrest and riots in 1981 and again in 2011. The bookies, kebab stores and nail parlours have replaced the glass smashed by looters in August 2011. This really is another world from Clapham.

CHANGING DECKS

Beyond Brixton, the 35 is best sampled from the hustle and bustle of the lower deck. Prepare to be barged by buggies, squeezed by shopping bags, and silenced by sirens – not a relaxing ride perhaps but the reality of **South London**.

Brixton street market (photo © Peeter Viisimaa / IS)

An Afro-Caribbean mood prevails along Coldharbour Lane towards **Camberwell** with numerous jerk chicken outlets and an improbable number of Afro hair and nail salons that, despite the plentiful competition, all seem to do a roaring trade. The notable exception is Sunday when the congregations of the area's many churches don their finest and you're more likely to hear a gospel choir than gossip from the salons.

Turning north at Camberwell, the bus jostles with cyclists, shoppers and other double-deckers along **Walworth Road**. The stop-start pace may frustrate the hurried traveller, but it gives time to survey the passing balconies, which are a window into the world of those who live in the apartment blocks. Some balconies are used as miniature gardens with potted plants and deckchairs, others double as bike racks or even laundry rooms. Coloured sheets flapping in the wind give a tapestry of colour to the estates.

CHANGING MOODS

Closer to **Elephant and Castle** new private apartments targeting students and young professionals start to appear, juxtaposed by the Heygate Estate which stands opposite. Sparkling new 40 years ago, the Heygate is now derelict, boarded up, foreboding and forgotten.

The stretch from Elephant and Castle to London Bridge takes only five minutes but a glimpse of the Shard – London's tallest building – hints at a shift in the economic and social mood. Gritty South London morphs into **the City**. Gone are the grey residential tower blocks, replaced by greyer, taller office blocks. Gone are the fried-chicken joints, replaced by corporate Britain and Starbucks.

Rufus, a regular driver on the 35, candidly remarks in his Caribbean twang that 'driving is hell' around here on weekdays – the lack of respect shown to him by passengers supposedly only matched by the disregard of cyclists for their own safety.

Beyond Monument, the bus tracks north along **Bishopsgate**, affording neck-straining views of Heron Tower and the Gherkin. These tall glass-fronted buildings stand alongside historic stone buildings. The Bank of England is just down Threadneedle Street, on the corner of which you'll see the engravings on the façade of **Gibson Hall**. They represent the industries and crafts for which finance is supplied. Take a look and see if you can spot the various trades, and statuary representing the arts, commerce, science, manufacturing, agriculture, navigation and shipbuilding.

Tourists slowly disembark at **Liverpool Street Station**, holding up the businessmen rushing to meetings at RBS's sparkling headquarters. The bohemian Spitalfields Market is a stone's throw to the east but Bishopsgate feels decidedly unbohemian with its endless glass-fronted offices.

Then the 35 crosses an invisible boundary line, this time into **Shoreditch**. Suddenly a pinstripe suit would look decidedly conspicuous as skinny jeans and vintage shirts dominate hipster cafés, where East London's traditional jellied eels have been usurped by organic fruit smoothies and soya lattes these days. Lively **Brick Lane** is a short walk from the last stop of the 35. It offers the best choice of curry houses in London. Barter well and you'll surely save yourself a couple of quid for the return trip to Clapham. ■

ABOUT THE AUTHORS | **FRANKIE RUSHTON** and **GREG GARDNER** are both development professionals who recently left their Brixton base to live and work in South Africa.

THE BUS THAT NEVER SLEEPS

Peter Sellars

Highbury Corner

Service no. 277 | Journey time 50–60mins | See map on page 9

OS Landranger 177. Daily, every 7–10mins (at night every 30mins).
Operator: Stagecoach London.

Leamouth

The 277 is a route for navigators, a journey for those who like tangents and meridians. The main roads to the northeast of London all track directly into the City. But the 277 defies that prevailing trend, **tracing an orbit** *around* the edge of London's business heart, to end bang on the Greenwich Meridian. Along the way, it maps the outskirts of Victorian London, tracking through territory that is now fashionably multi-cultural.

Cast back to the mid-fifties and the 677 trolleybus from Smithfield to West India Dock was a mainstay for dock workers and meat porters. It disappeared in 1959, one of a wave of trolleybus routes to be replaced in that year by noisy diesel buses. Thus the 277 bus route was born, although over the years its precise itinerary has varied, just like the trade routes of the sailing clippers of old, to reflect changing economic patterns. The dominant new magnet along the route is Canary Wharf, the thrusting office complex which has brought new life to riverside areas blighted by the closure of the docks.

Join me at **Highbury** for the journey to Docklands, a voyage through suburban doldrums that culminates on a little peninsula just at the point where the River Lea decants into the Thames. Along the way we pass cleaned-up canals, some fetching urban parks and myriad music and arts venues, cafés, pubs and street markets. This modest bus route has scope for an entire day out.

Before boarding the bus, make the most of **Highbury Corner**. Close by, but hidden, are the surprisingly extensive Highbury Fields, enclosed by elegant Georgian terraces and Italianate villas. Look for the plaque commemorating deaths from the flying bomb which destroyed the local station in 1944.

As we set off, we hear for the first time the staccato rhythm of the prescript that rules this route: '2 – 7 – 7 – To – Leamouth.' In the impersonal city, at least the buses still talk to you.

You'll find a mixed crew on the 277. On the lower deck, urban whippersnappers are still inclined to offer up their seats to any fellow passenger with a hint of grey. It is the upper deck, of course, that is the best place to keep watch. At each port of call a new crowd climbs aboard, but the mood of the passengers varies along the route. Sometimes it is Docklands commuters attached to their smartphones; elsewhere it is locals with all-terrain buggies and Hessian bags, or pensioners exercising their bus passes.

ALL STOPS EAST

We sail east at first, cruising past 19th-century terraces and 20th-century estates. The **New River Path** is on our right, an early candidate for a stroll south along the secluded bank of the aqueduct. It's a good way to see the Georgian houses of Canonbury. Then, suddenly, our bus hits the bustle of **Dalston**: Turkish, African and Caribbean restaurants, Irish pubs, Polish delis, arty coffee bars and sharp clothes shops. Hop off here for Ridley Road street market, with its colourful displays of meat, fish, fruit and veg – with a reggae soundtrack. In nearby Ashwin Street is the nicely idiosyncratic music venue Cafe OTO while just up the Kingsland Road are the venerable Vortex Jazz Club and the **Rio Cinema**, one of London's oldest, sensitively refurbished. This part of London has mightily changed since the days when Samuel Pepys remarked on its open fields and pretty character.

From the top deck, I spot **Eastern Curve Garden** where a cyclist's death is commemorated by a white 'ghost bike', just beneath the magnificent Peace Carnival mural. The route tracks the Victorian expansion of London into **Hackney**, once a royal village favoured by the Tudors, but subsequently sacrificed to the arrival of tram, train and industry. This is a part of London full of community energy. It boasts the revitalised Hackney Empire Theatre, the splendid Picturehouse, the fascinating Hackney Museum and the newly reopened Cock Tavern (☎ 020 8533 6369; open from 12.00 every day), home to a new microbrewery. Its bar boasts 16 handpumps all just begging to be pulled.

As we ride south down Mare Street, **London Fields** is hidden to our right. Once valued pasture for drovers' cattle on their way to Smithfield, it is now a pleasing park, with plane trees, a good pub, and a heated open-air lido (☎ 020 7254 9038; open all year). Stroll through the park to reach Broadway Market and the Regent's Canal.

The 277 sails on past Well Street Common, between a row of alms houses and the church of St John of Jerusalem with its distinctive copper spire. We cross the **Hertford Union Canal** near its junction with the Regent's Canal. You can get off here for a 45-minute towpath stroll to the Queen Elizabeth Olympic Park and its stadium. On the right is Wennington Green, with a free open-air gym, and another towpath leading to the Thames or Little Venice. After Roman Road (the street market is half a mile east) we continue south alongside Mile End Park.

ISLE OF DOGS

We cross to the Isle of Dogs, glimpsing the Thames as we negotiate the security gates at Westferry Circus. Alight here to take a speedy boat into the City. Buses may still be a staple for transport in London, but it's good to see how the city has rediscovered its river.

Canary Wharf is an astonishing redevelopment of West India Docks, providing ever more towering space for apparently

BILLINGSGATE MARKET

Billingsgate was originally a general market, but in 1699 an Act of Parliament gave it special status as 'a free and open market for all sorts of fish whatsoever.' It relocated from the City to **Docklands** in 1982. Come early to fish for bargains and then move on to **Canary Wharf** to breakfast with bankers. You can browse the fish stalls from 05.00 to 08.30 (the earlier the better) and mingle with the mongers and restaurateurs picking up their bulk supplies. Expect to emerge smelling fishy (Trafalgar Way; ☎ 020 7987 1118).

essential financial services. The one-time hub for worldwide trade of physical goods has become an electronic hub for trade of virtual money. Shopping malls lurk beneath the streets, but be sure also to pay a visit to **Billingsgate Market**.

The 277 turns round right on the **Greenwich Meridian** at Leamouth. Nearby, the Lea ends in a pair of tight meanders, creating isolated peninsulas within serpentine bends. Enjoy the view of Bow Creek Ecology Park across the murky river where grey herons stand alert in the deep mud. Before leaving, cross Lower Lea Crossing to the bird reserve at East India Dock Basin. Take to the hides to spot cormorants, teal taking turns on the rafts, shelduck, and the occasional kingfisher.

In many respects, **Leamouth** is an isolated and forgotten corner of Dockland. Yet it is also at the centre of things. High above is the cable car crossing the Thames to the Millennium Dome. Landmarks abound, Canada Tower nearby, the Crystal Palace TV mast in the distance. And just a short walk away is Trinity Buoy Wharf, at the confluence of Lea and Thames. Here is London's only lighthouse, a lightship, and a thriving community of artists (☎ 020 7515 7153; www.trinitybuoywharf.com). ∎

ABOUT THE AUTHOR | **PETER SELLARS** has lived on the 277 bus route for 30 years. Once part of his daily commute, the 277 and other local buses are now platforms for Peter's London explorations.

Encountering the Unseen
East London

Cila Warncke

 Romford

Service no. 86 | Journey time 40–72mins | See map on page 7

OS Landranger 177. Daily, every 6–10mins (every 30mins at night).
Operator: Stagecoach London.

Stratford ◄

In London, 'bus pass' is an epithet. It sets a tone. It's laden. Professionals, particularly young ones, and the bus-pass brigade don't often mix. I wanted speed and anonymity for my **regular journey** to work in central London. So I opted for the train from Romford. The bus is disconcerting. It pulls you into the suburban geography. The train, linear and often tucked away in cuttings and behind industrial estates, is estranged from geography.

One summer afternoon, however, a problem with the train in Stratford sent me to the bus station. It was a hot day and the 20-minute train journey stretched to over an hour as bus number 86 trundled through the rush hour, pulling in a fresh wave of sweating bodies at each bus stop.

The names I knew only from railway station platforms began to come to life. I noticed the **Forest Gate Mosque**, tucked away in a pair of converted terrace houses; Manor Park's red-brick turn-of-the-century library; Ilford's hollow concrete heart, which felt dark even in the sunshine; the Gothic gloom of the Cauliflower 'original gin palace' in Seven Kings; the take-aways, grocers, pawnbrokers, auto dealers, junk shops and nail salons that line the pavements of **Goodmayes** and Chadwell Heath. The occasional McDonalds or Tesco looked positively aspirational.

Later I discovered that the 86 passes the homes of perhaps half a million people as its cuts through a part of London that has remarkable ethnic variety. So recently I rode the route again, boarding the 86 at **Romford Station** for the ride into London – in the hope of learning more about this less familiar face of the capital's suburbs.

HIDDEN HISTORY

The 86 bus route is one where history is closeted behind mundane façades. Across St Edwards Way from Havering Town Hall, which is a flat-topped modernist building of grey Leicester brick, lies **Romford Market** which has been running since King Henry III granted its licence in 1247. This erstwhile sheep-trading fair is now home to 150 stalls selling everything from vegetables to jewellery and lingerie. From the heart of Romford, the 86 sets a straight course along the A118 (here called London Road) past Cottons Park.

In Chadwell Heath, the former police station is now a Weatherspoon pub named the Eva Hart in honour of a local woman who survived the *Titanic*. Minutes up the road in Goodmayes, the bus stops at St Cedd's Roman Catholic Church, which promises

WORKFARE 1920s STYLE

Cottons Park recalls the estate of Nicholas Cotton, a prominent local merchant during the reign of Elizabeth I. In 1920, the council bought the land for £4,500. England was in dire financial straits at the time and unemployment was high. A 1921 **Cabinet memo** urged that 'work of some description should be provided if for no other reason than that the "work-shy" could be distinguished from the genuine unemployed.' So local men were pressed into converting the **old Cotton estate** into a park. Unpaid labour helped to clear the land, erect fences, plant lime trees, build tennis courts and a bandstand. The space was officially opened as Cottons Park in 1927.

to give special attention to 'the alienated and estranged.' Mass and other services are in English, Polish or Latin. The 86 also stops outside the **Karamsar Temple**. Its pale-pink sandstone skin belies its past life as a Labour Party Hall before the local Sikh community converted it in the 1990s. One place of worship that hasn't changed is the Anglican St Mary's Church in Ilford.

WHO WE ARE AND WHERE WE LIVE

Religious buildings supply rare flashes of style in an **architectural landscape** dominated by shoddy low-rise commercial units. At first, the names of passing shops are delightfully eclectic: Aryana Halal Butchers is cheek by jowl with the Cockney Grub House which advertises 'Pie 'n' mash – all grub homemade.' But gradually the streets blur into sameness. **Seven Kings** is hardly different from Manor Park, though the former has more greengrocers and the latter more mobile phone shops.

Occasionally terrace houses interrupt the shop fronts, but they do little to lift the landscape. Paint peels from the trim and many of the **tiny concrete gardens** no longer have any hint of green. Now there is rubbish where once there were flowers. Blankets cover the front downstairs windows so even on the brightest summer day these homes are surely dark spaces. This is a very different London from that portrayed in the chic investment brochures. Living here is perhaps more a matter of necessity than choice. The view from the top deck suggests a community that has been worn down by circumstance.

There are rare new developments like **Pioneer Point** in Ilford. Its developers were keen to attract aspiring young professionals. If the developers succeeded, it seems that the high-income residents of Pioneer Point are not flocking to use their local bus services. The 86 carries school kids, mums, old-age pensioners and an assortment of shop assistants, cleaners, carers, labourers and job seekers – citizens economically and geographically estranged from London's prosperous centre. This is the realm of mothers herding

A CARNEGIE LEGACY

Scottish-born steel baron **Andrew Carnegie**, a passionate believer in self-education, funded over 2,000 libraries around the world. **Manor Park Library** was built in 1904 thanks to a £5,000 donation from Carnegie. Made of warm-red brick, it has high windows set in sweeping arcs, and a balcony that juts protectively over the **Art Nouveau** stained-glass window above the entrance. Bands of ruddy stone on its flanks bear the names of famous authors: Shakespeare, Tennyson, Dickens, Carlyle.

restless children. Teenagers squeal into their smartphones, while men sit with open knees, hands limp between their thighs, their eyes unfocused.

The 86 bears steadily southwest until Stratford where it takes a sharp northeast turn as it approaches its terminal in the shadow of the Westfield Shopping Centre and the London 2012 **Olympic Park**. That's a sore point among those who ride the 86. Many residents couldn't afford tickets to the Summer Olympics but now feel their taxes are filling a hole in the public purse. Shopping at Westfield is all that's left of the Greatest Show on Earth. The Olympic Village and sporting venues beyond are closed just now.

Standing at **Stratford** bus station, I have mixed emotions. It is churlish to resent progress. But it is also hard to feel kindly towards a culture that lavishes money on shopping malls and stadia while the houses around them crumble. Stratford's gleaming commercial facelift is one vision of what London should be, but the tired suburbs that surround tell a different story. Meaningful regeneration must unite these worlds and unity requires understanding. If you're looking for that, a ride on the 86 is a good place to start. ∎

ABOUT THE AUTHOR | American-born writer and journalist **CILA WARNCKE** has lived in various parts of east London for eight years. You can read more of her work at www.cilawarncke.com.

RED BUS AT NIGHT
CLUBBER'S DELIGHT

Rebecca Reynolds

5 Trafalgar Square 🚌

Service no. N91 | Journey time 62–70mins | See map on page 7

OS Landranger 176. At night, every 15–30mins.
Operator: Metroline.

Cockfosters ◄———

C ast back many years and London Transport promoted their night buses as 'a welcome sight on a dark night.' That old tag line still rings true for me after dancing late-night salsa in town, when the N91 is my preferred option for the journey back to my North London home.

The N91, a sort of nocturnal stand-in for the **Piccadilly Line**, departs from Trafalgar Square and ends up an hour later on the edge of Hertfordshire fields. But this late-night foray through London is no grit-your-teeth necessity – on the contrary, it is a marvellous opportunity to see another side of the city I call home.

It is two on a Sunday morning. From the bus stop in Northumberland Avenue (just off Trafalgar Square) I can just see the white cables of the **Hungerford Bridge** walkways and the illuminated dome of the National Gallery. I swap my plastic perch at the bus stop for a seat on the top deck. We glide along the Strand, the glitzy Savoy to the right and sparkling signs advertising musicals on the left.

Then we sweep past King's College and on to **Bush House**, one-time home of the BBC World Service. Even in darkness, Malvina Hoffman's classic sculpture above the portico of Bush House stands bold and clear, a striking silhouette in the London night. Now the N91 sails north up Kingsway – a road once judged so stately that Elgar wrote music to honour it. And so to **Bloomsbury**, which tonight is notable not for its literary connections but for the rickshaw rider who speeds towards the small-hours trade in Covent Garden or Soho.

We pass the dirty caryatids of St Pancras Church, the modern red-brick British Library and taxis waiting in a curve outside the cathedral-like **St Pancras Station** with its happily refurbished hotel. The famous clock above the great Gothic feast of Victoriana records the passing minutes of the night.

THE MOOD ON THE BUS

At **King's Cross** the bus takes on the biggest load of the journey. 'The only problem with London is that it's too far to walk,' I overhear. 'In Leeds, when one nightclub is dead, you can just walk to the next one.'

A **soundtrack of sorts** develops. There is the tinny rhythm from headphones, talk on mobiles, the scrape of a ring pull, along with the disembodied voice of an announcer reciting a litany of bus stop names. On the top deck, different languages mingle – three long-haired women flip between French and American

GOTHIC STYLE

The ghost of 19th-century train travel lingers in the **Booking Office Bar** (☎ 020 78413566; open daily 11.00–03.00) of the **St Pancras Renaissance Hotel**. The bar is part of the original neo-Gothic station building, and the menu includes intriguing Victorian-style drinks, some sounding like a cross between a cocktail and a cup of tea. Eat oysters and drink Charles Dickens Memorial Punch amidst leather armchairs, dark wood panelling and high ceilings and travel back to a time when a train journey was a **luxury adventure**. The staff are welcoming, and live music is played on Friday, Saturday and Sunday evenings.

English, an Indian language is spoken by two men behind me, and there's something that sounds like Turkish spoken into a mobile opposite.

I talk with 23-year-old Simon White, sitting at the front of the **top deck** with friends he has met at the airport. He tells me he often gets the bus after a night out. 'It's always a bit dodgy,' he says. 'By day no-one's going to get on smoking, with loads of beers. But the rules are different at night. It's sometimes funny to watch drunken people.'

So what about the hard-core clubbers, shift workers, transvestite DJs and other colourful denizens of London's dark underbelly? Well, I can only say that for me the N91 has always been a **distinctly unedgy experience**, and as a lone woman traveller I have always felt safe. That is an underrated aspect of London's night bus network.

We travel on. **Lights rule**. A ripped advert at a bus stop exposes fluorescent tubes beneath the plastic. A red back light flashes as a cyclist overtakes, high up are crane lights, traffic lights punctuate the journey. We go past Pentonville Prison, black pollarded trees outlined against its white bulk. Further on three blonde women cross the street, heading home with blue plastic bags. Men standing outside a restaurant turn their heads unashamedly. Looking back over the city from the top of **Crouch End Hill**, I can see the lights of Canary Wharf winking next to the newer vertical of the Shard.

Courting the Piccadilly Line

From Crouch End, we go down Turnpike Lane and emerge onto **Wood Green High Road**. This is a more desolate place than nearby Green Lanes, where jewel-like oranges are displayed outside Turkish and Cypriot greengrocers until the early hours. Here the stores include Poundland, downmarket jewellers, cinema multiplexes and, incongruously, an adventure travel shop with shadowy lumps of rucksacks hanging on the walls. Night brings respite from the crowds, and the shop windows are blank squares.

PICCADILLY HIGHLIGHTS

Night-bus travellers get to see **Piccadilly Line sights** missed by those who ride the trains. Southgate Station is one of several bold architectural statements on the Piccadilly Line route to Cockfosters. It, along with other stations north of Finsbury Park, was commissioned from architect **Charles Holden** by the visionary chief executive of the London Passenger Transport Board, Frank Pick. When the stations on this route were opened in 1933, they were promoted as affording **access to open countryside**. Now at three in the morning, the station at Southgate looks like a spaceship which has touched down by mistake among kebab shops and traffic lights.

From now on the bus calls at the Piccadilly Line tube stations. After **Bounds Green** we cross the North Circular, London's inner ring road, where power station rings frame the sky. At the top of the hill past New Southgate Station is a new, unfamiliar space where a dilapidated mock-castle pub used to stand.

We pause by London's most stylish tube station: **Southgate**, a perfectly circular Art Deco building standing on its own roundabout, banded in white, glowing in the dark, crowned by an audacious, illuminated, vertical stick with a white ball on the top.

The route becomes distinctly suburban. We quietly go past large homes where families are sleeping; a synagogue; a primary school. The occasional wall-wide plasma screen can be glimpsed through maisonette curtains. Then along **Cockfosters Road**, lined with banks, restaurants and slightly frumpy boutiques, the better-heeled cousins of the Wood Green stores. Shop signs call: Sweet Cherry; Moonlight; Anuraag; Kalamaras. The bright vertical spear of the Cockfosters tube sign appears. We halt here at the edge of the city, the dark **fields of Hertfordshire** beyond. ∎

ABOUT THE AUTHOR | **REBECCA REYNOLDS** is a freelance museum educator. She also teaches museum studies and creative writing at various universities.

NATURAL SELECTION
DOWNE YOUR WAY

Brian Grigg

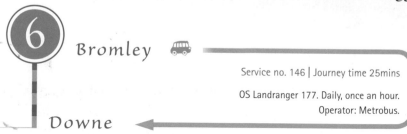

6 Bromley

Service no. 146 | Journey time 25mins

OS Landranger 177. Daily, once an hour.
Operator: Metrobus.

Downe

I don't know whether the former BBC radio programme *Down Your Way* ever went to the village of Downe. This community was surely a worthy candidate for inclusion in the show. For here is a **fragment of London** that has all the rural flavours so cherished by that perennial classic of the airwaves.

As London bus routes go, service 146 is one of the capital's shortest, yet one of the most extraordinary. It kicks off as just another red bus route in busy **Bromley**, but within half an hour morphs into a country bus journey along narrow leafy lanes. It is a route that dates back to before World War II – for many years numbered 146A but changing to 146 in 1952.

Londoners of a certain age will well remember the traditional colour coding of local buses: red for those that stayed within the city, green for those that bravely ventured out into London's rural hinterland. And this route from Bromley to Downe was always determinedly red, even though the southern part of the route was most decidedly green in character.

The starting point is Bromley North Station, definitely the lesser-known of the town's two railway stations. With its classical lines and copper-domed copula, it is a handsome piece of Southern Railway architecture from the 1920s, though nowadays sadly bereft of useful trains, having merely a weekdays-only shuttle service to Grove Park.

Bromley deserves a better press. Its most distinguished sons and daughters have fled, among them Enid Blyton and David Bowie. The **market square** has a blue plaque marking the birthplace of H G Wells who wrote none-too-lovingly of Bromley in his novels.

HEADING SOUTH

Visitors are more likely to board the 146 at **Bromley South Station** (17 minutes from London Victoria). The bus stays within the London Borough of Bromley, offering passengers a ride through what was originally Kent (and still is in postal address terms) before London became Greater!

With the hustle and bustle of Bromley left behind, some minutes are spent going through suburban commuter territory before reaching open country at **Hayes Common**. Keston village follows soon thereafter. When returning across Hayes Common on a clear day, there is a fleeting reminder, just before the traffic lights, of the approaching metropolis. Look north for a view over the great monuments to money at Canary Wharf. If you blink though, they will be obscured by trees and out of sight.

One can walk from **Keston**, using parts of the London Loop footpath over Keston Common with its Iron Age earthwork and large ponds. Once across Westerham Road, the path goes on to

---

KESTON

This village is also served by the 246 from Bromley, Biggin Hill and Westerham. **Fiona's Pantry** is a small café and delicatessen open daily (☎ 01689 638910). There are also two pubs and a restaurant by the green. I have enjoyed a couple of times meals at **The Fox Inn** (☎ 01689 852053; open daily from 11.00). Most conveniently, Bromley-bound buses stop immediately outside.

---

skirt Holwood Estate, now made up of luxury apartments, to the so-called 'Wilberforce Oak' and continues to **Holwood Farm**, a splendid barn conversion with a delicatessen and coffee shop specialising in quality produce (☎ 01689 638381; closed Mon).

The 146 has strong scientific and political credentials. William Wilberforce discussed the abolition of the slave trade with Prime Minister William Pitt the Younger under the **Wilberforce Oak** near Pitt's home on the Holwood Estate. Today an old stone bench with an inscription from Wilberforce's diary marks the spot, although precious little remains of the actual oak tree due to the ravages of the weather on this exposed location.

If you walked from Keston, you can reboard the 146 at Holwood Farm. This is lovely rolling countryside, wooded for some distance. Once out of Cuckoo Wood, flints can be seen in the soil.

THE DARWIN CONNECTION

Charles Darwin, author of *On the Origin of Species*, lived at **Down House** (no letter 'e') from 1842 to 1882. This followed a five-year world voyage as a young man aboard HMS *Beagle*, most famously including the Galapagos Islands. When London became a bit too much for Darwin, especially given health considerations,

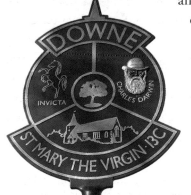

he chose Downe because of its quiet and rural nature – yet within reach of the capital. This description is still largely true although today occasionally light aircraft from nearby **Biggin Hill** can be heard.

Darwin was able to do his work in peace at Down House, observing flora and fauna and conducting many experiments

Downe village sign (photo © Brian Grigg)

while he and his wife Emma brought up their children in the area's idyllic surroundings. Nowadays those parts of Hayes and Keston Commons which Darwin explored are designated 'Sites of Special Scientific Interest.'

Bromley
12 mins
N
Hayes
6 mins
Keston
6 mins
Downe

Many local buildings along the bus route are constructed with flint stones, for example the churches at Keston and Downe and **Downe Village Hall**. In the centre of Downe, a tree with a circular wooden seat forms the turning circle for the 146. St Mary's Church, by the bus stop, has evidence of the Darwins. Emma and some of the couple's children are buried here. A sundial on the tower was placed here in memory of Charles, who is buried in Westminster Abbey.

Right in the centre of the village are **two pubs**, The Queen's Head with its Darwin Bar (☎ 01689 852145) and the George & Dragon (☎ 01689 889030). The latter has a nice old photograph of a double-deck London Transport bus on the Downe route. Just before its final stop, the 146 passes **a tea shop** called Cake which is well worth a visit – look out for the day's special sandwiches (☎ 01689 855044; open 10.00–17.00 Tue–Sun).

A little way from the village centre – and reached by the R8 bus from the middle of Downe – **Down House** is open to the public by English Heritage (☎ 01689 859119; www.english-heritage.org.uk/darwin). It makes for a rewarding visit, showing an insight into family and working life in authentic room settings.

I think readers will enjoy the 146. It is a London bus route with a difference. Return buses from Downe usually have some local passengers on board who are, no doubt, very pleased to have retained a regular bus service for their special village. ▪

ABOUT THE AUTHOR | **BRIAN GRIGG** has had a life-long interest in public transport. He travels at home and abroad by bus, coach and train.

LOVE ON THE 159

Sarah Taylor

7

Streatham 🚌

Service no. 159 | Journey time 50–90mins | See map on page 7

OS Landranger 176. Daily, every 5–10mins (every 20mins at night).
Operator: Arriva London.

Paddington ←

Monday morning. **Eyes half shut**. I sleepwalk past 159 identical Victorian terraces and then, and then, suddenly, I spot it. I wake. With a jolt. The 159 bus accelerates past me. Up towards St Leonard's Church. **I'm late**. Can't wait for the next one. I run. Faster than wind with my shower-damp curls. The blast of precious dawn air chills my scalp. Invigorates. My heart is beating out of my chest. And I chase that heart as it pursues the bus. I *will* catch this bus. I am invincible as I jump onto the open back of the Routemaster as the red light turns green and it pulls away. I leap straight into the arms of the conductor.

Take me away. My bus takes me away. From all this. From this cramped, Streatham flat that is home. I find my seat and my fingers squeak clear a patch in the steamed-up window. Trickles of condensation creep towards my shoved-up shoulder. Relax. I look through the window as **Streatham becomes Brixton**, as London stretches and yawns itself awake. Watch the swarms heading for subways to travel dark tunnels, dark fast tunnels that speed them to their work. I take the bus and I watch and I wait as the day decides what it will be. As the sky clears or stays cloudy. As the rain falls or doesn't. I watch a million pillow-creased, narrow-eyed, morning-after faces emerging from flats into this crisp, blissfully crisp, delicious December day. Watch the faces relax as the icy air banishes the night before. Whoosh. A new start. Eyes open, heads come up, lungs inhale, deep, deep, the pumping diesel life-force breath of London. **Catch the bus**. Run for your bus. For your life. You are alive here. Prove it to yourself as you run like the wind through these sweet litter-strewn, petrol-fumed South London streets.

SHARING

Stand or sit. We're all in this together. Reading borrowed words. Sharing. The *Guardian* on the row in front of you, *Time Out* next door, *Mills & Boon* behind. All life is here on the 159 as we head into town on **Kennington Road**. And on this cold, cold day, I bask in the tropics above the radiator where the searing heat of the heart of the bus burns through me. Defrosts. Penetrates my Doc Martens and my thick black tights and warms my toes and warms my body. And my feet are burning and my neck is freezing as fingers of this winter's chill come for me through the open platform. I'm hot and cold and so, so tired and I'm so awake as this journey jolts me into being. The bus shudders as it waits for passengers

to get on and off and we all shudder together as the pulse vibrates through our bodies. **We are one body**. One big living-breathing piece of life, coming from our nocturnal hibernations, our boxes in the suburbs.

Making space for the 159
(photo © Sarah Taylor)

Crossing **Westminster Bridge** we all glance up. Synchronised for a split second, we commune with the Thames. And on we go, past Whitehall's pomp and men on horses as we mouth our 'Good Mornings' or silent curses to our latest leaders. To Maggie, to John, to Tony; you come and you go. But we're coming now. We're coming into London. Our London. **We are the city**. We make it come alive. And by the time our 159 shudders past Piccadilly Circus and the neon billboards that need no sleep, we are flying up Regent Street and we can smell the searing heat of the burning engine of the Routemaster bus.

And **we are awake now**. And we get off our bus at our stops. And we walk into our offices, our shops, our recruitment consultancies, our schools, our hospitals, our banks, our pubs, our firms of chartered accountants, our sex shops, our hair salons, our photocopier sales offices, our production companies, our advertising agencies. And we are ready. We *are* London now. We are awake and alive and the bus has billowed life into us. And the noise and the traffic and the buzz of the people and the crowds on the street make our hearts sing.

I was looking for love for most of the nineties. Eyes watching from under the froth of my morning cappuccino as I leave Café Soho. Eyes looking right, looking left, then right again as I swig from my Evian and scurry down **Broadwick Street** for a quick fix of lunchtime Liberty, taking in the cut of their suits, the shine of their shoes. Eyes bright above the glass of Chardonnay in Shampers as I stand at the bar laughing with the girls from the office. Eyes bold, empty tequila glass in hand, eyes inviting the man in the striped shirt as we salsa towards midnight in Bar Madrid.

HEADING HOME

And later, on the night bus home, we're all so in love, me and this whole bus full of **post-party passengers**. And there's a man with bloodshot eyes who starts to sing a pitch-perfect *Danny Boy* and almost all on the lower deck join in. All but the boy with the paper-white skin and pinprick freckles on his forehead. He stares out through the window into the night's velvet blackness and in his reflection, I see **eyes as big as moons** and I watch as a glistening speck trickles from a tear duct towards his cheek. He does not wipe it off. I want to reach across and brush it away. It traces a thin salty trail and evaporates just before Oval. Where he gets off. I sing with the rest of them until I am spent.

I was looking for love for most of the nineties but it turns out, I was looking in all the wrong places. Next morning, on Streatham High Road, shower-damp curls meeting sharp morning air, cheeks pink, **I am alive again**. I am the wind, racing for the 159 Routemaster that is always just passing. I am a gazelle leaping, magnificent, onto the open back as the lights turn green. Dreadlocked, leaning against the winding stairs, the conductor bats me a wink and his face does not move. But I know his eyes are following me as I skip up the steps and sink, breathless into my front-row seat above the driver's head. My favourite seat. My favourite journey. And I'm feeling good! ∎

ABOUT THE AUTHOR | **SARAH TAYLOR** was a regular passenger on the 159 in the late '80s and '90s.

MOBILE BILLBOARDS

Buses are often surprisingly thought-provoking. We have been challenged to consider the mystery of the Resurrection while standing at a bus stop in Poland and to ponder the plight of caged animals while waiting in the rain in Spain. Buses are **poster spaces** on the move and lend themselves to advertising.

This is not always to the advantage of those inside the bus. The current craze for **wrap-around advertising** does not improve the view of the passing scenery. Instead of seeing glorious rural England slipping by beyond the window, travellers are condemned to a fractured view of the world. Lakeland writer Paul Buttle exploded a year or two back when buses on his local 564 bus route from Kendal to Brough suddenly appeared dressed in wrap-around advertising. 'That journey is one of the best in the region,' remarked Mr Buttle as he complained about having to view the scenery through a dark mesh of enveloping ads.

There was a time when buses carried ads for cigarettes and cheese. The side panels that a generation ago advertised soap or salt now **battle for the souls** of passers-by. Or, at the very least, for their hearts and minds. Buses have become prime vehicles for ethical or value-laden advertising campaigns. Motorists stuck behind a bus in busy city streets are invited to consider the evidence for the existence of God. London buses have carried hard-hitting atheist advertisements such as: 'There's probably no God. Now stop worrying and enjoy your life.'

It is no surprise perhaps that Christian groups have fought back with buses proclaiming a pro-God message. Nowadays the buses that jostle for space on our crowded streets carry legends that clamour for space in our **crowded lives**.

In New Zealand, we hear, the back of some buses carry words that promote a dating agency. But no single bus carries the entire slogan – 'Find Your Perfect Match.' But from time to time, two buses stand beside each other to disclose the entire legend. It is a lovely reminder that the human dating game is equally a matter of chance. Then the buses go their respective ways and the message slips away into the cityscape. **Love and buses** have so much in common. No surprise perhaps that the quest for some meaning in life is played out daily in bus advertising. ■

HOME COUNTIES

O ften densely populated, and seen by outsiders as an area of Britain where life is ever hectic, the counties that lie in **London's rural hinterland** offer immense possibilities for exploring by bus. The very fact that settlements nudge up against one another brings advantages. Bus services are usually frequent and routes so interconnected that there are often multiple ways of getting from A to B.

The region should not be dismissed for want of remarkable scenery. You won't find great swathes of wilderness but, in the gentle valleys of the **Weald** and the **Chilterns**, you find landscapes of delicate beauty. Move just slightly further away from London to discover Britain's newest national park. The South Downs National Park came into being in 2011 and is described in a Bradt guidebook by Tim Locke entitled *Slow Sussex*.

INDEPENDENT BUS OPERATORS

Sussex is also home to one of Britain's most creative bus operators: the Brighton & Hove Bus and Coach Company. That's quite a mouthful, so we'll call them **B&H**. It's a company that takes itself seriously and it stands out as one of the finest bus operators in the Home Counties.

Long before most other bus companies had even heard of the internet, those webwise guys at B&H picked up the simple domain name www.buses.co.uk – for a British bus company, there's no other address in cyberspace to top that. *Bus Times*, the **biannual magazine** of B&H, survives even in a web-savvy world, because it is invaluable. It includes bus times, naturally, but also notes and news on service innovations, days out and local attractions. In a grand gesture of corporate generosity, all too rare nowadays, B&H

even include the entire timetables of every competitor operator in their area. For those who live in or visit B&H territory, *Bus Times* is an essential part of the traveller's armamentarium. We included the Brighton to Eastbourne B&H route in *Bus-Pass Britain*.

In the Home Counties section of the current volume, we make space for two other independent bus operators who have a long tradition of serving their respective regions: Sussex-based **Compass Bus** (Journey 9) and **Stephensons of Essex** (Journey 11). Two routes in this section are particularly notable for their long history. Journey 12 picks up an old Alder Valley bus route – yes, there really was a bus company named after a non-existent valley – and the Kingston to Leatherhead bus route described in Journey 8. The latter has been running for over 80 years. Only its number has inflated (from 65 to 465), and of course the service now runs on through the Mole Gap to Dorking. Those who understand the high theology of Oyster and London Travelcards suggest that both these ticket options are valid on the 465 to Dorking. We suggest you do just check with the driver.

Even if you do not have a concessionary bus pass, you will find **rover tickets** that allow inexpensive explorations. The Arriva 'Explorer' ticket costs £6.80 for a day and covers not just Arriva buses in Kent, Sussex and Surrey but also the services of other operators (including B&H mentioned above). The area of validity extends west to include part of the New Forest and the Hampshire Downs. This is quite astounding value, and would in theory allow one to travel from Andover to Margate on a single, cheap rover ticket. A similar **day pass** covers a sweep of territory around the north of London, extending from Reading in the Thames Valley through the Chilterns to Hertfordshire and Essex. ■

MORE FAVOURITE JOURNEYS

The following Home Counties routes were included in *Bus-Pass Britain* (2011): Chatham to Grain, Dover to Hastings, Brighton to Eastbourne, Aldershot to Guildford, Guildford to Redhill and Luton to Aylesbury.

South through Surrey
By Bus to Dorking

Martin Stribblehill

8 Kingston-upon-Thames

Service no. 465 | Journey time 55–75mins

OS Landranger 176, 187. Every 30mins Mon–Sat, hourly on Sun.
Operator: Quality Line.

Dorking

I moved to Surbiton about ten years ago. Among the red buses I used when too lazy to cycle to and from the station was a clear interloper. Much of its journey is in **leafy Surrey,** yet the entire journey is still covered by a London Travelcard. Since then I've used the 465 bus for various journeys: getting home from work, shopping in Kingston, weekend jaunts to Box Hill and excursions to the pubs of Leatherhead and Mickleham. A recent change in operator means new plush seating and cleaner windows for an even better ride.

THE KING'S TOWN AND THE QUEEN OF THE SUBURBS

Board the bus in Eden Street in Kingston town centre. As the bus navigates the streets, you'll catch a glimpse of the busy marketplace, the old town hall and the 1930s-style Guildhall. In front of the latter is the **Coronation Stone**. The story is that seven Anglo-Saxon kings were crowned on it. You can see why later kings of England preferred a more comfortable coronation throne at Westminster instead.

The view quickly opens out, with the river on our right. This is the last run for the clean, flowing Thames before it hits the mud, salt and worse of the upcoming tide. On a summer's day it is full of boats – from kayaks to fake paddle steamers – on their way to Hampton Court Palace. This is where Jerome K Jerome's **three men in a boat** began their journey. In winter the river is a ribbon of calm belonging only to the swans and the coots.

The river setting is rudely snatched away as the bus turns left and weaves through suburban streets. This is the cue for the gleaming-white centre of **Surbiton life**: the railway station. In the nineteenth century, the people of Kingston didn't want the noise and fuss of the London to Southampton railway line going through their town. Instead, a village to the south found itself a short train ride from central London. The imposing **Art Deco station** building reflects its importance to the thousands who sigh and shuffle on the Waterloo-bound platform each day.

The bus ducks under the railway to emerge in leafy Southborough. A fellow passenger once saw me envying the grander houses, and assured me that while they look good, the roofs leak. You can peer up the side roads and speculate on which one might have been home to the 70s sitcom *The Good Life*. But you'll not spot it – the series was filmed in northwest London, though Surbiton got the credit. Accelerating south after crossing

TAKING A HORSE TO WATER

There are a number of good pubs, cafés and restaurants on the route. My favourite is the **Running Horse** (☎ 01372 372081; open 11.30–23.00 Mon–Sat, 11.30–22.30 Sun) by the river in **Leatherhead**. This is a traditional English pub with a low-ceiling, excellent beers and locally sourced food. Inside are pictures showing the history of the area, and an unexpected display of spigots. For something more gourmet, go plural. The **Running Horses** (☎ 01372 372279; open 12.00–23.00 Mon–Sat, 12.00–22.30 Sun) props up the bus stop opposite the church in **Mickleham**. The food in its restaurant is excellent (open daily from noon for lunch and supper, but closed between 14.30 and 19.00).

the A3, you may spot the blue plaque on the left marking where **Enid Blyton** lived as a governess in the 1920s.

LEAVING SUBURBIA

There is still plenty of suburbia before the edge of London's sprawl. The first clue to its end is the sight of wooded **Winey Hill** beyond the playing fields on the right, contrasting with the industrial estate on the left. After Malden Rushett, the bus then climbs and passes outside the control of the Mayor of London, but not of the Lord Mayor. The lightly wooded nature reserve on the left is Ashtead Common, owned by the Corporation of London.

You know you have properly escaped London's clutches as the bus crosses the eight lanes of the M25. The route into Leatherhead town centre isn't particularly picturesque. But after the crooked Running Horse pub, look right as you cross the **River Mole** to see the viaduct that carries the Leatherhead to Dorking railway. The company would have liked to keep it functional, but the landowner insisted on something more ornate.

Now the landscape becomes more three-dimensional and our bus climbs a steep hill. On the left is our first view of the **North Downs**, with their wooded heights overlooking the neat fields of Bocketts Farm Park. Generously, the bus almost turns back on itself, giving passengers a second look.

BETWEEN THE DOWNS

South from Leatherhead, we follow the ancient **Mole Gap** through the Downs, with our bus happily eschewing the main A24 and sticking to the old road through Mickleham. This narrow country

Kingston

12 mins

Surbiton N

16 mins

Chessington

12 mins

Leatherhead

9 mins

Mickleham

12 mins

Dorking

lane is a happy contrast to the earlier suburbs. On the right you get a quick peek at the red-brick mock-Tudor and Gothic grandeur of the **Box Hill School**. Then the white half-timbered sprawl of the village centre. Opposite is its Norman church. Some churches stand out because of their soaring spires, but St Michael's takes the opposite approach, squatting beneath the trees. The wooden grave markings are a local tradition in an area lacking suitable stone.

The next stop is at the bottom of the zigzag route up Box Hill. This road is Surrey's Alpe d'Huez, particularly popular with cyclists. It was so popular with the organisers of the **2012 Olympic road race** that riders had to haul themselves up it nine times. It is also a favourite for motorcyclists, and you often see rows of gleaming machines outside **Ryka's Café** at the following stop.

The bus rejoins the main road. The trees fall away and no longer hide the hills rising on either side. To the right are the regular rows of Denbies Vineyard above Dorking. As the bus enters the town, it has a final treat. A detour through the station car park means it turns for one last look north. There is a **panoramic view** of Box Hill's steep southern slopes. This is a far cry from the busy streets of Kingston-upon-Thames. ∎

ABOUT THE AUTHOR | Martin Stribblehill is a civil servant. He lives in Chessington.

A SUSSEX CENTURION

Brian Grigg

9 Horsham

Service no. 100 | Journey time 2hrs 15mins

OS Landranger 187, 197, 198. Hourly Mon–Sat, no Sun service.
Operator: Compass Bus.

Burgess Hill ◄

Sussex has its fair share of memorable bus journeys. The one-day 'Downlander' pass is a fine way of exploring routes over and around the South Downs in the Lewes and Beachy Head area. But as author Tim Locke reminds us in his book *Slow Sussex* (also published by Bradt Travel Guides), there is more to Sussex than chalk. The bus route from Horsham to Burgess Hill captures a great **variety of Sussex landscapes**, traversing a segment of the Weald that boasts sandy ridges, clay vales and culminating in some very fine views of the **South Downs**. In the latter part of the journey, the route dances along the northern border of England's newest national park.

You really have to be a bus enthusiast to ride the number 100 without a break

Steyning – definitely a worthy stopping-off point on this Wealden bus journey (photo © Brian Grigg)

of journey from end to end. It takes over two hours, and there are certainly quicker ways of getting from Horsham to Burgess Hill. The two communities are just 15 miles apart, but Compass Travel's service 100 contrives to cover over thrice that distance. The entire route is a charming ride **through the Weald**, but the real highlight is the section from Pulborough to Henfield where the South Downs are never far away to the south.

That part of the journey takes just under an hour, and with buses running along the route generally every 60 minutes, there is every opportunity to just hop off to take the pulse of some of the small Sussex villages along the route.

Take time before setting off to explore **Horsham**. The Causeway is the place to start. With its fabulous mix of traditional Wealden building styles, it is no surprise that this road is the most photographed in town. With its handsome lime trees, it is a lovely place to wander. On the Causeway you'll also find the town's visitor information centre and Horsham Museum and Art Gallery (☎ 01403 254959; open 10.00–17.00 Mon–Sat).

CENTURIONS OF YESTERYEAR

Our bus ride starts at a small modern bus station in cobbled Carfax by the bandstand and opposite the railway station. The single-deck bus slips out of town, crossing the **River Arun** and turning left onto the A29 at Slinfold. No ordinary highway this one, for

---

ARUN VALLEY WALKS

Visits to Pulborough Brooks or Parham House can be combined with an Arun Valley walk, perhaps venturing as far as the village of Amberley with its **Museum and Heritage Centre** (☎ 01798 831370; open 10.00–17.00 Wed–Sun mid-March till Nov). The museum is dedicated to industrial heritage and has some green-and-cream vintage buses of the old Southdown Motor Services. Walkers can return by train from Amberley to Pulborough to join the 100 again.

it traces the line of an ancient Roman road called **Stane Street**. So the 100 bus follows the ghosts of centurions of old, rumbling south through pleasant Sussex countryside. Indeed, we follow Stane Street all the way to Pulborough. The only place of any

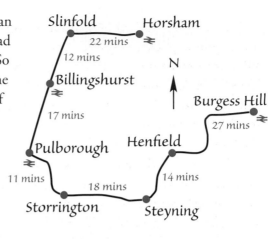

significance along the way is **Billingshurst** where, as often as not, the bus waits for a while by the level crossing. It is a chance to reflect on an unusually handsome green-and-white signal box just by the railway at that point.

Pulborough is a pleasant little town on the north bank of the River Arun. The bus gives a chance to see the town from all angles, running along the high street in both directions. We pause for a few minutes at the railway station, before heading east out of town. There are fine views of the River Arun, in rainy times often topping its banks and flooding the surrounding water meadows.

Now comes the finest stretch of the route, where it makes sense to grab a seat on the right side of the bus. We pass Pulborough Brooks Bird Reserve, which offers some lovely walks through the woods and down towards the Arun, with the possibility in spring and summer of hearing and even seeing the reclusive but vocal nightingale. Further along, shortly before Storrington, is the Elizabethan **Parham House** with its deer park and gardens (☎ 01903 742021; see www.parhaminsussex.co.uk for opening times). There are request bus stops near both these attractions.

Now heading more decisively east, we go through the heart of **Storrington**, then hug the foot of the Downs. Trees surround the Iron Age fort at Chanctonbury Ring high on the ridge above. There is evidence of the Romans having been here too and maybe more centurions. But beware: it is a formidably steep hike up to Chanctonbury from the bus stop.

The next place of any size is handsome **Steyning** (pronounced Stenning), surely the jewel in the crown of this route. This lovely old borough, so full of Saxon and Norman history, was once an inland port on the River Adur. The 100 stops by the clock tower. Walking along High Street, turning into Church Street, there are fine timbered flint-and-brick buildings. The road continues past the 12th-century **St Andrew's Church,** the library and museum leading to the River Adur and the Downs Link path.

From Steyning the 100 still has some way to go. The adjoining villages of Bramber and Upper Beeding are divided by an old brick and stone bridge over the River Adur. The ruins of the Norman Bramber Castle, seen from the bus, are looked after by English Heritage. Timber-framed **St Mary's House** dating from the 15th century is open to the public (☎ 01903 816205).

Then we detour to serve Henfield, before returning to the shadow of the Downs. There are fine views south to Devil's Dyke. But that's the last we see of the hills as the bus heads north through Hickstead, before ending its journey in **Burgess Hill**. It is a town that sprawls. The best that can be said of it is that it has a great range of onward bus and rail connections. ■

| ABOUT THE AUTHOR | Brian Grigg has had a life-long interest in public transport. He travels at home and abroad by bus, coach and train. |

EAST KENT BACKWATERS
THANET BOUND

Peter Shearman

10 Canterbury 🚐

Service no. 11 | Journey time 90mins

OS Landranger 179. Four journeys Mon–Fri, three on Sat; no Sun service.
Operator: Stagecoach.

Broadstairs ←

Life in Plucks Gutter took an enormous leap forward a couple of years ago when Stagecoach launched bus number 11. Though, even with a regular bus route, Plucks Gutter is still as much of a backwater as the name of the hamlet implies. It is tucked away on the **Thanet marshes** and certainly not a natural point to break a journey between Canterbury and the coast. Few people would instinctively opt for this bus for the end-to-end journey. But they should, for Plucks Gutter and a number of other oddball spots along the route of the 11 definitely deserve a visit. Along the way, there are wide vistas of fertile, **empty countryside** and marshland – plus a curiously unknown international airport.

If this journey appeals to you, don't delay. In these straitened times rural bus services are always at risk, and believe me, the quick and easy ways to Thanet on East Kent bus routes 8 and 9 are just not in the same league.

The number 11 was not designed just with Plucks Gutter in mind. For a swathe of Kent villages, this route is a lifeline allowing residents of rural areas to reach major shopping areas. Canterbury is the obvious **shopping hub** at the west end of the route where the delights of Primark, Debenhams and Marks & Spencer all beckon. Then, towards the eastern end of the route in Thanet,

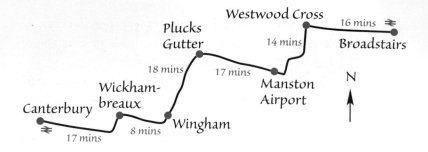

you'll find the area's new shopping temple: **Westwood Cross**. The undoubted success of the latter brings its own problems. Town centres in Thanet suffer and it is hard to get retailers in nearby Margate and Ramsgate to speak of Westwood Cross with any enthusiasm.

Evidently the (in)famous 'retail guru' Mary Portas, the quick-fix solution to all Britain's retail problems, has no answers, despite the government's confidence in appointing her to attend to Margate's woes. The top deck of the number 11 is a good spot to relax and reflect on the woes of a nation that has become a shade too addicted to shopping.

KENTISH VILLAGES

The shopping crowd, well-laden with their haul from Canterbury's stores, clusters on the lower deck of the bus. I'm on the top deck, and we are rolling up the valley of the **Little Stour** past a series of imposing Kentish clapboard watermills. Next stop: **Wickhambreaux**. I have learnt a lot on the number 11. The truth is that, prior to taking this bus route, I had never heard of Wickhambreaux and the discovery could not have been more rewarding.

As we enter the village, we pass another **watermill**, this one even taller than the others. Then we roll to a stop on the village green embraced by the manor house, 14th-century church, rectory, the historic Rose Inn and that distinctive watermill. This 'ensemble' is rural England at its best and you get to see it twice, as the bus continues on for a few yards before reversing to head back across the green and then eastwards to Ickham.

The bus dips back to the main road at **Wingham**, a mid-sized village with a trinity of decent pubs. My favourite is the Red Lion – excellent, medium-priced lunchtime food. But the number 11 is not about places on the main road. At the eastern end of the village it turns off northwards, passing hop fields and oast houses on its way to Preston, and then twists and turns through pretty **East Stourmouth**. On this section I love the views across towards the River Stour and the atmospheric marshland.

Now we are in **Plucks Gutter** country. The hamlet stands out on the local maps as the place where the Little Stour and the Great Stour meet. It is not exactly the ultimate picture-book community, but it is notable for its large, well-kept pub alongside the river and the equally well-kept and neatly ordered holiday chalet park. Here the River Stour is popular for boating, fishing and riverside walks.

These **low-key pleasures** provide the peace and quiet doubtless sought by the chalet owners, escaping from busy, noisy lives in the likes of Luton or Bexleyheath. Once at Plucks Gutter

PLUCKS GUTTER

This being Kent's version of Fenland, the **River Stour marshland** owes its present-day agricultural function – and the name of the hamlet – to the Dutch. A drainage engineer called Ploeg set about creating a network of ditches to reclaim the marshes, and he is buried at the church in nearby West Stourmouth – just off the bus route but on an easy three-mile circular walk. Follow the **Saxon Shore Way** westwards along the Little Stour, take in the beautifully restored Sarre Windmill in the distance, and after about 1.5 miles head back eastwards on the **River Stour Walk**, across fields to West and East Stourmouth. Plucks Gutter is then hardly a mile away, so drop in at the Dog and Duck and reflect on King Alfred's defeat of Viking invaders right here, and the early 19th-century smugglers who found this to be ideal territory.

they can switch off and enjoy the rural charms for a week or two, assisted by an occasional pint in the Dog and Duck. It would be nice to think that some also hopped on the bus for an afternoon in Canterbury or Broadstairs. However, I am told that normally the bus goes straight through without stopping. And that's a shame, because except in winter, visitors to the holiday park outnumber permanent residents and could help sustain the bus service.

If you have done the walk along the River Stour (see box on page 49), drop into the **Dog and Duck** (phone ☎ 01843 821542 to check seasonal opening times) before picking up the bus again. Whilst the building might be at home in a suburban setting, what it lacks in character is more than made up for by hearty, good-value pub food with friendly service and a riverside garden, all of which helps to make the watery setting of Plucks Gutter a pleasing stop-off.

To the coast

Beyond Plucks Gutter, we cruise over **Monkton Marshes** and around the edge of Manston airport which, despite a relative paucity of flights, boldly styles itself Kent's International Airport. A brace of good museums make up for the lack of flights. Neither the **Spitfire & Hurricane Memorial Museum** (☎ 01843 821 940, open 10.00–17.00 daily, or until 16.00 off season) nor the **RAF Manston History Museum** (☎ 01843 825224; open 10.00–16.00 daily Mar–Oct; 10.00–16.00 Sat & Sun from Nov–Feb) should be missed. From Manston it is but a short hop east to Westwood Cross and Broadstairs is not far beyond. The journey ends at Pierremont Hall, which has lost the lustre it surely had in the days when Queen Victoria would stay here when holidaying in Thanet. ■

ABOUT THE AUTHOR | **PETER SHEARMAN** lives near London. He is a retail development consultant but also an intrepid bus traveller. On a visit to Westwood Cross for work purposes he discovered the thrill of route 11.

GREEN
AND RED

bus stop

There was a moment in the opening ceremony of the 2012 Summer Olympics that nicely recalled the history of bus travel in and around London. **Isambard Kingdom Brunel**, played by the actor Kenneth Branagh, arrived in the stadium on a horse-drawn bus. The vehicle was in the **distinctive green livery** of the London General Omnibus Company (LGOC).

For those who know their buses, the symbolism was immense. Here was a London bus, presented in a scene rich in nostalgia, but the colour of the bus was a reminder of London's links with its hinterland. As Brian Grigg reminds us in Journey 6 in this book (page 28), the **colour coding** of London buses was for decades very clear. Buses that stayed in the city were red; those that ventured into the hinterland were green. Brunel arrived in a green bus.

LGOC had its fair share of 'red' routes, but the company was a pioneer in developing 'green' services that crossed the London boundary. The last horse-drawn LGOC vehicle ran in 1911. A brand-new fleet of LGOC motor buses were transforming bus travel. In summer 1911, LGOC launched a **monthly guide** highlighting the many places that could now so easily be reached by bus.

The following year, LGOC offered its first regular route into the Home Counties, providing a Sunday **service to Windsor Castle**. Other routes for excursionists quickly followed, and by September 1912, Londoners could take the bus out to St Albans on any day of the week. If there was a golden age of buses in London and the Home Counties, it was in these couple of years just prior to World War I. New routes were being launched every week.

These early LGOC ventures beyond the boundaries of London were the precursors of the **Green Line** network launched by LGOC in 1930, taking advantage of a period in which new services in the region could be introduced without prior permission from the Traffic Commissioners. Green Line developed into a **powerful transport brand**. There were some extraordinary routes that went right across London, eg: from Hitchin to Reigate and Harpenden to Great Bookham. They have long gone, but the name Green Line lives on in about a dozen bus services, mainly to the north and west of London. Happily, one of those routes is the 701 which still ferries Londoners every day of the week out to Windsor Castle. ■

A Ride Through THE DENGIE

Julia Hammond

Burnham-on-Crouch

Service no. D4 | Journey time 43mins

OS Landranger 168. Four journeys Mon–Sat, no Sun service.
Operator: Stephensons.

Bradwell Waterside

Ask most people what their opinions of Essex might be and the responses are unlikely to be complimentary to the county. Little over an hour from London's Liverpool Street Station, the remote and sometimes bleak **Dengie Peninsula**, sandwiched between the River Blackwater to the north and the River Crouch to the south, is a far cry from the orange tans and false nails that invite such parody.

The bus may be 21st-century, but my ride is not. Starting in the **Quayside café** (☎ 01621 783350; open 09.00–18.00 Mon, Wed, Sat, 09.00–22.00 Fri & Sat, closed Tue) next to Burnham's 500-year-old Anchor Hotel, I sip a morning coffee in the sunshine overlooking the Crouch whilst eavesdropping on conversations about boats. This is England's driest county, but if the wind is cold there are plenty of window seats to go around. Crowded during the regatta which takes place at the end of August, most days **Burnham-on-Crouch** is a sleepy town, perfect for mooching around the art gallery and taking a stroll along the riverbank towards the marina. In the main street, the 1877 clock tower stands in memory of the philanthropist Laban Sweeting. He made his money in oysters, which were in Laban's day much more a food for folk of all social classes than they are today. Oysters are still big business in Essex. This local landmark is a minute's walk from the quay and the bus stops right beside it.

NORTH TO SOUTHMINSTER

Leaving Burnham's traditional clapboard houses behind, the D4 bus takes me north towards Southminster. I pass **Mangapps Railway Museum** (☎ 01621 784898; www.mangapps.co.uk; open 11.30–17.00 Sat & Sun), a rescue centre for 18 steam and diesel locos and countless carriages. Originally a farm, at weekends the Jolly family and their team of volunteers have created a working railway with a museum and outbuildings housing an enormous amount of railway memorabilia and artefacts. Burnham Eve's Corner is the nearest bus stop, a third of a mile down the road, but smile nicely and the driver will let you alight at the museum gate.

Sweeting Tower in Burnham (photo © Julia Hammond)

At the end of the main-line railway, the tiny town of **Southminster** has a long history. Listed in the Domesday Book, it had 64 people and 13 slaves. It's scruffy now and the landscape is flat. A field of sheep gives way to fertile arable land punctuated by the occasional quarry or old folks' home. At Asheldham, the bus leaves the main road to take a lane to tiny Dengie – a mere slip of a hamlet that has lent its name to the entire peninsula.

Bradwell Waterside

N

11 mins

Tillingham

Dengie 3 mins

6 mins

Southminster

21 mins

Burnham-
on-Crouch

On the late-morning bus, I'm engrossed in conversation with a bunch of pensioners returning from an early shopping trip to Burnham. They are keen to find out where I'm from and dismiss my small south Essex town, a mere 15 miles away, as being far too noisy and built up. Midway through its journey, the bus reaches their beloved **Tillingham**, an attractive village, with clapboard houses and an imposing church dispersed around a well-maintained village green. Tillingham featured in H G Wells's famous novel *The War of the Worlds*; when the narrator's brother flees to the coast after the Martian invasion, this is the place where he heads to escape to the continent. The pensioners have a regular Wednesday lunch date in the **Fox and Hounds pub** (☎ 01621 779416) and invite me to join them. The landlord, Peter, welcomes us with honest pub grub and my new friends regale me with tales of the past. 'Bus is due soon, love, make sure you don't miss it,' they implore two hours later, and I reach for my coat.

ON TO BRADWELL

I board the next bus and head out to Bradwell-on-Sea. At the end of the road known as Mill End, travellers to the Hispanic world might be alarmed to see a sign proclaiming 'Bulls' eggs', for 'huevos de toro' as they are called in Spain, Argentina and Mexico, are bulls' testicles. Here though, Mr and Mrs Bull run the farm and their chickens lay prolifically in summer, meaning they are well known in this part of the county. The community shop, managed by the capable and jovial Janet, stocks them in season, or you can fill a box at the farm gate.

Bradwell has a long history and the main street, cars excepted, has changed little over the past century. The **King's Head** and St Thomas's church opposite are the two enduring landmarks. The driver curses the tiny gap inconsiderate drivers have left him on this narrow stretch. At the southeast corner of the churchyard be sure to look out for 'the cage', an 18th-century structure of brick with oak whipping posts where petty thieves and drunks would get their just desserts.

Sue Spiers's delightful, illustrated map is displayed in the church grounds to help me get my bearings. For the energetic, there's a six-mile walk along the coastal footpath; it will take a good three hours, so you'll need to be on the 09.30 bus out of Burnham or risk being stranded.

The Saturday timetable allows you an extra quarter of an hour to catch the last bus to Burnham; on weekdays, there is a later bus that will get you as far as Southminster from where you can catch a train back to Burnham should you forget the time. An easier two-mile hike along a flat path takes me to the chapel of **St Peter-on-the-Wall**.

From Bradwell-on-Sea, the bus squeezes up the main street and along Trusses Road before reaching its turning point at Bradwell Waterside. The hulking mass of **Bradwell Power Station** haunts the village as it goes through the decommissioning process.

THE MONSTER OF TILLINGHAM

A pamphlet entitled 'The Ranters Monster' was written in 1652 by a London journalist called George Horton, its subject a girl from **Tillingham** called **Mary Adams**. She was pregnant, unmarried and probably insane, claiming to be the Virgin Mary. The local vicar ordered that she be locked up and eventually the child was stillborn. Horton described the infant as 'an ugly misshapen monster with no hands or feet but with claws like a toad.' After giving birth, Mary was covered in hideous boils and scabs before committing **suicide** a few days later. Is the story true? No-one can prove either way.

A WALK ON THE WILD SIDE

Leaving **Bradwell** village, walk away from the King's Head and past St Thomas's along East End Road. Just before you reach the sea, you will come across one of England's oldest surviving churches. The chapel of **St Peter-on-the-Wall** dates from the 7th century. In AD653 St Cedd arrived from Lindisfarne and used stone from the abandoned Roman fort, Othona, to build a small chapel. Allegedly, in the 18th and 19th centuries, the chapel had a different purpose as the hiding place for **smugglers** and their loot.

Today, it's a church again. Services are held each weekend in summer and a pilgrimage convenes here each July. People even get married here – though they need permission from the Archbishop of Canterbury to do so. Continue your walk along the sea wall and past the **salt marshes**. In the dry Essex summer, this is the perfect place to get away from it all with a picnic; in winter, icy Siberian winds flick across the North Sea and cut through the thickest of fleeces. Bradwell Power Station looms large in front of the settlement of Bradwell Waterside before you double back past the **war memorial** to return to where you started.

Prior to 1992, it used to hum silently lest you forgot it was there. Time will tell whether a new power station rises from the ashes or whether Sizewell C will take its place; locals are divided but many are keen to see the jobs that a new power station will create. For now, it's all about the boats, whether the **smart yachts** of the packed marina or the sails of the restored barges tethered along the Blackwater Estuary.

Before catching the bus home, pause and ponder what life is like here at the end of Essex. Bradwell is just 45 miles from the City of London (as the crow flies). Once the pier was busy wish sheep being shipped to London and ports on the contient. Today it's a place of bleak and eerie isolation, relying on the D4 bus for a link to the wider world. ■

ABOUT THE AUTHOR | **JULIA HAMMOND** is an Essex native, a geography teacher and a passionate traveller. When home, she can usually be found planning her next trip with her two golden retrievers snoozing at her feet.

Three Counties
River Run

Kate Booth

12 High Wycombe

Service nos. 800 | Journey time 1hr 23mins

OS Landranger 175. Hourly Mon–Sun (no evening services).
Operator: Arriva.

Reading ←

Remember mild-mannered Mole? His spring-cleaning done, he ventured to the bank of the river. Kenneth Grahame captured the moment in *The Wind in the Willows*: 'He sat on the bank, while the river still chattered on to him, a babbling procession of the best stories in the world.' If like Mole you love the river, then this route that takes in part of **three counties** – Buckinghamshire, Oxfordshire and Berkshire – is most surely for you. Along the way, we encounter some delicious scenery as the River Thames nudges against the **Chiltern Hills**. With a high frequency of buses, there is ample opportunity to hop off along the way. The riverside towns of Marlow and Henley-on-Thames both warrant a stop.

We leave from the clean and modern bus station in **High Wycombe** and almost immediately the bus staggers uphill to the highest point of the journey where the Chilterns spread out before us. Look back for views of urban sprawl in the valley of the River Wye, and ahead for a glorious swathe of Chiltern countryside. The Arriva 800 bus dips down towards **Marlow**. Keep an eye open for red kites with their distinctive fork tail and six-foot wingspan.

Marlow is an amiable small town that attracts a moneyed crowd. No surprise perhaps that the first gastropub to secure

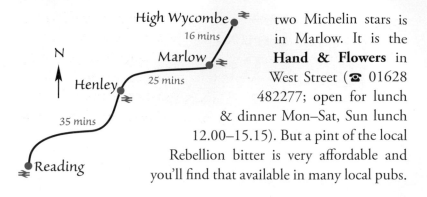

two Michelin stars is in Marlow. It is the **Hand & Flowers** in West Street (☎ 01628 482277; open for lunch & dinner Mon–Sat, Sun lunch 12.00–15.15). But a pint of the local Rebellion bitter is very affordable and you'll find that available in many local pubs.

OF BOATS AND TOADS

If you do stop, take a peek at Marlow's famous bridge over the Thames. Like Henley, a shade upstream, the river here is prime water for rowing, and the two towns vie for superiority. Both have produced **Olympic oarsmen**. Marlow is especially proud of Sir Steve Redgrave whose statue has pride of place in Higginson Park.

For the best views of the river, sit on the left as the bus heads west from Marlow. We pause by the entrance to Danesfield House Hotel, and a handful of regulars disembark. They look as though they are staff at the hotel. I guess that the guests probably don't arrive with Arriva. Indeed, I wonder if those guests even know what a bus is. As we set off again, don't miss a fine example of a wattle fence on the left, complete with a stylish thatched top.

When we arrive in **Mill End** and get the first proper view of the river, the more energetic might wish to break their journey with a walk in the picturesque Hambleden Valley. This gentle chalk vale tracks north from the river. It is much used in film and television productions.

Just beyond Mill End, you see an extraordinary road sign, one that advises of an upcoming **toad crossing**. Springtime is the season for the toad patrol. A toad tunnel under the road was designed to smooth the route of toads from woods on one side to their spawning ponds on the other. The tunnel has proved not to be to their liking, so a few weeks each spring volunteers escort toads across the road here. Over the last three years the **Henley Toad Patrol** has helped some 26,000 toads across the A4155.

The part of the run after the toad crossing is at its best in springtime when there are bluebells in abundance in woodland on the right-hand side. On the left there are fine views of **Fawley Court**, a country house designed by Christopher Wren with gardens landscaped by Capability Brown.

HENLEY-ON-THAMES

Once in Henley, the bus loops round the one-way system through town ending up by the side of the river – it's helpful if the traffic lights are red as it gives more time to absorb the views. Across the river is the **Leander Club** whose members have won more Olympic rowing medals than any other single-sport club in the world. It is Britain's oldest rowing club, founded in London in 1818 and then moving to Henley in 1896. Those who like to mock the Leander crowd are quick to note that the club's emblem is a hippo – the only other aquatic creature apart from Leander members to keep its nose permanently in the air!

Henley's famous **regatta** takes place over a five-day period in early July followed immediately by an arts festival, and in

EATERIES ALONG THE ROUTE

In Henley, the **River and Rowing Museum** has an excellent café serving a selection of homemade dishes throughout the day. For a quirky and intimate café, you can't do better than **Hot Gossip** (7 Friday St, Henley; ☎ 01491 414070; open 08.30–17.30 Mon–Fri, 09.00–17.00 Sat and 10.30–16.00 Sun) with its retro 1960s atmosphere, outdoor and indoor seating and a cosy log fire in the winter. In Marlow, **Burgers** is a must (The Causeway; ☎ 01628 483 389; 08.30–17.30 Mon–Sat, 11.00–17.00 Sun). It has been family run for three generations since 1942. Everything is freshly baked on the premises and you might as well abandon the diet for the day.

A HENLEY HIGHLIGHT

The **River and Rowing Museum** in Henley is certainly worth a visit (Mill Meadows; ☎ 01491 415600; www.rrm.co.uk; open daily 10.00–17.00, until 17.30 May–Aug). The building itself has won awards and the museum has a constantly changing calendar of exhibitions, adult lectures, workshops and children's events. The **three galleries** are dedicated to rowing, rivers and the history of Henley. Visit the magical 'Wind in the Willows' exhibition (more toads of course), which brings to life the much-loved story with 3D models, lighting and music.

September there is a hugely popular literary festival with many daytime events. For those wishing to emulate the regatta's rowers, boats can be hired from Hobbs of Henley (☎ 01491 572035).

The current bridge was built from 1776–86 by Thomas Hayward who died before it was finished, supposedly having caught a cold after giving up his place inside a coach to a lady.

Leaving Henley on the A321, the 800 bus gives us a good view of Victorian terraced cottages before heading towards **Shiplake** which featured in Jerome K Jerome's *Three Men in a Boat*. The river disappears from view, but the ride through the village is attractive and continues so as the bus takes us past agricultural land through Binfield Heath, Playhatch and on to Caversham where we cross over the river into Berkshire. It's a short ride over the bridge to journey's end at Friar Street in **Reading**. This is a town which has happily rediscovered its river in recent years and some imaginative urban renewal has opened up walks along the canalised River Kennet which joins the Thames here. Reading deserves a better press than it often gets. If you are inclined to linger, Reading Museum on Blagrave Street is a first-class diversion (☎ 0118 937 3400; open 10.00–16.00 Tue–Sat, 11.00–16.00 Sun). ∎

ABOUT THE AUTHOR | **KATE BOOTH** has spent almost all her life in the Chilterns. Now semi-retired, she is equally happy continuing to explore the area on foot or by bus.

SOUTH & SOUTHWEST ENGLAND

L et us plot an imaginary journey, one that
starts on the shores of Poole Harbour and
ends over 200 miles away in the village of St
Agnes on the wild north coast of Cornwall.
This is a journey where many travellers might
naturally look to the train as their first option. St Agnes is not
on any rail route, but it is just half an hour by local bus from the
nearest railhead in Truro. It is perfectly possible to leave Poole
Station just after noon, change trains twice along the way, then
connect onto a bus at Truro, and reach St Agnes at 19.45. With
an off-peak single ticket for the train costing £84, plus a small
add-on for the short last leg on the bus, this stacks up to being a
very pricey journey.

CHEAP BUT SCENIC

Now consider the alternative. It does take a little longer, to be
sure, for you'll need to leave Poole two hours earlier – at 10.05 in
the morning on the X53 from Poole to Exeter. This route is one of
Britain's finest bus adventures – so good in fact that we devoted ten
pages to it in *Bus-Pass Britain*. It takes in the remarkable coastline
of Dorset, an area so intimately associated with the early history
of geology that in 2001 it was inscribed on the UNESCO World
Heritage List.

At Exeter bus station, which is no worse but also no better
than most British bus stations, there is a comfortable 38-minute
connection onto the second bus. This is a Western Greyhound
service to Cornwall, a journey which also includes some fine
scenery. Following the A30 west from Exeter, it skirts the northern
edge of Dartmoor National Park. The bus from Exeter sets out

as the 510, changing its identity at Wadebridge into the 594. It travels on via Truro (changing numbers there yet again) and arrives in St Agnes at 19.45.

The fare for this remarkable bus journey from Poole to St Agnes is just £15.50 single, though of course you can ride for free if you hold an English concessionary bus pass. If you do not have a pass though, just buy tickets from the driver of each bus. It is £7 single from Poole to Exeter on the X53 and £8.50 for a Day Explorer ticket on the 510 onward service from Exeter.

Within south and southwest England there are many routes where journey segments that appear to be different routes can in fact be completed as a through journey without any need to change buses. Some versions of the printed timetable for the X53 (often dubbed the Jurassic Coast route) suggest a change of bus might be necessary at three intermediate points: Weymouth, Bridport and Seaton. Similarly, many Wadebridge-bound Western Greyhound services from Exeter in fact continue beyond Wadebridge to more distant spots in west Cornwall.

Of course, the real delights in exploring south and southwest England by bus lie not merely in unusually long journeys but in less demanding explorations. In this section, we present eight very varied routes. All are journeys that take less than two hours, and in Journey 20 we have the shortest journey in this book. Just 17 minutes, but when you buy a ticket on the St Mary's Community Bus (on the Isles of Scilly) you are also buying a slice of island life. That's not the only island route in this section of the book, for we also include the Isle of Wight. ■

MORE FAVOURITE JOURNEYS

The following routes from this region were included in *Bus-Pass Britain* (2011): Newbury to Andover, Trowbridge to Swindon, Wells to Taunton, Bournemouth to Swanage, Exeter to Poole, Minehead to Lynmouth, Plymouth to Dartmouth, Helston to Penzance and the Haytor Hoppa service on Dartmoor.

INTO THE MAGIC FOREST
PONY COUNTRY

Jane Westlake

13

Southampton

Service no. 6 | Journey time 70mins

OS Landranger 196. Hourly Mon–Sat daytime, five journeys Sun.
Operator: Bluestar.

Lymington ←

O n this bus trip it is the ponies that have the right of way. The West Quay shopping mall in Southampton, often with a visiting ocean liner as backdrop, is our starting point. Along the way, we delve right into the heart of the New Forest, once a royal hunting ground where commoners still exercise their rights and the animals roam free. **Wonderland** continues with the opportunity to see the original Alice's grave and once out of the woods we're deposited in the yachting haven and former smugglers' port of Lymington.

The good-natured queue at the bus stop just outside **West Quay** is growing steadily as it's a Saturday – market day in Lymington. If you are here at the right time you may hear a hymn by local lad Isaac Watts sounded by the Southampton Civic Centre clock. It is the old favourite 'Oh God, Our Help in Ages Past.' However, there's no need for divine intervention as Bluestar has laid on one of their finest blue double-decker buses. So today there's room for everyone and with a flurry of shopping trolleys we clamber aboard.

Once we're clear of the scruffier part of the city, where I used to live as a student in the 1970s, a glance to the left reminds me that **Southampton** is still a major passenger and cargo port.

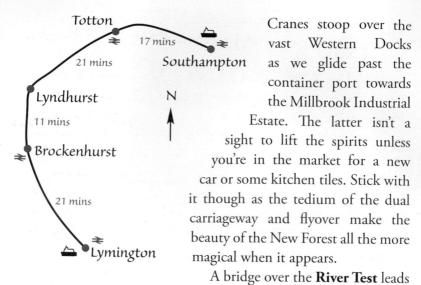

Totton

17 mins

21 mins

Southampton

Lyndhurst

N

11 mins

Brockenhurst

21 mins

Lymington

Cranes stoop over the vast Western Docks as we glide past the container port towards the Millbrook Industrial Estate. The latter isn't a sight to lift the spirits unless you're in the market for a new car or some kitchen tiles. Stick with it though as the tedium of the dual carriageway and flyover make the beauty of the New Forest all the more magical when it appears.

A bridge over the **River Test** leads us to Totton where we exchange a few passengers opposite the church of St Theresa. The soft yellow building with a statue of the 'Little Flower' seems out of place next to a Chinese take-away.

Into the Woods

The bus is now weaving on and off the A35, here and there serving the **edgeland sprawl** of estates of bungalows. This land of one-storey dwellers gives way to big trees, long drives and smart homes hidden away in woodland glades.

Bob, a fellow passenger who makes full use of his bus pass, is on his way to Lyndhurst to top up his stamp collection. He tells me about his old job delivering furniture, before the days of mobile phones. 'Addresses in the New Forest were often a challenge,' he recalls. 'We couldn't find them. It was just a house name, no street or number.'

We've passed the New Forest Hotel at **Ashurst** and woods are now hugging either side of the forest road. We're looking out for ponies and deer but instead we spot walkers appearing and disappearing like a magic trick among the oak and beech glades. A group of them hail the bus and scramble upstairs. The woodland then morphs into **heathland**, which changes colour with the seasons: vibrant yellow gorse, purple heather or burnt orange as the bracken dies down.

Bob is on his feet as we pass on the left a Lyndhurst landmark, Bolton's Bench, a handsome yew-topped hill. Hop off at the Lyndhurst Park Hotel bus stop if you want to visit the village. Don't miss **St Michael and All Angels**, the village's Victorian red-brick church. It has a large painted fresco recalling the parable of the wise and foolish virgins by Frederic Leighton and glorious stained-glass windows. Behind the church you'll find the grave of a woman who as a little girl was the inspiration for Alice in *Alice's Adventures in Wonderland*. She grew up to be Mrs Reginald Hargreaves and that's the name on her grave.

If you fancy a tea or coffee while curled up on a big settee, opposite St Michael's is **Crown Manor House Hotel** (☎ 02380 282922) where non-residents are welcome in both the lounge and the bright restaurant. The **Greenwood Tree** café and restaurant down the other end of High Street (65 High St; ☎ 02380 282463; open daily 08.30-17.00, and additionally 18.00–21.00 Thu–Sat) is a good place to refuel whether you want a homemade main course, cream tea or their speciality, waffles, before you're back on the number 6, heading south towards the coast.

This next stretch of the route is one of my favourites with the Lymington River flowing nearby. We pass the Balmer Lawn

NEW FOREST INFORMATION

Whatever information you seek or activity you wish to follow the **New Forest Visitor Information Centre and Museum** with its well-informed staff is a good place to start (Main Car Park, Lyndhurst; ☎ 023 8028 2269; www.thenewforest.co.uk; open daily 10.00-17.00). They have books, maps and walking guides for sale and free leaflets including one with details of an **eight-mile circular walk** around Lyndhurst Parish. There is also information on horse riding and cycling and there's a gift shop.

VERDERERS AND AGISTERS

There are ten Verderers who regulate and protect the commoners' interests and preserve the natural beauty of the **New Forest**. They appoint five Agisters who help with the management of the commoners' livestock in the Forest. The Verderers sit in open court on the third Wednesday of each month at the **Verderers' Hall** in Lyndhurst. The hall isn't open to the public except on court days, but the Clerk to the Verderers (☎ 023 8028 2052) is often willing to give visitors access on weekdays if advised in advance. Look out for the **Rufus's Stirrup**, used to determine whether a dog would be a threat to royal hunting. If a dog couldn't pass through the stirrup the animal's toes were cut off, or the owner paid a fine.

Hotel which was used during World War I as an army hospital for wounded Indian and New Zealand troops. As we draw into **Brockenhurst**, we see a pony trimming the grass around the war memorial.

We pass, and some may be tempted to stop, at a pub with a story. **The Snakecatcher** at Lyndhurst Road in Brockenhurst was originally called the Railway Inn, but was renamed after Harry 'Brusher' Mills who used to drink here (☎ 01590 622348). He lived in a charcoal burner's hut in the New Forest and made his living from catching snakes, some of which he was said to have sold to London Zoo.

We're now driving slowly across heathland under the watchful gaze of the **ponies**. They're mooching about in convivial groups and although they appear to be wild they are owned by commoners exercising their rights to use the common pasture. Another common right, called Mast, lets the owners turn out their pigs to gobble up acorns and beechmast. There are about 700 commoners; the rights attach to the land they own or rent.

A mother and foal meander across the road and our driver breaks gently. A child who's been kicking the back of my seat is thankfully transfixed by them. The **deer** are more skittish and tend to occupy quieter parts of the forest. Sadly there's a problem throughout the forest with drivers who hit animals but fail to stop. **William the Conqueror** designated the New Forest a royal hunting ground more than 900 years ago. It's now a National Park but still maintains its tradition of Verderers and Agisters (see box opposite).

There's a small detour for the modern Lymington New Forest Hospital which is set next to a retail park. It's a shock to the senses after the soft lawns, forest glades and heath. Ultimately, though, it is a reminder of the appeal of the New Forest. It is an area of England which has not kept modernity at a distance. It's there but in its place. So there's still space for ponies.

GEORGIAN DELIGHT

Daniel Defoe described the main commercial activities of the people of Lymington as 'smuggling and rogueing.' There's little evidence of this as we pass **St Thomas's Church** with its elegant cupola. The bus is making slow progress and restless passengers, keen to enjoy the market, descend before the final stop. The wares reflect local concerns and pastimes: fishing rods and waders, golf clubs, local fish, meat and cheese, beautiful handmade crafts and of course – there being lots of dog owners – items for their pets to chew, eat or sleep in.

The last stragglers and I thank the driver as we descend at the compact bus station. **Lymington** is ever pleasant but positively bustles on market days. Much of the architecture is Georgian. The high street slopes down to a cobbled area, Quay Hill, where many shops have bow-fronted windows. Just beyond is Town Quay by the Lymington River which is still used as a base by commercial fishing boats and the town's a popular sailing centre. ■

ABOUT THE AUTHOR | **JANE WESTLAKE** is a former BBC producer. She used to travel this route regularly with her mother who, like Jane, enjoys a good piece of cake.

Beautifully Bleak
Visiting West Wight

Emily Bullock

14 Newport 🚌

Service no. 12 | Journey time 48mins

OS Landranger 196. Four journeys daily Mon–Sat, three on Sun.
Operator: Southern Vectis.

Totland

Tourists are attracted by the Isle of Wight's sandy beaches, local ice cream, adventure parks, and water sport activities. But my quest is rather different. Southern Vectis's bus number 12 goes to **West Wight** – and that's the part of the island where I was born. Ignoring warnings about the possible dangers that attend trips down memory lane, I found myself queuing for the bus and realised how times have changed. Nowadays, you have to get there early if you want a front window seat on the top deck.

This is a journey that **recalls my childhood**, holidays and family visits. We would get the bus from the brick-and-stone sprawl of Newport; head out along the salty rush of the Military Road to the Needles at the westernmost extremity of Wight. It has an end-of-the world feel with its lighthouse and white rocks, threading sea and sky together.

I have moved away, grown older, but the island hasn't changed. It is still populated with tea rooms and ice cream vans. Taking my seat on the top deck, I imagine I'm wearing long socks and hand-knitted cardigans again, mouth itching for a lick of sugary rock. The Isle of Wight is often both praised and dismissed for being **wedged in the 1950s** – austerity Britain and technicolor hopes for the future. So this is the perfect moment to revisit my childhood. But nostalgia comes at a price. Almost a fiver for a 48-minute journey.

Island roads are different. Street signs remind drivers of this but it isn't until the bus starts that I remember it really is so. The driver isn't off-roading or aiming for cars on the other side – he is avoiding potholes. Perhaps the ride is rougher upstairs, but sit downstairs and the only view would be high hedges and cycle helmets. The bus leaves **Newport** bus station, leading me through the town like a giant in a miniature village. The top floor of the buildings have evidently not changed over the centuries while the high street shop façades reinvent themselves every season.

My first disappointment comes as the bus climbs west towards Carisbrooke and I realise none of the schools I attended still exist. But not everything has changed. We pass Spring Lane which leads to **Carisbrooke Castle**. The ford on that lane was the perfect place to float in an upside-down umbrella!

Cutting through the Downs

It is a cold day but sun fills the upper deck, the heating is pumping, and coats are coming off. This is the scenery I remember: **patchwork downland** on all sides as the bus travels the Bowcombe Road between Carisbrooke and Shorwell. There are aerodynamic displays by low-flying seagulls as we glide past working farms and forgotten farms. Although not completely forgotten, the route passes through many small villages ending in 'stone' – a suffix declaring it is a farmstead. Maps don't forget.

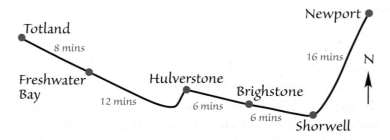

LOOKING SOUTH

West from Shorwell, the bus follows the B3399 through Brighstone to Hulverstone. There are useful pubs along the way. You might try the **Three Bishops** on Brighstone Main Road (☎ 01983 740226) or the **Sun Inn** in Hulverstone, a hostelry for over 600 years (☎ 01983 741124; open daily from 12.00) Both pubs offer varied menus featuring local produce and seafood. The bistro and bar **Seven** by St Mary's Church in Brighstone has B&B accommodation. The menu offers everything from a full English breakfast to Thai Red Chicken Curry, using locally sourced food and drink (☎ 01983 740370; open daily from 9.00 Jun–Sep, and daily exc Mon from 10.00 Oct–May).

The winter scene outside the window has the faded feel of a bleached-out photograph. Perhaps the memories are a little older than I would want to admit. Can I still claim to be a true islander if I haven't lived here for over 18 years? No-one knows me on the bus, but a few faces have nodded recognition to each other. Have I finally become a grockle (an island word for a holidaymaker)?

Cheverton Farm comes up on the left, open for lambing days and cycle events. I am taken back to summer holidays: driving along these roads, the bus smelling of wild garlic as it brushed past the hedgerows. Going under the wooden footbridge at Shorwell Shute feels like entering a fairytale land: thatched cottages and stone walls mark the way. The bus also stops for its first walkers, carrying wooden sticks as they come down from Brighstone forest.

On the horizon above the village of **Shorwell** the coast emerges, reminding me this is an island. Sea running into sky until it is hard to tell which is which. A buzzard watches from a tree, then flies off towards Limerstone; the bus follows.

To the seaside

Brighstone with the old St Mary's Church, village shop, local museum and small cottages, conforms to most people's imaginary village of the 1950s: the shop has goods stacked outside in baskets and an array of primrose plants for sale – a nice hint that spring is on the way. I want to stop just to touch such brightness. A chalkboard lists island produce for sale: honey, milk, cheese, garlic. Plenty to fill a lunch box before setting off along a footpath; with names like Hunny Hill or Strawberry Lane.

We pass **Mottistone Manor Garden** (☎ 01983 741302), a place for floral magic with herbaceous borders and hidden pathways. The bus reaches Hulverstone and I get my first glimpse of the white cliffs of Tennyson Down. This is a journey full of literary connections. Moments later we pause at Brook, one-time home to J B Priestley: novelist, playwright, and broadcaster.

The bus turns right at Brook Chine onto the **Military Road**. The Chine itself is worth a visit, with the chance to see surfers, dogs chasing big waves, and children hunting in rock pools. I remember the smell of coconut from summer days here, rising off the sun worshippers stretched out on the beach.

The Military Road sounds like a harsh place to be; the twisted trees whisper of icy winds and thundering rain. The bus slows as it climbs the downs; rabbit warrens have eaten into the sandy earth. But as it reaches the top, Freshwater appears, rolling green down to the pebble beach. The sun comes out and sparks across

Lighthouse at the Needles (photo © Simon Greig / DT)

the sea on my left. This road and these rocks will work their way out there too; there is only so long the Isle of Wight can hold onto this route. **Frequent landslips** can result in road closures. When we were young, my sister and I thought lying in the middle of the road (when it was closed, of course) was the funniest thing to do, made even more ridiculous by sharing a box of *After Eights* at the same time. So if the bus is diverted you might like to try this out; I can recommend it. But for now, the Military Road spreads itself out along hills and knolls.

Standing sentinel above **Freshwater Bay** is Tennyson's Monument, a stone cross pointing up through the blue. The grockles decant, evidently keen to see the coloured sands and rocket launch test site at the **Needles**. Our bus continues to Freshwater town centre, with its tiny parade of shops, such as Val's Collectables and the Rock and Rose tattoo parlour.

The last stop is Totland War Memorial where I am the only person to get off the bus. End of the line. The woman occupying the front seat since Newport is in no mood to give it up and stays on board. The driver wishes me a good day and circles around the memorial heading back to Newport.

As a child, I recall many a bright afternoon on **Totland's pebbly beach**. I turn right down Madeira Road towards Turf Walk and the promenade. Battered by winter storms and the economic downturn, Totland stands precariously, like the pier that for years has been crumbling into the sea, on the point of being bypassed by tourists. Perhaps this is its aim because the tranquillity of grass and sea and pebbles and nothing else, is peaceful – beautifully bleak indeed. Perhaps I am still an islander because when I close my eyes I smell sea salt on wood. And still I hear the beat of the waves against the struts of Totland pier. Yes, this really is like coming home. ∎

ABOUT THE AUTHOR | **EMILY BULLOCK** is a writer and university lecturer. You can find out more about her work at www.emilybullock.com.

THE WIMBORNE FLYER

June Webber

15

Poole

Service no. 3 | Journey time 33mins

OS Landranger 195. Twice hourly Mon–Sat.
Operator: Wilts and Dorset.

Wimborne Minster

Sometimes, the corporate world manages to get things just right. Managers actually listen to their clients. And the operators of the number 3 bus from Poole to Wimborne Minster did just that a year or two ago when this short but undeniably useful bus route was **peremptorily axed** from the schedules. Local councillors led the charge and aggrieved bus users turned out *en masse* to a protest meeting in a local school hall.

The bus company is a well-established local name: Wilts and Dorset. Note the 'Wilts.' Not Wiltshire, but Wilts. Only recently has the company adopted a more modern demeanour by branding itself *More*. Very minimalist, very chic, very brand-conscious. Just check out www.morebus.co.uk. *More* buses are now a common sight in and around Poole on the south coast of England. And Poole is the starting point for the ride to Wimborne Minster.

It is a **picturesque route** from Poole covering countryside, coast and town, with superb views over Holes Bay, before turning inland following the old railway track to Broadstone. It meanders around Corfe Mullen, and then runs through the Dorset countryside to the pretty market town of Wimborne Minster.

The bus is popular with pensioners and mothers for shopping, appointments or leisure activities, and at peak times with commuters and school children. It is a bus route for all ages, and a **journey for all seasons**. No surprise perhaps that so many folk breathed a mighty sigh of relief when the decision to withdraw the service was reversed. I live in Broadstone, and as the proud owner of a bus pass, I am a regular on the number 3. The bus makes sense, and it avoids the knotty issue of finding a parking place in Poole or Wimborne Minster.

EXPRESS STYLE

The journey begins at **Poole** bus station, conveniently outside the Dolphin shopping centre. A full brigade of bright blue *More* buses with their red trim and white lettering stand in formation at the bus station. *More* in waiting, ready to advance, ready to fan out in many directions. To Swanage and Sandbanks. There are shoppers heading home to Waterloo, a pair of lovers heading for Alderney – a district northeast of Poole rather than the island off the coast of Normandy – and a very tall man asking for the bus to Lilliput. Yes, we have our fair share of **oddball toponyms** around Poole.

Bang on time, we pull away from Stand D. *More* works to the minute. I prefer the left side of the bus. It affords fine views of **Holes Bay**, an inlet on the north side of Poole Harbour. This is the liminal zone where land and sea meet. A modern block of flats on the edge of the shore is built in the shape of a ship. Bright orange lifeboats can be glimpsed outside the RNLI headquarters and college, and small boats are moored in the bay.

At low tide, one can see wading birds searching for worms in the mud, and ducks swim amongst the reeds and patches of grass. To the left are Pergins Island and **Creekmoor Viaduct** which carries the railway line from London to Weymouth across the bay. The Purbeck Hills can be seen in the distance. Walkers and cyclists follow the path around the bay, between the road and the shore. On the bus, pensioners are chatting and teenagers texting or listening to music.

TURNING INLAND

At a roundabout displaying a huge anchor, the bus turns inland and follows the route of the old railway track from Bournemouth West. The bus does not stop again until it reaches **Broadstone**, taking only twelve minutes from Poole. It is this short, fast stretch

Wimborne Minster Church of St Cuthburga
(photo © Ian Woolcock / DT)

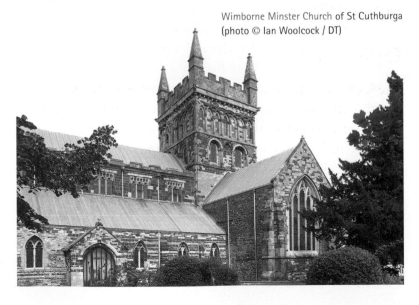

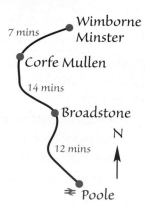

7 mins — Wimborne Minster

Corfe Mullen

14 mins

Broadstone

N

12 mins

≈ Poole

that prompts us locals to dub the bus 'The Wimborne Flyer.'

We pause at the Broadway in Broadstone, a place that, although now really part of Poole, still has a village-like atmosphere with a strong community spirit. Beyond Broadstone the pace is slower. We cross the line of an old **Roman road** that was once used to haul goods from the coast to the interior of Wessex. The bus winds through the straggling village of **Corfe Mullen**, stopping frequently. We loop round quiet residential roads and past shops, churches, a pub and the village hall. A menswear and hat-hire shop is curiously isolated, with no other shop nearby.

The next stage is flat, open country with meadows and trees. Approaching **Wimborne Minster** from the southwest there is a view of the solid square towers of the **Minster Church of St Cuthburga**. We reach the town centre by crossing the River Stour on Julian's Bridge – a sturdy seven-arched structure that's been carrying traffic for almost 400 years. The Green Man to the left is covered in hanging baskets and window boxes in the summer. This pub is a good place to relax and watch the world go by.

The bus stop is in West Borough, just off the square in the centre of town. On the corner of the square is the King's Head, a grey 18th-century coaching hotel which serves good food in elegant surroundings. Ahead is the Tivoli, a charming **Art Deco theatre** which doubles as a cinema. It had been threatened with demolition in 1979, but was saved, and is now largely staffed by volunteers. It is a nice reminder that community action is a great asset in preserving England's infrastructure. ∎

ABOUT THE AUTHOR | **JUNE WEBBER** is a former teacher. She has lived in Broadstone with her husband since 2006. They have four daughters and seven grandchildren. June is a keen walker.

THREE TOWNS AND A LOAF OF BREAD

Jacqueline Suffolk

Wimborne Minster

Service no. 83 | Journey time 75mins

OS Landranger 195, 194, 183. Six journeys daily Mon–Sat, no service on Sun.
Operator: Damory Coaches.

Shaftesbury

Ah! So you made it to Wimborne Minster. That's good. Came in on the number 3 from Poole, did you? That's the previous journey in this book. Well, I'd like to invite you on a journey upriver. We'll catch the number 83 for a **classic Dorset rural ride** that will take us up the River Stour to the Georgian town of Blandford Forum.

Then we'll follow a little left-bank tributary of the Stour called the Iwerne up into the hills. There's a **touch of theatre** in this journey and the final act of the play is quite something: our route ends in the hilltop town of Shaftesbury, a place with a

---

A DASH OF RURAL HISTORY

The **Priest's House Museum** in Wimborne Minster tells the story of changing times in the Stour Valley and this region of eastern Dorset. It has an eclectic range of artefacts from Roman frescoes to Victorian Valentine cards. But the real strength of the museum is the manner it brings **rural history** to life. There's a Victorian school room and a working Victorian kitchen where the aromas evoke memories for me of my grandmother's cooking (☎ 01202 882533; www.priest-house.co.uk; open daily 10.00–16.30 exc Sun from Apr–Oct).

---

strong medieval heritage that for an older generation is intimately associated with a celebrated series of **Hovis advertisements**.

But let's not rush. Wimborne is a place to linger. My family has done just that. Lingering here on the banks of the River Stour for generations. **Wimborne** is a place for any time of year, but perhaps best in autumn when the various deciduous trees around the River Stour sweep through a rich palette of russet and ochre. Watch the wash of the Stour under the bridges and past watermills. Explore the Minster and listen out for the Quarter Jack which has been ringing out the quarter hour for over 400 years.

THE STOUR VALLEY

The Quarter Jack sounds and our bus pulls away on the morning ride to Shaftesbury. The service is run by Damory Coaches, a local operator based in Blandform Forum. Nowadays the company is part of the multinational Go-Ahead Group, but the Damory team wisely play the local card. That goes down well in these parts. The first section of the journey retraces the final portion of the preceding route, as we leave Wimborne by **Julian's Bridge**.

We pause at the riverside village of Sturminster Marshall, a five-syllable mouthful that is abbreviated locally to Stur. We Dorset

Hints of Hovis at Gold Hill in Shaftesbury
(photo © Jacqueline Suffolk)

folk don't waste our words. It has a pretty village green with an old maypole. Around the green are well-kept thatched cottages once inhabited by local farm workers.

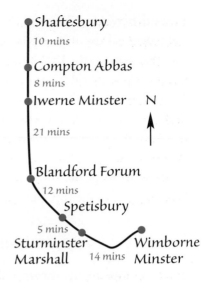

With Stur behind us, we continue along the A350 through **Spetisbury**, a riverside village which straddles the main road. It is remarkably popular with Dorset's discerning swans. They arrive each year in spring and rear their young in Spetisbury. They clearly recognise the village as a good spot for family life. And Spetisbury is good for walks too. Alight at the crossroads for a choice of two well-marked footpaths: either over the bridge to follow the Stour northwards or trace the route of the disused railway line (now the **North Dorset Trailway**). Both take you into Blandford three miles distant.

The town of Blandford is the pivot of our Dorset transect – the midpoint of our journey. It is hugely more attractive than the approach from the south on the bus might suggest. There is more to **Blandford Forum** than the Tesco car park. The tourist information office is on the right just before the bus stop in West Street, from where it is a stone's throw to the Georgian marketplace with its Corn Exchange and the Greyhound Inn. The latter was an important stopping point for stagecoaches. Blandford's good fortune to have such a fine range of **Georgian architecture** arose from a disaster. After a fire in 1731, which began in a candle-maker's shop and destroyed most of the buildings, the town was completely rebuilt in the Georgian style. The only buildings to escape any damage were the almshouses in Salisbury Street and the Old House in the Close, both worth a wander past. The new town was designed and rebuilt by the brothers John and William

Bastard between 1732 and 1760. Many of the buildings retain their original decorative plasterwork interiors. At the end of the market square is the Parish Church of St Peter and Paul, rebuilt in 1732 in the classical style and similar in design to Derby Cathedral. It retains its original box pews, galleries and mayoral seat.

Now it's time to continue north towards Shaftesbury. The hills gradually close in around the narrowing valley of the Stour. If you've the energy for a stiff walk, hop off the bus at the White Horse in **Stourpaine** and walk up Hambledon or Hod Hill. You'll be breathless at the top, but it's worth the effort for the fine views.

THE IWERNE AND BEYOND

As we climb up the **Iwerne Valley**, there is a happy litany of double-barrelled place names: Iwerne Minster, Sutton Waldron, Fontmell Magna and Compton Abbas. I can only marvel at how enormous lorries negotiate their way along this road between the hedges and high walls that mark the boundaries of rural estates. Climbing up the steep hills to either side of the main road are ancient rutted drove ways – the avenues of history that snake tantalisingly up into the creases of the rounded hills.

Reaching the highest part of the journey the views in all directions are spectacular. This is north Dorset at her glorious best. But today we seem to be not quite in luck. The low cloud that dances on the ridges is dropping down to envelop us.

Shaftesbury is the wonderful end point for this dramatic journey. It is every bit as Ridley Scott's iconic Hovis ad suggests. That advertisement used Dvořák' *New World Symphony* as its music. Take a look and you'll find Shaftesbury is in fact a very old world – some would suggest the **finest hill-top town** in England. But take a look for yourself. ∎

ABOUT THE AUTHOR | **JACQUELINE SUFFOLK** was born and raised near Wimborne. She is well known by friends and family for wandering off. This habit began about the age of two.

VINTAGE SEASIDE
OFF TO SAND BAY

Fraser Balaam

Weston-super-Mare

Service no. 1/100 | Journey time 20 to 30mins

OS Landranger 182. Two to five times hourly Mon–Sat, once or twice per hour Sun.
Operator: First and Crosville.

Sand Bay ⟵

When I was a boy, few things felt quite as daring as dangling an arm over the edge of the top deck of the **open-top bus** in Weston-super-Mare. Knowing that there was nothing but air between my fingers and the ground so far below added a frisson to the ride. Twenty years ago, as the wind whipped the curls of my hair across my eyes, my dad would clasp the toggles of my coat to rein me in as my spread hand reached for any overhanging branches that flicked by. Before my attention was stolen by trains, rockets and race cars, nothing was quite as captivating as sitting on a bus that exposed me to the summer drizzle. Nowadays, I'm dusted with a light nostalgia whenever an open-top bus rattles by, its passengers craning out of the upper deck, and that boyhood fascination belongs to the coastal route between my home town of **Weston-super-Mare** and its sedate neighbour, Sand Bay.

Departing from the railway station, the service winds quickly through Weston's town centre and onto the sea front. Weston's **waterfront and promenade** have had a thorough makeover since the turn of the century. Brushed stonework, new sea walling and a new gleam to the pier help undermine the common perception that the traditional seaside town is little more than peeling paintwork and crumbled paving. On a summer day, when the route to Sand Bay has open-top buses, this is a journey that is fun for all on board – and for me it is a journey that excites a few good memories.

Excited children on the seafront trade in the prospect of a donkey ride on the beach for a ride on the open-top bus. That the queue for the bus is so much shorter than the queue for the donkeys surely plays some part in the calculus. Up the top deck, life is a treasure. Childhood is shorter than the kids realise. They smile, and so too do their parents and grandparents. For all on the top deck, this is more than merely the bus to Sand Bay. It is a journey through childhood, one that for older travellers invites reflection on summer holidays of yesteryear.

A BUS WITH A VIEW

Slowly we get beyond the garish bars and penny arcades of the town centre. As **Knightstone Island** and **Marine Lake** appear, many passengers turn to take a look back towards the town, catching the smack of salty sea air in their faces. This is the classic view of Weston. Old picture postcards catch the sun creeping over the **Grand Pier** and Brean Down. The latter is the rocky peninsula which juts out into the Bristol Channel well south of the town. The grey, wave-like structure of the pier, much closer to hand,

THE GRAND PIER

Stretching for 430 yards out to sea, **Weston's Grand Pier** dominates the promenade and is arguably Weston's statement to the wider world (☎ 01934 620 238; www.grandpier.co.uk; open from 10.00 each day except Christmas Day). Well that, and the fact that this is the home town of **John Cleese**. Ripples of laughter from Weston-super-Mare have certainly made the world smile. First built in 1904, devastated by fire in 2008 and reopened two years later, the new-look pier squeezes in a **medley of attractions** from 4D cinema to go-karting. Admission to the pier is free.

WESTON WOODS

Weston is lucky to have a fabulous spread of woodland so close to the centre. The 130 hectares of Weston Woods make it easy to escape the fever of the town. **Footpaths** snake through dense woodland; some of them are wheelchair accessible. For younger visitors there's an **adventure playground** in a clearing with wooden fixtures including a particularly jerky zip line (tested in the name of research, of course). The conifers of Weston Woods were used to shore up the trenches of the Western Front during World War I, and in the heart of the woods are the remains of an **Iron Age hill fort**, with its crumbled ramparts and deep-storage pits visible. On many of the paths you'll be able to hear the sound of waves smoothly folding against the nearby shore.

gives a sense of scale. It's bold and almost overbearing in the way it overlooks the town and demands attention (see box opposite).

Passing **Knightstone Island**, the bus breaches a gentle crest and Birnbeck Pier comes into view. Opened in 1867, Weston's largely derelict pier has long lost its seaside charm. It recalls the heyday of Victorian seaside tourism, when visitors to Weston would often make a day trip by steamer over to the Welsh coast. Birnbeck rusts in isolation. Beyond the old pier, the Bristol Channel is interrupted by Flat Holm Island which edges above sea level like a rising submarine. **Flat Holm** has an intriguing history. It was, for example, used as an isolation hospital to protect mainland Britain from cholera in 1883. Sixty years later it had been fortified to provide protection against potential invasion in World War II. Its hump-shaped sister island Steep Holm, five miles from Weston, is also visible.

THE TOLL-FREE TOLL ROAD

Quickly leaving the town behind, the atmosphere changes as the bus approaches **Kewstoke Road**, which is commonly referred to locally as the toll road. A cliff-top stretch, the toll road is flanked on the left by a steep drop to the sea and on the right by the brooding dankness of **Weston Woods** – a place that in my imagination as a lad was definitely full of all manner of wild things (see box on page 83). We have swapped one Weston for another. The hue and cue of the brash seafront has been eclipsed by imposing nature. Occasionally, the toll road – which, incidentally, no longer charges a toll – gives views across Sand Bay. When I was young, it seemed so huge and I surely gasped at the sight. But beaches shrink as a boy turns into a man.

Thus, catching views and reaching out for overhanging branches, we weave our way through Kewstoke to reach **Sand Bay** – which is both a beach and a community. It is however a timid neighbour to bold Weston. It is a place to look across the water to Wales and to be battered by the winds that sweep up the Bristol Channel. The north end of Sand Bay is Sand Point, owned by the National Trust. It is an easy half-hour walk from the bus terminus to the grasslands of Sand Point from where one can look up the **Severn Estuary** to the two Severn bridges. To the northwest, there are clear views to the South Wales coastline, with the spikes of Cardiff's Millennium Stadium punching the horizon.

From bitter personal experience, **Sand Point** is a lousy place from which to launch a message in a bottle with any prospect of receiving a reply. I tried many times. But my most positive memory of that bus journey, beyond the breezy dangers of life on the top deck, is just the moment of arrival at Sand Bay. The mustard shore unfolded by the roadside. We'd run downstairs and hop off. My dad would put me on his shoulders and carry me down to the water's edge, where I'd meekly skim shells at the surface and collect sticks as if they had a resale value. Sand Bay is surely a good place to think about yesterday. ∎

ABOUT THE
AUTHOR

FRASER BALAAM grew up on the Somerset coast. Once, he was fined $100 for riding without a ticket on a bus in Sydney, Australia. He has learnt his lesson.

BRITAIN'S RAREST BUS

As bus stops go, the one at Dawlish Green on the coast of Devon is pretty handsome. There is the **salty tang of sea air**, and a cosy bus shelter that affords a little protection when a sharp east wind comes in off the bay. It is at this bus shelter that every afternoon a National Express coach decants the Midlands holidaymakers who come to Dawlish for a few days of sun, sea and sand.

The 337 is the most distinguished arrival of the day at Dawlish Green. 'That one is Rugby to Brixham. Quite a long haul,' says Fred who used to work on the buses and now sits in summer sunshine to watch the comings and goings at Dawlish Green. The 337 pauses at the bus shelter just after four every afternoon – an hour shy of the end of its long journey across England.

On this summer Saturday, there are many new arrivals. A single mum attends to a mountain of luggage, while one of her three charges makes a bid to escape. Fred helpfully goes to the rescue, restraining the toddler who is keen to catch a **glimpse of the sea**. The newcomers disperse, and we start to head off too.

'Don't go yet,' calls Fred. 'You'll miss the 113. She's due off the Green at half past four.' So we wait. And the 4.30 departure to **Tavistock** is indeed a rare sight to behold. For this is Britain's least-frequent bus service. It runs from March to October – but only on the fifth Saturday of each month. So in 2013 it ran just thrice – on 30 March, 29 June and 31 August.

The two-hour journey to Tavistock crosses the very heart of **Dartmoor**. The 113 is run by **Tavistock Country Bus**, a community transport association founded more than 30 years ago by Tavistock locals who felt that their area deserved better bus services (www.tavistockcountrybus.co.uk). Nowadays the association runs routes around the town and to nearby villages in the Tavy Valley. They run a route from Tavistock to Launceston in Cornwall. And from March to October they run special Saturday routes to Exeter, Truro, Plymouth, Torquay and – when there is a fifth Saturday in the month – to Dawlish.

This suite of Tavistock services are run entirely by **volunteers**. Concessionary passes are accepted on all services. All services are advertised as regular scheduled bus routes, so they run even if nobody turns up for the ride. ■

DIPPING INTO DEVON'S PAST

Janice Booth

Okehampton

Service no. 178 | Journey time 1hr 50mins

OS Landranger 191. Once daily Mon–Sat, no service on Sun.
Operator: Dartline Coaches.

Newton Abbot ←

I love the **rural Devon roadsides** on this route! Hedges and verges vary with the seasons, from scatterings of snowdrops in early spring through primroses, daffodils, foxgloves, wild roses, to nettles and bramble blossom. Finally we get the blackberries, hips and fading foliage of autumn. Here and there a gnarled tree survives in a hedgerow, an ancient stone wall underlies a bank, or a stream bubbles beside the road. Sheep and red Devon cattle graze in the fields, and crops ripen through deepening shades of green to dusty gold. Between gaps in the trees, the hills and tors of Dartmoor appear as a distant backdrop.

Landscapes of this kind have endured for millennia, and are so **rich in history**. In this case the medieval thatched cottages, centuries-old inns and much-loved little village churches are in areas where prehistoric monoliths, hut circles and burial cairns once stood, and the footprints of their early people stretch back a long, long way.

The 178 bus is a rare visitor to Market Street in Okehampton. It runs but once a day (and never on Sundays). It is the back-lane route to Newton Abbot, and for most of the journey the bus is within the boundaries of Dartmoor National Park. The lunchtime departure gives opportunity for exploring **Okehampton** before setting off. Some high-street shops have closed, but several small independent shops are flourishing, so there's every chance to buy a **homemade snack** for your journey (just follow the smell of fresh baking). Some attractive old buildings still survive and a little shopping arcade that replicates London's Burlington Arcade, but in miniature, is an unexpected treat.

Okehampton — 12 mins — Sticklepath — 12 mins — South Zeal
21 mins
Chagford — 15 mins — Moretonhampstead
15 mins
Lustleigh — 12 mins — Bovey
Tracey
23 mins
Newton
Abbot

N

GETTING UNDER WAY

The route is operated by a Devon company called Dartline Coaches. At its starting point in **Market Street**, the single-decker bus fills up quickly with local passengers, some of them shoppers and others off to visit friends. We head east out of town, quickly gaining open countryside, with fine views across Dartmoor to the right (the best views are on this side on the journey).

Soon we are plunging downhill into the valley of the infant **River Taw**, which we cross in Sticklepath, an attractive village with some fine thatched cottages. It's one of Dartmoor's four 'beacon villages' (South Zeal, South Tawton and Belstone are the others) located at the base of Cosdon Beacon, a broad 1,804-feet hill where signal fires were lit in medieval times and on which are many prehistoric remains. **Sticklepath** is also home to the Finch Foundry (☎ 01837 840046; open daily 11.00–17.00 mid-March till Oct), the last working water-powered forge in the country, now managed by the National Trust with a shop and café.

From Sticklepath, the bus heads for South Tawton and stops near its surprisingly large church of St Andrew. South Tawton was a royal manor at the time of the Domesday survey and its fertile land made for successful farming. Wealth from the wool trade expanded a smaller, probably 11th-century chapel into the mainly 15th-century granite church that dominates the village today. The picturesque thatched **Church House** beside it was built soon after 1490 as a parish centre where communal feasts and functions could be held (☎ 01837 840418; open on Sun May–Oct or phone to make an appointment).

More narrow, winding roads and thick hedges lead on through open country until the bus dips sharply down into **South Zeal**; watch out for the 16th-century King's Arms on the left and then, on the right, the 14th-century market cross in the churchyard of little St Mary's Chapel, with its distinctive turret for two bells. Directly after these comes the Oxenham Arms (see box on South Zeal below), where Charles Dickens stayed while writing *The Pickwick Papers*. Then soon you're climbing steeply out of the village again, with the outline of Dartmoor emerging distantly on the right. Sharp, blurred, misty, grey, calm, menacing – it's never the same two days running.

Heading more purposefully south, we cross the watershed into the **Teign Valley** and then descend into Chagford. On the way, we take in lovely open roads with views of gentle countryside

SOUTH ZEAL

There's so much history here. Long ago, the village was on the main road from Exeter to Cornwall, and back in 1298 was granted a royal charter for a weekly market. The **Oxenham Arms**, an imposing listed building looking more monastery than pub, was probably built by lay monks in the 12th century. It is one of Devon's oldest inns. Extraordinarily, set into the wall of one of its inside rooms is a huge **prehistoric standing stone**, supposedly about 5,000-years-old. Another room has a similar stone supporting the ceiling. The menu is somewhat more modern – I've had an **excellent meal** there – and the bedrooms are beautiful (☎ 01837 840244).

BREAKING YOUR JOURNEY

With only one daily 178 service running the full length of the route in each direction, you can't hop off to explore a village *en route* and then continue on the next bus. But other buses operate in the area. **Chagford**, for example, is served by a sister service from Dartline. That's the 173 which gives a link with both Exeter and Moretonhampstead. If you leave the 178 at **Moretonhampstead** or Bovey Tracey, you'll have even more onward connections to choose from. **Bovey Tracey** has an hourly service to Exeter (every two hours on Sundays). So, although the 178 takes in some pretty remote villages, if you choose your stopping-off point with care, you'll certainly not find yourself stranded.

Devon County Council produces a wonderful set of printed timetables that cover the county. If you are at all webwise, play with the **interactive bus map** at www.journeydevon.info. It is a wondrous tool, one which allows to bring up the current timetable for every route in the county at a mouse click.

and Dartmoor's rounded hills; glimpses of **Chagford** ahead show how tightly it is cradled by the moor to which it leads. It's a delightful little town, with twisty streets, a mix of old and new buildings and some good independent shops and eateries, including the **Devonshire Dairy** which offers honey and local lamb, an extensive hardware store selling far more than just hardware, handicraft shops and a busy central market. The striking 13th-century church of St Michael the Archangel, built with wealth from the tin trade, has been considerably restored but retains some appealing carvings, such as an angelic St Michael with flowing locks slaying a rather small demon.

Southward bound

Back on the main road beyond Chagford, the journey is faster and less strikingly rural for a while, although the traditional countryside still unfolds pleasantly. **Moretonhampstead** is a busy small town mixing old-world charm with modernity; it has some attractive old buildings and an atmospheric centre, but the bus only allows a few glimpses as it rattles through. After some rather tatty industrial buildings on its outskirts, the scenery becomes prettier, with flowers in the verges, open views, woods, and – when I last was there – a lone buzzard surveying the landscape from a treetop. Then the bus veers round a very sharp right turn and down a steep lane as it heads towards **Lustleigh**; don't miss the beautiful thatched cottage crouching on the right at the top of the lane.

To Lustleigh's benefit, although not to yours, the bus stops well short of the centre. After a switchback approach along narrow roads it drops passengers and turns round at two small restored gatehouses. Thus you'll miss a true picture-postcard village, with an array of thatched cottages, a 13th-century church and the yellow-painted Primrose tea rooms. If you're energetic, tired of the bus and have a suitable map, there's an easy walk (roughly three miles, along lanes) from Lustleigh to **Bovey Tracey**.

DRAWING TO A CLOSE

Back on the A382 after retracing the route from Lustleigh, the 'village' part of your journey is over, although the views are still pleasantly rural. Bovey Tracey is a friendly town, part traditional and part modern, notable for the wonderful gallery of the Devon Guild of Craftsmen at the Riverside Mill (☎ 01626 832223; open daily 10.00–17.30) and the House of Marbles with the world's longest marble run. I would be inclined to end the journey here, rather than continuing to Newton Abbot – which is nice enough, but much busier and noisier than the places you've been visiting. However, **Newton Abbot** does offer you rail links to Plymouth or Exeter (sit on the right for Exeter to get wonderful views across the Exe Estuary) and good bus services in either direction. ∎

ABOUT THE AUTHOR | **JANICE BOOTH** lives in Devon, within sight and sound of the sea. She has edited over 20 Bradt guides to various far-flung countries and co-written the Bradt guide to Rwanda.

By Bus Along the Atlantic Highway

Nicky Gardner

19

Barnstaple 🚐

Service no. 319 | Journey time 70 to 90mins

OS Landranger 180, 190. Four journeys daily Mon–Sat, no service on Sun.
Operator: Stagecoach.

Hartland ←

B uttered toast and crumpets are staple fare at the bus station in Barnstaple. Edith opts for a cuppa ('two sugars, please') and a round of toast ('extra butter if you don't mind, love'), then points out the sign that recalls the **Barnstaple elephant**. 'They dug up the poor beast over there. Just where that 319 to Hartland is waiting,' says Edith with evident Devon pride.

Actually, it was way back in 1844 that workmen unearthed a fossilised elephant, long before Barnstaple had buses. Long before the 319 ever ran out to Hartland. The story of Barnstaple's most **famous fossil** done and dusted, Edith turns her attention to the destination of the 319. 'I cannot imagine who goes all the way to Hartland,' she reflects. 'I've heard say it's like the end of the world out there. Very wild, so they say.'

My idea had been to head northeast from Barnstaple to the Exmoor coast. Odd, isn't it, how a chance meeting at a bus station can change your plans? Were it not for the elephant and Edith, I would never have boarded bus number 319 bound for **Devon's Atlantic extremity**.

Since then, I've thoroughly explored that route to Hartland, which several times each weekday is served by one of the smart double-deckers operated by Stagecoach. There are bus routes in

England which distil greater social magic, and there are journeys which take in more dramatic scenery. But the 319 captures quite perfectly the sense of heading out to the end of the world. Hartland is just as Edith suggested: very wild.

CROSSING THE TAW

North Devon has two great tidal estuaries, the Torridge and the Taw. Route 319 takes in both of them before sweeping west to Clovelly and Hartland – high ground to port, the sea off to starboard. Grand stuff, but the departure from Barnstaple is more prosaic. The bus tussles with **Barnstaple** traffic, eventually making its escape from the town centre across Long Bridge which has for over 700 years escorted travellers across the River Taw – though presumably medieval man did not plan the original structure with double-deck buses in mind. No doubt the bridge's sixteen masonry arches have been many times widened and strengthened over the centuries.

'An ancient and respectable market town,' I read of Barnstaple in a 200-year-old copy of *Crosby's Gazetteer*. The editors then go on to praise the town's 'handsome piazza, ornamented with a statue of Queen Anne.' Cast a glance back, as the bus purrs over **Long Bridge**, and Barnstaple looks handsome enough. Look forward to the far bank of the Taw and I am confronted by quite another Barnstaple. Where once the woollen industry was diligently prosecuted, now there is an urban wilderness of vast supermarket sheds and DIY stores. Come, come now! This is not the Devon of the tourist brochures, but rather a soulless Tescoland, a triffid sprawl impertinently casting a maze of modernity over the banks of the River Taw.

Our bus driver rather depressingly follows the road sign marked 'superstore', though this turns out to have one building of interest. Buried away amid the shopping park (a scarred wasteland that is anything but park-like) is **Barnstaple Station**, a little gem of antique railway architecture that is mightily inconvenient for travellers bound for the middle of Barnstaple.

Bideford and beyond

A few more passengers join at the station, and we are now on our way. The driver manoeuvres the double-decker into the fast flow of traffic on the Atlantic Highway, a road so over-engineered as to defy the warp and weft of Devon topography. It is a fast dash, and those on board are distracted by their mobile phones. 'No Tipping' proclaim the signs in a lay-by. No-one notices **Kittymoor Brake** or Huish Moor: the cool analytics of cartography are reduced to a blur on the top deck as our driver rushes to reclaim minutes lost in that loop through Tescoland.

You meet all sorts on the top deck. Today, the star of the show is a retired engineer from London, on holiday in Devon, who is making a quick hop from Barnstaple to Bideford. 'Just to see the Torridge Bridge,' he says. I make the dreadful mistake of assuming that the **Torridge Bridge** is the venerable old stone bridge that crosses the Torridge in the heart of Bideford. 'No, no. That's the old

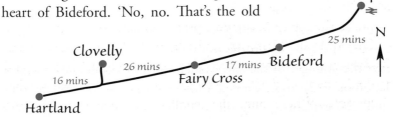

one,' he says. 'I'm more interested in new bridges.' He tells us how back in the eighties he helped design the Torridge Bridge. 'It perfectly combined aesthetics with economy,' he adds with a smile and proudly recounts how the new bridge won an award from the Concrete Society.

Within a few minutes we are cruising over that new bridge. It is wonderful, a delicate span over a silken estuary. Downstream there are views over tidal sandbanks towards **Appledore**, while upstream there is a glorious vista of Bideford, hugging the west bank of the river. There the old stone bridge is the centrepiece.

Bideford is as good close-up as that first glimpse from the new bridge promised. The bus route nicely contrives to reveal Bideford from all angles. The 319 stops on the quayside, where there are signs for the ferry connection to the Isle of Lundy. It sweeps past the town hall, a fussy mock-Tudor creation, then up through back streets to regain open country.

We pass through a medley of Devon villages and then, back on the A39, head west to Fairy Cross. A few years ago, few travellers on the A39 even noticed Fairy Cross. It was just one of dozens of inconsequential hamlets on the Atlantic Highway. That was before the inhabitants of **Fairy Cross** hit on the inspired idea of embellishing their village with the finest bus shelters in England. Each side of the road, there is a striking **hexagonal stone shelter** with a slate roof. Those waiting for the bus to the coast at Hartland enjoy aquamarine décor. Move to the other side of the road for buses to Bideford and Barnstaple and the design theme is orange. The latter shelter is dedicated to the memory of local farm manager Robert Davies who died in an accident in 2005. 'Make time to stand and stare. Bob Davies would have appreciated this,' reads the inscription.

I am in luck. Two villagers are waiting for our bus. They climb aboard and join us on the top deck. 'Ah, yes, the bus shelters,' says the younger of the two women, sensing my interest in these fabulous structures. 'Caused a lot of problems hereabouts, they did,' she explains, going on to recount the story of how other villages on the A39 thought they might copy the example set by Fairy Cross. I wondered if armed brigades went out from Fairy Cross by night to destroy rival bus shelters. 'There was talk for a while of bus-stop wars,' says the woman but declines to elaborate.

TO THE COAST

The bus dips down past **Hoops Inn** (☎ 01237 451222). This old pub, a labyrinth of a place, makes a good spot to break the journey to Hartland for a couple of hours. Then it detours to the coast to serve Clovelly, a wee slip of a village that tumbles down to the coast. It is mightily popular with tourists, and levies a hefty entrance fee. Its crowded car park suggests that there are plenty of visitors willing to pay to see **Clovelly**.

The route of the 319 beyond Clovelly seems almost to have been designed as a reaction to the village. Now it is time to really get off the beaten track. We leave the A39 for the last time and take to back lanes for the final part of the journey to Hartland. The landscape suggests that Cornwall cannot be far away. It is suddenly altogether bleaker. This is territory where, over the centuries, life has often been a struggle. Farmers and peasants turned to God for support, and this corner of Devon boasts large churches that once gathered huge congregations. The Church of England and

The 319 in front of Hoops Inn (photo © hidden europe)

BUS NOTES

Hartland may seem like the end of the road, but there is a good connection into the **Jackett's Coaches** service that runs south across the Cornish border to Bude. The last bus of the day from Barnstaple to Hartland continues through to **Bude** without any need to change vehicles. The short hop onward from Hartland to Bude takes an additional 30 minutes.

Methodism tussled for the souls of folk in and around Hartland, both leaving a strong imprint on the landscape. Devonians in the remote northwest of the county were seduced by neither, looking instead for a compromise. They discovered in the **Bible Christian Society** a home-grown Church that took elements of Anglican and Wesleyan liturgical practice and threw in a dose of Quaker piety to create a uniquely local religion.

Our bus slows to allow a passenger to alight at the **Providence Chapel**, built in the 19th century by the Bible Christian Society. The stern building bears the bold inscription 'I believe in Church and State and all other religions that do good.' No mention of God, strangely.

We roll down into **Hartland**, the village's irregular main street made all the nicer by the raised pavement on the north side. What did Edith say back in Barnstaple? 'It's like the end of the world out there.' And it is. A fierce west wind funnels through Hartland. Undeterred, I take to footpaths to explore the old port and the imposing cliffs. Offshore lies Lundy, serenely beautiful. 'Make time to stand and stare,' was the wording on that dedication to Bob Davies on the bus shelter back at Fairy Cross. Here, at the very **edge of England**, where Devon meets the sea, that maxim seems like very good advice. ■

ABOUT THE AUTHOR | **NICKY GARDNER** is a Berlin-based travel writer and great devotee of Slow Travel. She is co-editor of *hidden europe* magazine and also co-editor of this book.

COMMUNITY SPIRIT IN THE ISLES OF SCILLY

Jenny Byers

20 St Mary's

Service unnumbered | Journey time 17mins

OS Landranger 203. Five to eight times daily Easter to Oct.
Operator: St Mary's Community Bus.

circular route

If you want to know what's going on in the skies above the Isles of Scilly, then the **bus driver** is the man to ask. For Steve Sims, who runs the community bus service on the largest island in the archipelago, is more than just a bus driver. He is a part-time astronomer, a regular presenter on Radio Scilly and has latterly even turned his hand to writing a pantomime. Steve deftly combines these many trades, so listeners to **Radio Scilly** can enjoy Steve's regular chats with passengers on his community bus service. The series is called *Request Stop* – true evidence, if ever it were needed, that buses are close to Steve's heart.

The community bus service on St Mary's was much improved in spring 2013 when Steve took delivery of a **new vehicle**. Steve is quick to qualify the description. 'To say brand new is pushing it a bit,' he admits. 'It's a Mercedes 790D that worked the streets of Plymouth for many years.' But for the residents of St Mary's it's a big change.

'I quite liked the old bus,' commented one local as the new vehicle made a debut tour of the island, Steve at the wheel and ready with a cheery wave for anyone along the road. That old community bus was homely, unreliable and carried ancient advertisements for a solicitor's practice in Burnley. The fading ads surely outlived the business they promoted. The new bus is pristine, clean and betrays no hint that it has over the years ferried passengers around Plymouth.

There are no regular scheduled bus services on the Isles of Scilly. Boats are a mainstay for travel between islands. Once ashore, everything is pretty walkable. On **Tresco**, the second largest island in the archipelago, the casual visitor might hitch a ride on the motorised golf carts that roam the island's few lanes. On **St Mary's**, the dial-a-ride Buzza Bus offers a pre-bookable door-to-door service for the elderly and infirm. That apart, islanders look to their legs, bicycles or Steve's seasonal community bus to get around St Mary's. Bus passes are not valid. Steve wants cash on the nail. Fares are cheap, so no-one quibbles. Islanders get a modest discount, and Steve has the knack of knowing precisely who is and who is not an islander.

Leaving Hugh Town

On the face of it, this is a **no-frills bus service** that loops around St Mary's, starting and ending in Hugh Town. But that's not to reckon with Steve – a master of witty asides and a fabulous source of information on everything to do with the Isles of Scilly (and the skies above the islands). He tailors his commentary to whoever

---

ISLAND CAPITAL

To say that St Mary's has a capital is perhaps to over-egg the grandeur of **Hugh Town**. But it does the administrative biz for the islands, and it is here that the daily ferry from Penzance arrives. The boat, run by the **Isles of Scilly Steamship Company**, is a lifeline link with the wider world. It is a passengers-only affair, so you'll not find the roads of St Mary's crowded with tourists' cars. That, for many visitors, is the strong appeal of the Isles of Scilly. Pick up the current timetable for **Steve's bus** at the tourist information centre (☎ 01720 424031) in the middle of Hugh Town.

---

happens to be aboard on any particular journey and is especially adept at catering to specialist needs. 'Ah, here for the birds, I guess,' says Steve as a trio of twitchers climb aboard in **Hugh Town**. As we head towards Telegraph, Steve follows through with a few tips on where might be the best places to spot some of the island's wonderful birdlife. So even if you are not heading anywhere in particular, the St Mary's community bus is a good place to learn about the island.

From the moment we leave Hugh Town, there is a feast of **beautiful scenery**. Much of the journey is along narrow country roads, bounded by drystone walls, dotted with wild flowers, remnants of dark fir trees, pittosporum and gorse. We pass fields of heavenly scented flowers in early season, for which the islands are renowned, and pockets of habitation. There are no fixed bus stops, but Steve will gladly pull in whenever there's the prospect of a passenger. And even when there's not! He'll often pull over just to have a chat with an islander standing at a front gate. One of the first clear landmarks is **Carreg Dhu**, a subtropical community garden a mile out of town along Telegraph Road. It's an exotic place to have a picnic, or play hide-and-seek with the kids. A minute or two later we pull up for a couple heading out to lunch at Juliet's Garden (☎ 01720 422228). It is a popular licensed restaurant with an outdoor terrace café. Next stop is at McFarlands Down, where there is a little cluster of houses.

Onward to Old Town

Steve drives back past the **Telegraph radio mast** and the old coastguard tower which is the highest point of St Mary's, at 165 feet above mean sea level. Passing the mast, Steve cannot resist the chance to plug the virtues of the local radio station which uses this mast to beam its signals across the archipelago. Now we are approaching the eastern extremity of St Mary's – about as far as one can get from Hugh Town. **Pelistry Lane** is a good place to break your journey. You can follow the road down to a beautiful secluded bay. The bus then returns to Hugh Town, sticking to a clockwise pattern, with stops at **Carn Vean Tea Gardens**, the indoor public swimming pool at Normandy and Old Town.

The penultimate stop is opposite Old Town Café by a lovely south-facing beach and cove which is flanked on one side by the 12th-century Old Town Church where evening services are still held by candlelight. This small community has **Old Town Inn**, which serves local ale and homemade bar food, and where folk nights and line dancing are held (☎ 01720 422301). Beyond the church you can take the coastal path to Peninnis, a rugged promontory off which many ships have been wrecked and where weather and sea have sculpted the rocks into remarkable formations. With its springy turf, heathland and some stimulating scrambling, **Peninnis** is another of nature's playgrounds for children. You can continue around the coast to Porthcressa beach, or return to Old Town and wait for Steve's next circuit on the bus. Three minutes on the community bus is all that's needed to whisk you from the sedate charms of **Old Town** back to the only slightly less sedate bustle of the island's capital. ∎

ABOUT THE
AUTHOR

JENNY BYERS is an islander who returned to the Isles of Scilly permanently in 2005. She volunteers for the Memory Café, Theatre Club and League of Friends and dabbles in art.

WALES & THE MARCHES

Wales packs more of interest to bus travellers in a compact area than many mid-sized European countries. Yet bus travel to and within the Principality can be **a real bargain**. An 'Arriva Day Saver' ticket for Wales and northwest England costs just £6.50 and covers an area that extends from Manchester to Anglesey and Ceredigion. The company offers a weekly ticket for the same area for just £19.

For us, the real delight of bus travel in Wales lies less in the routes operated by big mainstream operators but in travelling with smaller, **locally based operators**. And there are dozens of them. Life suddenly takes on a different feel when you shift from one of the big players (like Arriva or Stagecoach) to a service run as a family business. Journey 26 in this book is run by **Richards Brothers**, a family-owned company that has for seventy years provided reliable transport around southwest Wales. The three brothers alluded to in the company name are Marteine, Malcolm and Nigel. We've travelled many times on their buses through the Pembrokeshire Coast National Park, and every journey is a treat. There is a real sense of a company that thrives on its links with the local community.

SPREADING WINGS FROM LLEYN

Some Welsh local bus operators can trace their roots back to the earliest days of rural bus travel in Wales. The villages of Clynnog and Trefor on the **Lleyn Peninsula** of northwest Wales felt they were being bypassed by the revolution in mobility which swept Britain in the early-20th century. So in 1912, they clubbed together and purchased a bus. Their initiative was called Moto

Coch (the Welsh for 'red bus'), but over time the name of the company evolved to reflect the names of the two villages where it was founded: **Clynnog & Trefor**. The original vehicle was a single-decker, but had a roof rack that could be used to transport small animals to market in Pwllheli.

Today Clynnog & Trefor run a web of school bus services across Gwynedd but still operate just one scheduled bus route. Fittingly, it is the service across the Lleyn Peninsula from **Caernarfon to Pwllheli** via Clynnog and Trefor. It is the very same route that the company served when it started business in 1912.

Holders of free **concessionary bus passes** in Wales can of course use their passes on the buses of any operator – large or small. The Welsh scheme long predates its English equivalent and is in some respects superior to the English initiative. Passes are still available from the age of 60 and they may be used for travel at any time of the day (whereas in most areas of England travel may not commence until after the morning peak).

Visitors to Wales can benefit from a number of **great-value passes** beyond the company-specific Arriva bus passes mentioned at the start of this section. The 'Explore Wales' pass offers eight consecutive days unlimited travel by bus in Wales. The pass is accepted by many of Wales's colourful local bus operators including those mentioned in this section. On any four days of your choice (within the overall eight-day validity of the pass), you can *also* use train services within Wales and make **cross-border rail journeys** to Chester, Crewe, Shrewsbury, Hereford and Gloucester. The pass also gives discounts on museum entrance. The cost for an adult is £94 (or £62 with a railcard and £47 for children). ∎

MORE FAVOURITE JOURNEYS

The following routes in Wales and the Marches were included in *Bus-Pass Britain* (2011): Ludlow to Hereford, Hereford to Llandrindod Wells, Wrexham to Barmouth, Mold to Ruthin and Aberystwyth to Tregaron.

OFFA'S COUNTRY
WESTWARD TO WALES

Les Lumsdon

Ludlow 🚐

Service no. 738/740 | Journey time 60mins

OS Landranger 137. Four services daily Mon–Sat, no service on Sun.
Operator: Arriva.

Knighton ⬅

A driver once mentioned to me that he loved doing the runs through the Marches as there are so many beautiful chimneys to admire. I know what he means. In **Ludlow** for example, the streets are rich with Georgian town houses, almost every one possessing an ornate brick flue, standing tall above the roofline. But Ludlow is essentially a Norman town wrapped within the old walls; witness the narrow streets that the bus has to negotiate. That's where you'll catch a glimpse of fine examples of **half-timbered houses**, many of which lie between the ruins of Ludlow Castle and the parish church dedicated to St Laurence. These are remarkable survivors of the Middle Ages much loved by the locals.

The half-timbered façade of the Feathers Hotel in Ludlow (photo © Deniskellyson / DT)

There have been changes, of course. I overhear two older men on board talking about a cinema that once stood in Old Street, which they refer to as the 'flea pit.' It was evidently the place to be in their youth. Lamentably, it has gone now the way of many small-town cinemas. The bus eases up to the lights at the **Bull Ring**, a traditional crossroads where bulls might well have been tethered in previous decades – but not now. Well not today at any rate. There are more passengers to be picked up in Corve Street but the bus soon leaves Ludlow **bound for Wales**. This is the only international bus route in this book!

The first stop on our cross-border journey is at Bromfield, where the Ludlow Food Centre makes and sells fresh produce, most of it grown on local farms. Now begins the climb, gently at first, but then in a determined manner towards the wooded scarp slope known as **Mocktree**. If you're lucky you'll spot fallow deer to the right where pockets of woodland give way to pasture. There's often a change of mood on the bus at the summit. The bus falls quiet. People stop conversing in order to concentrate on the view – and what a view it is! Look over the hedgerow to the Wigmore Rolls, a succession of low-lying hills that surround the village and castle of Wigmore. But it is the higher and more foreboding Radnor Forest ahead that catches the eye, miles of rough moorland plateaux where hardy sheep such as Hill Radnor, Beulah Speckled Face, Clun Forest and Kerry Hill graze in all weathers.

CORACLE COUNTRY

The bus arrives at the ancient Roman settlement of **Leintwardine** (Bravonium), a strategic bridging point over the River Teme. There's no evidence of the Roman camp above ground but it is a good place to stop off awhile. The village is known for its coracle making and a local man, known as the Oracle of the Coracle, still practises the ancient skills using locally grown willows, hazel rods and cow hides from Griffiths, the village butcher. He even runs courses for those who want to make their own under the

THE SUN INN

You'll find the Sun Inn in **Leintwardine** on Rosemary Lane (where the bus pulls in). This is one of the few remaining Victorian parlour pubs in Britain, a pub where people used to sit in the parlour and be served beer from jugs directly tapped from the cask! The pub was for decades in the hands of **Flossie Lane**, the oldest landlady in England at the age of 94, until her death in 2009. The greatest tribute to her, however, is that one of her regulars, Gary Seymour, and a local brewer, Nick Davis of Hobsons, have brought new life to the pub, while at the same time maintaining the character of the two **19th-century rooms**. They have done this with panache and it is a fitting place to take refreshment; they'll even serve you beer direct from the cask if you want! Open every day from 11.00 except Monday when the pub opens at 17.30 (☎ 01547 540705).

supervision of his expert eye. The **parish church** of St Mary Magdalene stands at the very centre of the village and is two minutes' walk from the bus stop.

The bus route in Leintwardine can be confusing to the uninitiated. Some buses (the 738 and the Castle Connect) continue ahead across the stone bridge to Brampton Bryan, where the ruins of its ancient castle are open to the public but once a year – and that during the scarecrow festival in early August.

Anyway, back in Leintwardine, the other service (the 740) sweeps round to set down passengers underneath the tall shady oak opposite the Lion Hotel, then runs back on itself through the village before branching off to **Clungunford**. This was one of A E Houseman's 'quietest places under the sun'. The village is home to the award-winning Rocke Cottage tea rooms (☎ 01588 660631; open 10.00–17.00 Wed–Sun). Next stop is **Hopton Heath**, which is where you can alight for a one-mile walk to Hopton Castle, recently restored by local residents. The castle harbours the story of one of the worst atrocities of the English Civil War. But those planning to explore this area might also consult the train timetable as there's a railway station at Hopton Heath in case return bus times don't suit.

Whichever route is taken, all buses end up in the sprawling village of **Bucknell**; it has grown up around the sparkling waters of the River Redlake. Bucknell has, in recent times, become a mini-mecca for walkers and the 'Walking with Offa' project encourages walks from here, including a route through to Knighton, about six to seven miles by way of woods and sheep pastures. Fortunately, there are also two pubs in the village, the Baron at Bucknell (☎ 01547 530549) and the Sitwell Arms (☎ 01547 530213) so it is a good place to enjoy refreshment.

The bus crosses the track of the **Heart of Wales railway**, a stubborn survivor if ever there was one. With a number of stations on or close to this bus route, there's a lot of scope for creating fine bus-rail itineraries (more on www.heart-of-wales.co.uk).

Approaching the border

The bus begins to complete the last leg of the route into Wales. The **changing landscape** hints of the border. Suddenly there is a sense of wilderness. The gentle familiarity of Shropshire is being challenged by something different. The Teme Valley narrows and the high hills hold a greater presence now than hitherto. They are, in part, shrouded with dense woodland which in some respects makes them look more striking, most particularly in autumn.

Between these beckoning hills sits the classic gap town of **Knighton** where England meets Wales. It is with some irony that the railway station is actually in Shropshire but the remainder of the town lies well and truly in Wales. Its Welsh name is Tref-y-Clawdd, meaning 'town on the dyke,' and this refers to its significance as a trading post on Offa's Dyke, said to have been built by the Mercian King Offa to hold back Welsh tribes.

The situation was far more complex than can be told here and it is not unreasonable to conclude that this border dyke allowed multi-directional trade between communities. Visit the **Offa's Dyke Centre** (☎ 01547 528753; open daily 10.00–17.00 during summer, with a short break over lunch), about a 10-min walk from Knighton

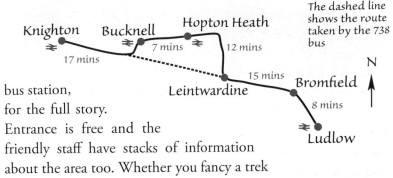

The dashed line shows the route taken by the 738 bus

Knighton — Bucknell — Hopton Heath
17 mins   7 mins   12 mins
N

15 mins   Bromfield
Leintwardine   8 mins

Ludlow

bus station, for the full story. Entrance is free and the friendly staff have stacks of information about the area too. Whether you fancy a trek on **Offa's Dyke Path** or one of the other paths weaving in and out of Knighton, the centre has the low-down on them all. And it's a place to learn about the history and archaeology of this part of the Marches. It also doubles as the visitor centre for Knighton.

Knighton bus station is somewhat of an exaggeration in terms. It comprises one draconian shelter and a raised curb, sandwiched between recycling bins and the cattle market. It is not surprising then that it rarely gets nominated for any bus awards. Yet there are some redeeming features, such as a public toilet nearby and, for those with an interest in farming, an almost ringside view of the livestock in the auction pens. You'll certainly hear and smell them!

Probably the best way into town is to walk along Bowling Green Lane, past the market, towards the small supermarket and then to turn right for the centre. This is marked with a **Victorian clock tower**, a landmark that cannot be missed. Leading up from here are the 'Narrows,' a network of narrow streets, distinctly medieval in layout, that rise to the top of the town, where there's an old castle mound (not open to the public).

If you are out to discover Knighton and the Offa's Dyke Centre then the time available between buses is about right before returning through a part of the borderland that too few visit. ■

ABOUT THE AUTHOR | **LES LUMSDON** lives near Ludlow and spends much of his time exploring the Welsh Marches on foot, by cycle or by bus. He is author of *A Guide to Slow Travel in the Marches* (Logaston Press).

CUTTING ACROSS THE
BRECON BEACONS

Tudor Thomas

22 Newtown

Service no. T4 | Journey time 3hrs 45mins

OS Landranger 136, 147, 161, 160, 170, 171. Thrice daily Mon–Sat.
Operators: Stagecoach for TrawsCymru.

Cardiff

With a route length of over one hundred miles, this is no ordinary bus journey. This is a trip on a local bus with an express feel, and a ride comparable to a magic carpet with an ever-changing vista. It covers a great swathe of countryside – sometimes revealing **quiet pastoral beauty**, sometimes dramatically wild – before ending at the capital city of Wales. Along the way we take in rivers, reservoirs and rich industrial heritage. Today's buses on the TrawsCymru T4 are easy access, have leather seats, and Wi-Fi – so you could in theory update your Facebook profile or tweet your way through Wales. But only the most unromantic of travellers would miss the opportunity of gazing at the landscapes that slip by beyond the window of the bus.

We start at the Back Lane bus station in **Newtown** (Y Drenewydd in Welsh) in the county of Powys. So we're off, and almost immediately we have a sense of the journey to come. Although the route south follows a trunk road (the A483), it is formidably twisty and has a switchback quality. Soon we are looking down onto the rooftops of Newtown.

There are views that hint of a wilder Wales that lies away to the west. Plynlimon in the **Cambrian Mountain range** is discernible as a modest pimple on the horizon. But Powys is wild enough for now and we should be grateful that our driver evidently knows the dangers that might lurk in every dip and bend of the road ahead.

A WELSH SPA ROUTE

Talk of spas today and most folk think of five-star chic. But the spa towns of central Wales are from another era – one that was less cosseted, not so relentless in the pursuit of luxury. And, less than an hour out of Newtown, we are cruising into our first spa stop: **Llandrindod Wells**.

Time for a five-minute break, and a handful of passengers hop off for a quick smoke. Across the way stands the bright red Sargeants Brothers bus, ready to set off on its run to Hereford. That cross-border route is described as Journey 18 in *Bus-Pass Britain*.

Llandrindod's annual Victorian Festival in August recalls the town's heyday when the supposed healing qualities of the local waters pulled visitors from far and wide. Back on board the bus, we pass the Metropole Hotel – once the largest in the country. It is a mark of how Landrindod's reputation has waned.

Leaving Llandrindod, we run parallel to the **Heart of Wales rail route** which was so important in building Llandrindod's trade. We sweep south through rolling countryside, the rugged ridge of Carneddau edging up towards us on the left and suddenly we reach the River Wye. Close by the road is the Royal Welsh showground. Here is **Builth Wells**, a town that draws the crowds for its four-day agricultural show each July.

Newtown

50 mins

N

Llandrindod Wells

19 mins

Builth Wells

26 mins

Llyswen

9 mins

13 mins / Felinfach

Brecon

16 mins

Storey Arms

16 mins

Merthyr Tydfil

55 mins

Cardiff

Heading south from Builth on the A470, we follow the partly wooded **Wye Valley** downstream. Every now and again, the hills open out to give a glimpse of the Black Mountains ahead. For the most part this is a stretch of route where the focus is close to the bus with riverside scenes of rare beauty in the right light. Unexpectedly, the landscape opens out and we stop at the village of Llyswen, where the bus stop is by the 17th-century Griffin Inn, which has accommodation (☎ 01874 754241). It is a good spot to just stop for a day and take the tempo of Welsh life. This is not a country to rush through.

Just a few minutes later we stop at another pub with a similar name, the **Felin Fach Griffin** (☎ 01874 620111; rooms available). It has garnered accolades from national media for its high-quality restaurant. This old drovers' inn was acclaimed as 'Inn of the Year' in the 2013 *Good Pub Guide*. The last time I was there it had a large roaring fire which set the tone for a very good lunch. Don't get the two Griffins confused! Both are equally deserving of a visit, and each attracts many well-heeled visitors from across the border.

It is a fast run south to **Brecon** (Aberhonddu in Welsh). The town is the midway point on our journey. I'm not the only one to give thanks for the fact that there's a brief toilet stop at the bus station. If you follow the call, just let the bus driver know and he'll

---

BRECON BEACONS NATIONAL PARK

Webwise travellers can start **exploring the national park** before leaving home by going to www.breconbeacons.org. 'One of Britain's breathing spaces,' reads the tagline on that website and it's a good reminder that there is **fresh air aplenty** in this gorgeous sweep of mountains and moorland. For accommodation options, check with the tourist information centre in Brecon (☎ 01874 622485).

If heading to the summits or into remote valleys, dress for the conditions. **Weather** can change suddenly. Mobile phones may not always have any reception, so always tell someone where you are going and when you'll be back.

surely wait for you before driving off. If you are tempted to stop off, Giglios Coffee Shop on Bethel Square (☎ 01874 625062) is much to be recommended. Leaving Brecon, we cross the **River Usk** and head determinedly south with the dark summits of the Brecon Beacons rising up in front of us. From the bus stop at Libanus, it is a stiff half-hour walk up to the **Brecon Beacons Mountain Centre** (☎ 01874 623366), where there is a café and viewing interpretation area.

The Beacons and beyond

Gathering pace on an empty and well-graded road, we move into wilder territory. The road clings to the edge of the hillside, passing waterfalls on the right, and here and there giving glimpses of the old drovers' route which nowadays is part of the **Taff Trail** – a route that takes walkers and cyclists to no great heights but gives wonderful views of the national park.

We have already seen the potential for confusion over those two Griffins. Now comes another puzzle in similar vein. 'Next stop, Storey Arms,' calls out the driver to two young women with rucksacks who are clearly bound for the summits. It sounds for all the world like a pub. But the old Storey Arms was demolished in the 1920s, and nowadays there is an **Outdoor Education Centre** on the site. So it's not a place to stop for a pint. And be warned: it is a wild spot and there is not even a bus shelter.

Into industrial Wales

Over the summit at Storey Arms, our driver shifts down a gear as we roll south towards Merthyr. The road dips and dives, taking its cue from the surrounding hills. We pass **three reservoirs** in quick succession: Beacons, Cantref and Llwyn-on. It's good to be on board the T4 on a bright day. Drivers on this route tell tales of fearsome winter storms and the snow fences above the road lend credence to those accounts.

MERTHYR'S INDUSTRIAL LEGACY

The Merthyr Tydfil Tourist Information (☎ 01685 727474) is a good spot to find out more about the place. **Cyfarthfa Castle Museum & Art Gallery** (☎ 01685 727371; open daily 10.00–17.30 Apr–Sep; 10.00–16.00 Tue–Fri and 12.00–16.00 Sat & Sun Oct–Mar) is well worth a visit. This area at the heads of the Welsh valleys has a rich heritage. **Dowlais Iron Company** started in 1759 and, over the following 50 years, pioneered many new techniques in iron working. In 1802 a tramway was built. Two years later, Cornishman Richard Trevithick invented the first working **steam engine** to run on rails.

There is a palpable sense of a change in the landscape as we return to more settled terrain. On the left there is a glimpse of Cyfarthfa Castle (see box above) and a minute or two later we are in **Merthyr Tydfil**. This is a town that was shaped by industry, growing by the mid-19th century to become the largest community in Wales. It was eventually betrayed by the very industries that it had nurtured – with the coal seams worked out, the iron and steel industry moved towards the coast. From here we follow the Taff Valley down to **Cardiff**. I'll bow out here, for you can catch the flavour of the valleys in the next journey in this book.

But if you are staying on board, keep a lookout on the right-hand side as you travel south down the valley. You'll see the village of **Aberfan**, scene of the awful disaster in 1966 when a hillside spoil heap collapsed, engulfing the village school. 144 people perished in the disaster, robbing this part of the Taff Valley of an entire younger generation. It is a reminder that the Welsh landscapes which give so much character to this extraordinary cross-country bus route has been, for some, a source of trial and tribulation. ∎

ABOUT THE AUTHOR | **TUDOR THOMAS** is a marketing and transport specialist currently working for Bus Users UK in Wales. He lives near Cardiff and is a regular user of the T4 TrawsCymru bus service.

Barry Hankey

23

Brynmawr 🚐

Service no. 30 | Journey time 55mins

OS Landranger 161, 171. Hourly Mon–Sat. No evening services.
Operator: Stagecoach South Wales.

Newport ⬅

D eclining the option of a cuppa at one of the cafés clustered
around the small bus station, I settle for a more potent
caffeine fix in the coffee shop at the top of the main street. Then I
join the few people on board the bus as it pulls out of **Brynmawr**
for the short run to Newport (Casnewydd in Welsh). This route
is a reminder that local buses in Britain are still generally spaces
for local voices. Buses are deeply rooted in communities. A glance
around the bus suggests that everyone on board today comes from
the immediate area. This route takes less than an hour, but it's a
spectacular tour through a landscape which played a pivotal role
in world history – the birthplace of the Industrial Revolution.

Brynmawr is one of the highest communities in Wales. To
the north are the lovely Brecon Beacons, while the country to
the south was once every bit as beautiful but has been scarred by
200 years of intensive industrial exploitation. From Brynmawr, we
start by heading uphill to the bleak, brown **moorland watershed**.
At 1,400 feet, this is the highest point on the route. On the
right, Coity Mountain rises another 500 feet. It is a scarp much
populated by paragliders when the wind direction is propitious.

Below the scarp the reed-covered bog swallowed a Halifax
bomber in 1944, though thankfully not its crew. The bog is the

source of the **Afon Lwyd**, one of the steepest rivers in the region. It has carved a deep valley into the underlying geology and it is that valley that we now follow for the entire journey down to Newport. It was down this valley that iron and coal were transported on their way to all parts of the world. Latterly, it is the direction in which entire industries have migrated, forsaking the valleys and moving south towards the banks of the River Severn.

COAL: BLESSING AND BLIGHT

The industrial history of this valley has brought it **World Heritage status**. UNESCO agreed the designation in 2000, and the focal point is Blaenavon's Big Pit. So I hop off the bus at Whistle Road and follow a good waymarked trail to the Big Pit Mining Museum. It takes less than an hour, passing *en route* through the Garn Lakes Nature Reserve, an area of reclaimed colliery workings now offering diverse wetland wildlife habitats.

Back on the bus, we make a hither-and-thither circuit of Blaenavon. This stage of the journey is not for those in a hurry. Instead of going straight down the valley, the bus heads off to **Forge Side**, a small urban village and once the world leader in iron working. That is the curious thing about these old industrial settlements. Miners and labourers lived close to their work and you'll find isolated housing terraces on mountainsides, as often as

---

INDUSTRIAL LEGACY

Big Pit was sunk in the mid-1860s to supply the Forge Side ironworks. Coal production ceased in 1980 and the site reopened as the **National Coal Museum** in 1983, offering tours to the former coalface 300 feet underground led by miners who previously dug the coal. Quickly becoming one of the major visitor attractions in Wales, it gives an eye-opening insight into working conditions underground dating back to the days of pit ponies (☎ 029 2057 3650; open daily 09.30–17.00; underground tours 10.00-15.30).

---

not with conical spoil heaps as the backdrop to the housing.

The bus loops around the narrow gridiron streets of 19th-century steelworkers' terraced cottages, some bearing the original no-nonsense names Row C, Row D, Row E, others with more aspirational names like Oxford Terrace or Clapham Terrace. It was here that the scientific experiments of two cousins, **Thomas and Gilchrist**, in the 1870s pioneered a method of removing phosphorous contaminants from iron ore by using local limestone. Serendipitously, iron ore, limestone, wood for charcoal and plentiful supplies of coal, were all found close to Blaenavon. The Gilchrist-Thomas technique was patented and soon copied worldwide. Ironically, this led to the decline of steel making in Blaenavon as ores in other parts of the world were more plentiful and economical to mine.

Blaenavon richly repays a visit. One 'must see' is the Ironworks the most comprehensive 18th-century iron-working complex in Britain, with furnaces, water balance and casting houses. The whitewashed cottages of Stack Square next to it are hugely evocative of a lost way of life in the valleys. The Blaenavon World Heritage Centre in Church Road is an excellent starting point

Brynmawr
10 mins

N

Blaenavon

15 mins

Pontypool

25 mins

Newport

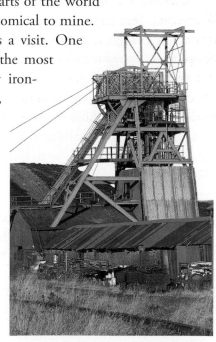

Colliery at Big Pit, Blaenavon (photo © Barry Hankey)

for finding out about the place (☎ 01495 742333; open daily exc Mon from 09.00–17.00 Apr–Sept and an hour less Oct–Mar).

Leaving Blaenavon the bus passes through **beech woodland** rising steeply up the valley sides, fresh green in spring, golden brown in autumn, the bubbling river just below. Then it shoots upwards again on winding roads past terraces of small stone cottages with tiny front gardens. Anything bigger than the Optare Solo buses used on this route would get stuck.

Once back on the valley floor the route is more direct. I often leave the bus in **Pontypool** to walk through the magnificent park in the town's centre, redesigned by Capability Brown in 1801. My favourites are the gnarled 200-year-old sweet chestnut trees. Better known is the famous rugby ground once home to the Pontypool Front Row. At one entrance to the park is a small museum with a display of 'Japanware,' a method of corrosion-resistant decorative lacquering of iron pioneered in Pontypool in the 17th century.

If I have time, I take my favourite walk to the **shell grotto** at the top of the hill and then along the ridge to the Folly Tower which, at 1,000 feet, offers great views over the Vale of Usk and across the Severn Estuary to the West Country. Alternatively I drop down from the grotto to catch the bus again in New Inn at the foot of the mountain.

From Pontypool town centre the bus makes rapid progress through New Inn, skirts the edge of Cwmbran and then, express-style, on to its destination, the centre of **Newport**. The town originally owed its existence to Blaenavon – exporting its iron and coal – but then the steel industry moved to the coast and the huge Lanwern steelworks were built. Now the last vestiges of steel making have all but disappeared from the city and moved overseas just as inexorably as it migrated to the coast. Another irony on this bus journey through history. ■

ABOUT THE AUTHOR | **BARRY HANKEY** has lived for 35 years at the midpoint of the route of bus number 30 and uses it frequently in both directions.

GOWER BOUND

Elisabeth Parsons

24 Swansea

Service no. 14/14A/114 | Journey time 35 to 45mins

OS Landranger 159. Hourly Mon–Sat, five services on Sun in summer.
Operator: First.

Pennard Cliffs ←

I've been travelling this route for about 30 years. Bar for a spot of urban redevelopment, it is a journey that has hardly changed in all those years. Yet no two journeys are the same. The **variations in light**, weather, tides and seasons provide a new experience every time. This journey evokes a thousand moodscapes.

The chief appeal of this route lies in the many opportunities it offers for good linear walks. It also provides access to some beautiful coves and beaches – rocky, sandy or multicoloured shingle. But if you don't have the energy or mobility for a walk, the bus ride itself is diverting. We set off from a city that is struggling to redefine itself in a new post-industrial era – **Swansea** (Abertawe in Welsh) is no longer a city delimited by the copper industry. And we end our journey on the cliffed coast of the Gower Peninsula. Look on Welsh maps and you'll see the peninsula marked as Penrhyn Gwyr. English or Welsh, that knobbly peninsula is a magic escape from the city. And yet it seems to be an area that is only provisionally part of Wales. You'll not hear a lot of Welsh spoken in villages on the peninsula. From the bus, on a clear day, there are **dramatic views** across the Bristol Channel to the cliffed coast of Exmoor. The English counties of Somerset and Devon thus figure strongly in the Gower imagination.

Setting off

The first part of the route passes through the Swansea district of **Sandfields**. We slide past rows of neat two-up-two-down terraces. At first sight, they present an image of unremitting uniformity. But look more closely to discover the ingenuity of residents who imaginatively mark their space with individual touches: a Welsh flag here, a statue on the window sill there, even a little welcome sign by the front door.

As we leave Oxford Road, Joe's is on the right. Joe and his family are a Swansea institution. It was a hundred years ago that the family arrived from Italy, bringing their taste for ice cream with them. Swansea is hooked on Joe's ice cream. We slip past the **Art Deco Guildhall** and turn onto Oystermouth Road. This is a grand moment: the full sweep of Swansea Bay comes into view. That vista captures the spirit of this part of Wales. Look east across the bay to the flames and stacks of Port Talbot steelworks. Closer to hand and straight ahead is **Mumbles Head** with its twin islets and lighthouse.

For the next few minutes we follow the curve of the bay, until it disappears behind the embankment which now hosts a cycle path – quicker than the road in rush hour – and a fitness trail, which seems to offer an appealing challenge to inebriated students from the nearby University of Swansea. The main uni buildings

SWANSEA BAY

Two worlds unite in this **broad bay** that boasts an unusually large tidal range. The tide ebbs and flows to reveal great swathes of sand (and, it must be admitted, sometimes a little mud too). In warmer weather the sands are used by kitesurfers, sand yachters, kite-flyers, dog walkers, beach-football players and men pursuing the **mysterious art** of metal detecting. Odd, is it not, how the metallurgical industries have shaped the region? At one side of the bay that huge steel works and here men searching for fragments of metal buried in the sands.

are in the grounds of
Singleton Park. The
Park Lodge, on the
corner, was designed
by Henry Woodyer
for John Henry
Vivian (1785–1855),

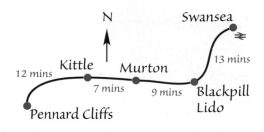

the industrialist and politician whose copper mining and smelting
works contributed a great deal to Swansea's wealth – and air
pollution – in the 19th century.

There is a pitch-and-putt course on the left. No pitchers or
putters today so pigeons hold sway on the first hole, but cut to
the middle of the course for crows or oystercatchers. There is
more scope for entertainment at **Blackpill Lido**. It's packed with
local families in summer, but it's a good stop for a coffee in colder
weather – you can walk back along the seafront to Swansea.

Turning away from the sea

Now we cut inland through territory that is less given to seaside
enjoyment. This is a gentler, more sedate Swansea with grand
Victorian villas set back from the road, mature trees shadowing
the verges. As we reach the top of the hill, we leave the suburbs and
the view opens out across the green breadth of **Clyne Common**.
I always find the next few minutes are great for clearing the mind.
The sheep and grazing ponies bring their own therapy. It's an easy
run along an empty B-road to the Gower villages of Murton and
Bishopston.

We dip down and cross Bishopston Valley before climbing
up to the next village: **Kittle**. But do take a look at that valley.
It's a classic piece of Gower *karst* – fresh white limestone that is
riddled with caverns. You can follow it downstream to the coast,
and you'll see what a perverse thing the river is here. It comes and
goes as it pleases, often flowing underground for a spell before
popping up for air.

GOWER WALKS

Ask the driver to stop at Brandy Cove Road for an adventurous coastal walk. Follow the lane down to **Brandy Cove**. It slims down into little more than a path before dropping steeply down the beach. From there you can walk west to **Pwlldu Bay** and Southgate, rejoining the number 14 bus at its terminus at Pennard Cliffs for the ride back to Swansea. There's also a nice walk east from Brandy Cove to **Caswell Bay** from where you can continue around the coast to Langland Bay, Mumbles, or all the way to Swansea. Go prepared for changes in weather, check tides and take along OS Explorer Map Sheet 164.

Our driver pauses outside the Beaufort Arms in Kittle. Just a minute or two as he chats with a couple of men standing by the side of the road. But drivers are beholden unto schedules and soon we are on our way again, heading west through **Southgate** village to **Pennard Cliffs**, where the route terminates besides two coffee shops and a dozen footpaths.

The only decision now is how long to stay – one hour, two, or until the last bus back. There are B&Bs, a caravan site (no tents), and even a retirement home so you could stay for days, weeks, or the rest of your life! However, wild camping is not an option – the land is National Trust owned.

You'll need strong legs to access the beaches, but there are some level, quiet tarmac roads you can roll or stroll along if mobility is limited. The buses are usually modern ones with easy access for wheelchairs and pushchairs, but be aware that many bus stops are low-level without a kerb – ask the driver for advice. If you can access the coves, you'll be rewarded with some **truly stunning beaches** – but keep an eye on the tide, and don't get cut off! ∎

ABOUT THE AUTHOR

ELISABETH PARSONS is a part-time Open University lecturer. She moved to Swansea in 2003. She favours pro-environmental transport choices and has visited places as far afield as Turkey and Moldova by bus and train.

SPEAKING IN TONGUES

It is rare to speak of Wales, and more particularly the more rural parts of the Principality, without the issue of **place names** being raised. Most English visitors judge Welsh to be formidably complicated. For English speakers, the orthography looks curious and the language sounds immensely challenging. Yet there is a **real beauty to Welsh** and that shines through in the poetry of the bus timetables. Ystrad Meurig and Llanafan are every bit as lovely as the lilt in their names suggests.

But tucked away amid the Welsh place names are a few surprises. We caught the bus from Blaenau down to the coast some years ago, and were astonished when the driver said that for Pwllheli we should hop off at Australia and wait there for the onward connection. Sensing that we were not quite up for an Antipodean adventure, the driver reassured us that the **bus stop** took its name from a pub in Porthmadog. And on subsequent travels we came to appreciate that Australia was a nodal point in the bus network of that part of North Wales.

Australia slipped from the timetables when the pub changed its name to Y Gestiana, a move that stemmed the tide of curious visitors from Sydney but left the premises with a name that evokes powerful local connotations. In the last days of sail, **Porthmadog** developed a considerable reputation for the three-masted topsail schooners built in the local shipyards. The last of these ships, launched in 1913, was *Y Gestiana*. Sadly, she was wrecked on her maiden voyage. This detail does not seem to trouble the locals who stand and chat at the bus stop as they wait for transport to villages and towns across Gwynedd and beyond.

The issue of language on **cross-border bus services** between England and Wales has occasionally given cause for debate. Bus operator Arriva ruffled English feathers in May 2013 when it introduced bilingual announcements on some of its services from Wales to Chester, a city that is just two miles from the Welsh border. Some aggrieved English passengers were reportedly unhappy to hear **announcements** still being made in Welsh on the English side of the border – as well as in English, of course. Yet how would the same passengers react if on-board announcements were made *only* in Welsh on the Welsh side of the border? ■

THROUGH SNOWDONIA
WILD WALES

Julie Bromilow

Bangor

Service no. T2 | Journey time 3hrs 15mins to 3hrs 35mins

OS Landranger 115, 124, 135. Twice daily.
Operators: Lloyds Coaches and Express Motors.

Aberystwyth

Bangor is a town on the edge. Scruffy, bitten by wind and the Menai Straits. As the last spot on the mainland, only Anglesey beyond, it's a transient place for students, for those heading for Ireland via Holyhead and for Bardsey-bound pilgrims.

To me **Bangor** is exciting, as edgy places often are – rough and rich in music and poets. I like to head down **Garth Pier** before the bus leaves to see the oystercatchers race the Straits and read the sweet-sad tributes on the memorial benches – 'he loved to sail, we loved to see him smile.' The bus depot is a shifting mix of vehicles vying for space outside Debenhams but is so close to the museum and cathedral you can visit them both in a 20-minute wait.

I used this bus many times when my work in Machynlleth took me to schools on Anglesey or the north Wales coast. On the way I'd be deep in teaching thoughts but the return journeys south were an indulgent ramble through Snowdonia, ruled by clouds and mountains.

The bus climbs south from Bangor and before long you see across the Straits to **Anglesey** and Newborough Sands stretching soft into the sea. Caernarfon is the first major stop. Do not be fooled as I was by the undignified entrance through back streets where the bus comes to sulk a few moments between Argos and a multistorey car park – Caernarfon is a pretty, cobbled town with a continental feel when the sun shines on the great castle by the sea.

MOUNTAINS AND SHADOWS

From here to Porthmadog the **landscape is wide**: west to the sea over wild fields dashed with bent hawthorns and lichen-scored walls, and east to the Snowdon range – snow-stricken, brooding in cloud, or dissolving into blue distances. The sky dominates this highland, chasing shadows across peanut-butter hills and rusted heather, wind ravaging the Welsh dragon flags around Penygroes – and then we descend.

At sea level **Tremadog** is quiet and stately in slate, a genteel introduction to Porthmadog a minute along and more gregarious – 'Darren pays more for your gold!' writ large by the harbour. **Porthmadog** is a steam town, home to both the Ffestiniog and Welsh Highland narrow-gauge railways.

There are gentle beaches nearby at Borth-y-Gest and Morfa Bychan but I love to walk along the Cob, an embankment built to form a deep harbour from where slate was shipped round the world, now carrying the A487, the **Ffestiniog Railway**, and the Wales Coast Path across the Glaslyn Estuary. The best views are from here. The estuary flutes with birds, the sand flats are riven

Porthmadog – home of the Ffestiniog Railway (photo © Gail Johnson / DT)

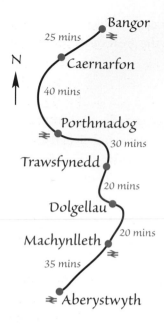

N

Bangor
25 mins
Caernarfon
40 mins
Porthmadog
30 mins
Trawsfynedd
20 mins
Dolgellau
20 mins
Machynlleth
35 mins
Aberystwyth

serpentine with silver water and framed by mountains, and you can watch curlews from behind the buddleia.

The lady behind me is also excited by the views, and we begin sharing them. She has come especially for the scenery. 'A bus ride is the best way to forget your troubles,' she says. Passenger chat flows in Welsh and English and the bus is busy. We call at green bus shelters in Penrhyndeudraeth, Gellilydan and Trawsfynydd, the green paint bright like the scarlet phone boxes in dark slate streets.

In **Penrhyndeudraeth** – where the mighty pylons stand serene in Afon Dwyryd before marching up the creek – Rob and I spent a rose-gold night at the end of summer. We were hungry for food and beer and drawn to Y Dderwen ('The Oak') (☎ 01766 770652; open daily from 13.00), but there was no menu to be had that night on account of a christening. The landlord was rueful, but instead there were piles of sandwiches and onion bhajis to eat while a grandpa and little boy crashed the piano and everyone was jolly. Penrhyndeudraeth just seemed the right place to be.

Welsh black cattle shelter, and sheep graze the marshy fields. The landscape changes towards **Trawsfynydd** where the nuclear power station sits square and peculiar in the pewter lake – the hills are closing in and the brisk windscape is replaced by woodland and slate. Trees, stone walls and dripping rocks by the road are all moistly resplendent in moss and the air is wet and silver. Across the wilds to the west are the craggy blue **Rhinogs** – sometimes Rob and I get off at Ganllwyd to walk across them to the coast.

There are woodlands in this damper climate, and from Ganllwyd you can also visit Coed-y-Brenin (Kings Woodland)

Forest Park (☎ 01341 440747). It has bike tracks, a café, and a 'Go Ape' adventure centre, but for me it's the **waterfalls** Pistyll Cain, Rhaedr Mawddach and Rhaedr Du that make it special, particularly in autumn when beech leaves whirl copper over the spray. These falls and rivers once powered wheels for the gold mines of which you can still see the relics – John the Rock, a friend of ours, once found a nugget on a rock after heavy rain.

SAUSAGES AND SLATE

The bus waits in **Dolgellau** for a few minutes, so there's time to walk round Eldon Square or buy sausages perhaps from the Roberts Bros butchers by the bus stop – pork and leek, sage and red onion, or pork and black pepper chalked up on the board, and today homemade faggots for £1.10. Dolgellau dwells beneath Cadair Idris glowering craggy to the south and is at the mercy of its weather.

Cadair Idris backdrops the T2 for some distance yet and walkers alight at Minffordd or Talyllyn. The landscape here has a ragged glacial beauty. I like to get off at the gates where sheep are herded across the road to hike left up to Crach Fynydd pass with

EATING AND DRINKING

This route is rich in good food and drink. Try the **Tap and Spile** at Garth Pier in Bangor (☎ 01248 370835) – it is full of character and characters. In Porthmadog the **Station Inn** (☎ 01766 806517) otherwise known as 'the pub on the platform,' is home to locals guffawing at old British sitcoms. Steam fans head for **Spooner's** bar and café (☎ 01766 516032; open daily from 09.00) at the Ffestiniog Railway Harbour Station.

    Y Sospan (☎ 01341 423174) in Dolgellau was a court house in 1606 and is now a café – head through the old jail door to cosier tables upstairs. In Machynlleth **The Wynnstay** (☎ 01654 702941), a grand old hotel both luxurious and cosy, has slow food reasonably priced.

views back over the Rhinogs and south to the Cambrians. I've picked gluts of whinberries there and lain in yellow grasses under the great sky bowl.

But not everyone comes here for quietude – across the moor that faces Cadair Idris and down on to the ribbon of A487, men from the Midlands gather to spot fighter jets from Anglesey screaming down the valley.

Perhaps my favourite view on this beguiling route is at the top of the Talyllyn Pass when the bus crests the final peak before plummeting down, the waters of Talyllyn shining below. 'Oh how I do wish an artist would get off here and paint that,' says a woman on the bus.

Now we roll through slate country: Upper Corris, Lower Corris, the Centre for Alternative Technology (www.cat.org.uk) – the eco-centre developed on a derelict slate quarry – and into **Machynlleth** the small market town where I live and where the bus pauses a moment by the clock tower.

THE DYFI BIOSPHERE

UNESCO has awarded International Biosphere Reserve status to the **Dyfi Valley** in recognition of its **biodiversity**. It is the rich coastal waters, salt marsh and peat bogs which make the valley special. But biosphere reserves are about more than wildlife – they should also be places where people care for and cultivate language, culture and sustainable development.

Three nature reserves at the heart of the biosphere are within easy reach of the T2 – ask the driver to stop at Morben Isaf caravan park to visit the **Dyfi Osprey Project** (☎ 01654 781414; open daily 10.00–18.00) run by Montgomeryshire Wildlife Trust, at Cors Dyfi Nature Reserve, or at Eglwys Fach to visit the **RSPB Ynys-hir Reserve** (☎ 01654 700222) – this will be familiar to BBC *Springwatch* fans.

Get off at Bow Street and take a Mid Wales 512 connection to Ynyslas to visit the **Dyfi National Nature Reserve** (☎ 01970 872901) managed by the Countryside Council for Wales and home to spectacular sand dune, estuary and peat bog habitats. You can read more about the Dyfi Biosphere at www.dyfibiosphere.org.uk.

THE DYFI VALLEY

The route beyond Machynlleth is another chapter in my history. We are now in the Dyfi Valley, indeed the **Dyfi Biosphere** (see box opposite), and heading for Aberystwyth where I spent my student years. The bus here is always busy despite the route being well served by frequent buses and trains, and we are joined by students, shoppers, men going to watch the rugby and Rob for the final stretch. Still on the A487, the route kisses the river and is gentler than in the highlands but just as beautiful. It is the **Tarren Mountains** that backdrop the Dyfi, often glowing in a richer light than reaches the road – keep watch for ospreys and in summer water buffalo that graze Cors Dyfi.

At **Taliesin** you glimpse the sea and Aberystwyth with Pen Dinas hill fort on the skyline, and the glorious peat bog which is Cors Fochno, a raised bog rich in sundews, raft spiders, and rosy marsh moths. And suddenly we're on the edge of Bow Street (where you would be unlucky not to see red kites wheeling above the road), the start of the final descent into **Aberystwyth**, where the mountains meet the sea.

It's a lively town, lovely at the castle and the old college, dignified at the National Library of Wales, quiet and wild towards South Beach and the Ceredigion coast. It's where we come to hide in coffee shops or the cinema, or watch the starlings whirl over the pier. And sometimes like today, we come to find a pub and watch the rugby. The Ship and Castle (☎ 01970 612334) is still my favourite, as good for cider and folk music as it is for real ale. Ultracomida on Pier Street is a great delhi and tapas restaurant, and it would be remiss of me not to mention the Dolphin (☎ 01970 624081) by the castle – an excellent chip shop where I worked one summer guzzling many delicious chips. ■

ABOUT THE AUTHOR | **JULIE BROMILOW** recently left her career in sustainability education to become a writer. She lives in mid-Wales and loves to travel – slowly!

A ROLLER-COASTER RIDE
YELLOW GALORE

Julie Bromilow

Aberystwyth 🚐

Service no. X50/550 | Journey time 80mins

OS Landranger 135, 146, 145. Six times daily Mon–Sat.
Operators: Richard Brothers.

Cardigan ◀

I was once a student in **Aberystwyth** and in love with the town where mountains meet the sea. This is where Led Zeppelin recorded early albums, and where I pulled pints in the Fountain on Sunday afternoons with the curtains closed – when Wales was still dry on Sunday afternoons. There were more chapels than pubs here – or was it the other way round? It's a romantic town, and I love it still. The X50 heads down a road I think of as new – this was countryside till they built a supermarket and moved the police to the suburbs. Welsh Government buildings are here now too, we pass them and the roundabout and out-of-town stores – and head for the south.

The driver is jolly and the bus is plush; it even has Wi-Fi and tables, but there's no chatter this early – my **fellow passengers** are all young guys who slump into seats, pull hoods over their heads, and go to sleep. But I'm awake and excited – this was the bus I took as a student teacher, changing in Aberteifi for connections to Pembrokeshire to inflict my new skills on baffled pupils.

I simply can't pass the radio mast at **Morfa Bychan** without remembering the scent of summer grasses. I used to scramble about these hills and coves, emerging scratched and feral. 'Cofiwch Dryweryn!' – 'Remember Tryweryn' is daubed on a roadside rock.

It's been there for years as a tribute to the village flooded in the '60s to provide Liverpool with drinking water. And suddenly we're in Llanrhystud, a pretty village and home to **Felin Ganol**.

I think of this, the A487, as the roller-coaster road; not a comment on the driving, but it's more the impression of speed as we climb to the sky, then roll to the coast, swooping through green fields and brown fields that meld and blur with the sky. The landscape's not intriguing although the **sky is wide** – the hills are distant, and the roadside farms are weathered, the sheep fields endless; but it's the sensation of something, of day dreaming, cloud watching, a sense that the sea is so close and sometimes you come to a great heart-in-mouth view of it, that makes me love this route.

But best of all is its yellowness. Gorse bushes race the road – as hedges with chamfered edges, dotted up hillsides in clumps, or random in fields. In spring daffodils march along the banks, in summer there's laburnum past Aberaeron – but it's the bright gold gorse which is constant, for as the old saying goes, 'when gorse is not in bloom, kissing is out of season.'

SMACKS AND SLOOPS AND PAN-FRIED HAKE

I get off in **Aberaeron** – though I'm suspicious of this very pretty harbour town. Surely these neat bright houses in lilacs and fuchsias and blues must hide dark secrets? I've never found any, nor any scruffy edges – even the £1.20 shop is receiving an attentive polish

---

FELIN GANOL WATERMILL

The Parrys bought this old mill on the River Wyre in **Llanrhystud** because of its pretty garden and granny annex. On finding the mill parts were all still there, they felt duty-bound to return it to working order. Felin Ganol is the only restored water-powered cornmill in Ceredigion. It mills organic flour just as it did more than 100 years ago. The mill is open for **tours** and flour sales by prior appointment – call ☎ 01974 202272.

---

this morning. Maybe it's the £1.20 shop that sums up Aberaeron for me – no bargain basement, but not too posh either.

A graceful **wooden footbridge** spans the harbour. Yachts and dinghies crowd the water, but an information board tells of a more industrial past, listing the dozens of brigs, brigantines, ketches, sloops, schooners and smacks that were built here in the 19th century. There's no industry now and not much fishing, though fish play a big role in Aberaeron's gourmet reputation. The Hive ('Y Cwch Gwenyn') (☎ 01545 570445; open daily 09.00–21.00) is always busy. I used to know it as the 'honey ice cream place' before discovering the hot food was just as good. I read the menu on the door – 'fishcake with mustard mayo' … and 'honey-smoked brisket ends.'

The Harbourmaster Hotel (☎ 01545 570755) opens early. I tiptoe past the Michelin awards in my scruffy boots but the welcome is warm from the owner whose grandparents owned the building when it was an aquarium. I sip cappuccino, read the papers, and gaze out at the boats from my Welsh wool banquette – before jumping back into my normal world and onto the bus.

The fields are strewn with molehills, the **gorse is gold**, and some of the barns are broken. There are mechanics and farm shops and cows (but mostly sheep) and barbed wire aflutter in bale-wrap. The passengers now are women we collect from the end of farm tracks, with shopping bags and daffodil lapel pins. They know the driver by name (Dave) and compliment him on his royal blue shirt which is clearly a hit – 'the new Richards Brothers uniform' explains Dave.

'Don't get off!' he says, when I ask if he recommends alighting anywhere. 'Wait till Aberteifi and have a walk there.' He's keen to suggest the 554, a circular route from Aberteifi that takes in

Aberystwyth
20 mins
Llanrhystud
Blaen-porth   12 mins   20 mins   N
16 mins   18 mins   Aberaeron
Synod Inn
Cardigan / Aberteifi

Ferwig and Aberporth on the coast near to Mwnt and Gwbert. He has a point – the X50 turns inland at Llanarth, though the 550 (which shares a timetable with the X50) does make a quick run to Aberporth beach and back. But I sit back to enjoy the rest of the gorse – there are other ways to experience the coast.

WHAT'S IN A NAME?

Cardigan County is Sir Ceredigion in Welsh, yet Cardigan town is Aberteifi – mouth of the Teifi. Whatever the name, **Aberteifi** has both charm and scruffy edges. Bedecked in fairy lights and ragged bunting, I sense there's often a party round the corner. **Small World Theatre** (☎ 01239 615952; www.smallworld.org. uk) hosts puppet nights and music in its magical timber theatre, and the Teifi Marshes Nature Reserve (☎ 01239 621600) also boasts a fine wood-and-glass structure overlooking the wetlands, which today are whirling in swallows. But my day is made complete at the cattle market where an auctioneer in the shadows sings sheep bids in English and Welsh like hip hop, like poetry, like the melodic chants of Mongolian monks. ∎

ABOUT THE AUTHOR	**JULIE BROMILOW** is a Shropshire lass who loves to live in Wales and writes about her blissful life in the valley in her blog at www.theyellowcaravan.wordpress.com.

COTSWOLDS & THE MIDLANDS

One hundred years ago (in July 1913), Birmingham Corporation made their debut in the bus business. It was a cunning piece of Brummie ingenuity, for the prevailing legislation was designed to preclude the city authorities from running omnibuses. Trams were the business of the corporation. But a loophole allowed Birmingham Corporation to run an omnibus in lieu of a tram service due to building work or where a tramline was being extended.

During spring 1913, maps in the corporation offices were embellished with many 'new' tram routes. New lines were plotted, extending the network out to the edges of the city and beyond. Most of these ambitious routes were never built. It was merely a pretext to run buses in lieu of trams on routes under construction. The ploy worked. The tram lines were never laid. The maps had served their purpose and were quickly forgotten. The corporation buses transformed travel on the streets of Birmingham. One of the greatest municipal bus undertakings the world has even known was in business.

The city authorities have long since handed control of buses over to other agencies, and nowadays services in the entire West Midlands area are co-ordinated by brand-conscious Centro. Yet Birmingham still remains a place where buses matter. The city's Outer Circle bus route featured in *Bus-Pass Britain*. For decades it had a place in the record books as the longest urban bus route in Europe. Eclipse Gemini double-deckers are in constant orbit on this circular route that has been a feature of the Birmingham bus map since the 1920s.

In June 2013, Coventry stole a march on Birmingham and launched its own circular route – one that, like its peer in

Birmingham, orbits through the leafy suburbs, but stays within the urban boundary. Local company Travel de Courcey runs the Coventry 360 service, which is rather longer than its Birmingham counterpart. So, in a new rendition of a familiar inter-city rivalry, Coventry has ousted Birmingham from the record books. Brum will surely bite back. That's the way things are in the Midlands.

Cut out of the city (as Nigel Roberts does in Journey 28 in this section), and there is some stunning countryside around the West Midlands conurbation. Nigel's journey leads us out of Birmingham towards the Lickey Hills, while in Journey 29 we skirt the edge of Cannock Chase, another area of open space that has long been a favourite escape for city dwellers.

Explore a little further from the major urban hubs and you'll find some wonderful countryside in a region that includes the Cotswold Hills. Edward James escorts us on a transect through the Cotswolds in Journey 30. This is a part of the country that matches all the stereotypes of rural England: thatched-roof pubs and cricket on the village green. It is a dream of England, a rather different dream from the one played out on the late-night buses that ferry clubbers home to the suburbs in the wee small hours.

The Cotswolds are rightly celebrated in tourist brochures. But this region includes a lot of other fine country. Make time to explore the valley of the Severn around Bridgnorth, the Forest of Arden in Warwickshire or Charnwood Forest which rather impertinently interrupts the Midland Plain northwest of Leicester. Further east, Leicestershire grades gracefully into Rutland, a county which hedges its bets in terms of regional identity. It is into the lanes and villages of Rutland that we venture in the first journey in this section of the book. ∎

MORE FAVOURITE JOURNEYS

The following journeys from this region were included in *Bus-Pass Britain* (2011): Banbury to Chipping Norton, Northampton to Leicester and the Outer Circle orbital route in Birmingham.

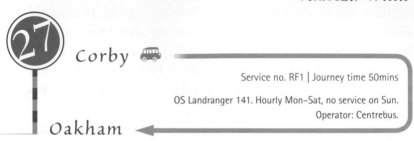

THE
RUTLAND FLYER

Alastair Willis

27 Corby

Service no. RF1 | Journey time 50mins

OS Landranger 141. Hourly Mon–Sat, no service on Sun.
Operator: Centrebus.

Oakham

What's in a name? The Rutland Flyer title is official, but it sounds more like a stylish 1930s express train, than a bus journey on a veteran Optare Solo, negotiating **country byways** in the rolling East Midlands. It is a bus route that compensates for lack of a decent rail service. There *are* direct trains from Corby to Oakham, but they run just twice daily.

This bus journey is **full of contrast**, leading from a one-time steel-making community, through honey-coloured ironstone villages, to charming market towns in England's smallest county. I like the RF1 most on clear winter days, when the unfolding landscapes and succession of fine churches can be observed through as well as over the tidy hedgerows.

In the centre of **Corby** a group of schoolchildren, gathered round the town's Steelworker statue, are learning about the area's industrial heritage. After the British Steel closures in 1981 local people suffered unemployment rates of over 30%. Today it's more of a boom town, in the top ten of up-and-coming places to live. In the 1930s Stewarts and Lloyds started up their first blast furnace here, employing many migrant workers from Scotland. Generations later 'Glaswegian' accents continue to be commonplace around town. Corby's Highland Gathering is the largest outside Scotland and residents have a legendary affection for the Scottish-made fizzy drink Irn-Bru.

THREE COUNTIES IN 15 MINUTES

I like my memento bus ticket, with 'The Rutland Flyer' printed at the top. My fellow travellers are shoppers and students, and as they board several have chats with Mark, the driver. Initially we head west out of Corby, passing the popular boating lake and parkland. Soon we're off the main road and head north through **Cottingham**, where it's good to see the village's thriving community shop and café. As we go over the River Welland there are glimpses of two striking country houses up on the valley sides, Rockingham Castle to the south and Nevill Holt to the north.

We've crossed from Northamptonshire into Leicestershire. Swiftly we drive through **Bringhurst**, which stands on an isolated hill. Its 'high street', a side road, is the shortest and most peaceful high street that I know. Soon follows Great Easton which is particularly attractive. Many of the buildings lining our route are of locally quarried ironstone, with thatch or slate roofing.

At **Caldecott** we reach Rutland. In 2012 the Office for National Statistics declared the county's citizens 'the happiest in England.' I'm surprised there isn't a queue of grumpy people just before the border seeking a better life in happy **Rutland**. We veer off the A6003 and on to Lyddington, one of the prettiest villages in Rutland. Buildings again are mainly ironstone, including St Andrew's Church and the adjacent Bede House, a medieval Bishops' Palace turned Elizabethan poorhouse, now an English Heritage property.

As we climb out of **Lyddington**, a handsome red kite hovers low over the

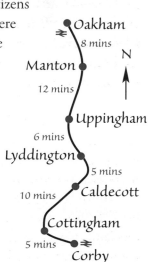

Oakham
8 mins
N
Manton
12 mins
Uppingham
6 mins
Lyddington
5 mins
10 mins
Caldecott
Cottingham
5 mins
Corby

fields. Their re-introduction to Rockingham Forest, by the Royal Society for the Protection of Birds, has been very successful. In Uppingham we pass the Church of St Peter and St Paul and the compact market square, which has held a market since 1281. Then we cross the elegant high street, once the main road from Leicester to Peterborough and the line of an ancient ridgeway.

UPPINGHAM TO OAKHAM

It is worthwhile spending an hour or more looking round **Uppingham**, and rejoining the Flyer in North Street for the onward journey. I like the town's old-fashioned charm and its range of independent shops and galleries. The west end of the high street is dominated by Uppingham School, established in 1584. Baines is a family business, opened in 1867 as a 'fancy bread, biscuit and muffin baker,' and has a relaxing tea room next door.

The bus needs several manoeuvres to turn at the end of North Street, providing an opportunity to view the school's 1923 Arts-and-Crafts-style cricket pavilion. Back on the A6003 we dash through **Preston**, and then straight on to the turn for Manton. At the east end of the village we make another U-turn, and there's an excellent view to the north across the expanse of Rutland Water.

Heading north, we skirt the western edge of this **Anglian water reservoir**, one of the largest man-made lakes in Europe, and a globally important wetland site for wildlife. Since the 1970s,

A WALK TO THE WILD SIDE

The **Leicestershire and Rutland Wildlife Trust** (☎ 0116 272 0444; www.lrwt.org.uk) manages both the Anglian Birdwatching Centre at Egleton and **Lyndon Nature Reserve**. Buy a day permit and look out for thousands of waterfowl and other species. It's a rewarding 1.5-mile walk to Lyndon Reserve from Manton. The **Birdwatching Centre** is nearer Oakham, accessed by a shorter walk from the Egleton Lane End stop. Come prepared with binoculars and appropriate clothing.

OAKHAM HERITAGE TRAIL

Following this trail is an excellent introduction to Oakham. Free copies of the **Heritage Trail leaflet** and map are available from various information points and the **County Library** (☎ 01572 722918; open Mon-Sat from 09.00) in Catmos Street, at the south end of High Street.

Rutland County Museum (Catmos Street; ☎ 01572 758441; www. rutland.gov.uk/museum; open 10.00-16.00 Mon, Wed, Fri, Sat; free admission) is a good starting point. It is very welcoming, and has a focus on rural life and farming. The Oakham Gallows, first used in 1813, are a chilling local history exhibit.

Back along the high street, turn into the marketplace, past the town pump and butter cross to **Oakham Castle** (same contact details and opening times as Rutland County Museum). The **Great Hall** is all that remains of a fortified Norman manor house. It has an impressive display of 238 decorative horseshoes, the earliest dating from 1470.

water has been pumped into it from the Rivers Nene and Welland. Rutland Water is a great place for cycling, fishing, birdwatching, sailing and other water sports, especially along the southern and northern shores.

On our way into **Oakham**, we pass Rutland County Council's HQ, which serves the needs of less than 30,000 inhabitants. There is a strong sense of community and independence hereabouts. After 23 years as a district answerable to Leicestershire, Rutland battled to become a unitary authority again in 1997.

Oakham is an attractive English market town, and we drive in along its bustling high street. Bus services terminate in John Street, a side street behind the Wilkinson store. For those who have not quite had enough of the Rutland Flyer, there is a chance to connect at Oakham onto the RF1's sister service. The RF2, also operated by Centrebus, tracks northwest from Oakham through more Rutland and Leicestershire villages to Melton Mowbray. ∎

ABOUT THE
AUTHOR
| **ALASTAIR WILLIS** lives in Leicestershire and enjoys rambling in the region where the counties of Leicestershire, Northamptonshire and Rutland converge.

Nigel Roberts

Birmingham

> Service no. 144 | Journey time 1hr 45mins
>
> OS Landranger 139, 150. Every 30mins Mon–Sat, hourly on Sun.
> Operator: First.

Worcester ◀

It is hard to imagine two more contrasting cities than the pair which mark the start and end of this journey. **Birmingham** once styled itself 'the city of a thousand trades.' Today it is a vibrant representation of modern multi-cultural Britain. Worcester has never lost its archetypically English county qualities, with associations to the Middle Ages, the English Civil War, cricket, fine porcelain, Worcestershire Sauce and Edward Elgar.

This route is thus a bridge from the metropolitan bustle of Birmingham to the more sedate pace of Worcester. Every bus on this service *should* be a double-decker, but the reality is that some are singles. You don't need me to articulate the panoramic delights of the top-deck front seat, so try to be amongst the first in the queue to board the bus.

PULSE OF THE CITY

I readily acknowledge that Brummagem (as we Brummies know it) isn't everybody's cup of tea; but it's my home town so for me, it's a steaming mug with two sugars. You'll need to save its riches for another (bespoke) visit, but do return for 32 miles of canals, the Jewellery Quarter and the **Balti Triangle** (look that one up!).

So it's a scramble for seats and we're off, tackling the traffic and heading southwest on the **Bristol Road**. The carriageway is broad at this point (as it is most of the way to the fringes of the city), with a central reservation of grass and trees. This was formerly the line of a major tram route serving the suburbs for commuters and day trippers alike.

'That's where I used to get off the tram to visit Aunty Alice,' says the woman in the seat behind me to her husband.

We sail past the striking Art Deco apartments of Viceroy Close, and then a few minutes later glimpse Birmingham University's **imposing clock tower**. If you've made an early start and have the time, alight for a stroll through the Victorian splendour of the university campus. Selly Oak now has a bypass to ease traffic congestion, but the 144 winds its way slowly up the old high street. This is **student land**, and most of the Victorian terraced houses along the many roads off the main drag are in multiple undergraduate occupation. Aficionados of Devon will smile fondly at the names of some of the roads off on the left.

'That's where we came for our tap-dancing lessons,' says the voice behind me. For some on board, the 144 is evidently a trip down Memory Lane.

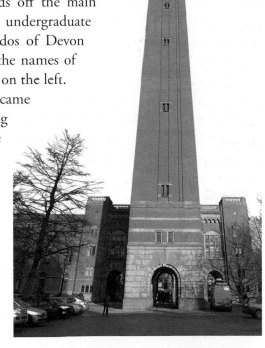

Clock tower of Birmingham University (photo © hidden europe)

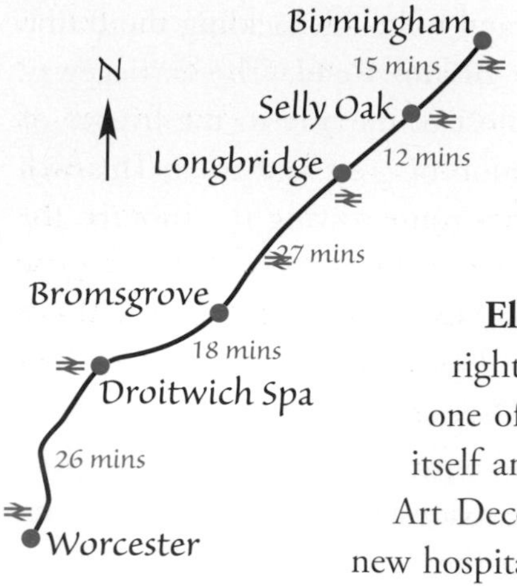

Birmingham

N

15 mins

Selly Oak

Longbridge

12 mins

27 mins

Bromsgrove

18 mins

Droitwich Spa

26 mins

Worcester

As we climb the steepening gradient, there are more glimpses of the university campus. After the road levels out, a full view of the stunning new **Queen Elizabeth Hospital** appears on the right-hand side, standing adjacent to one of the former hospital buildings, itself another beautiful example of the Art Deco style. The architecture of the new hospital is impressive on its own, but the statistics take it into new territory. It has the largest critical-care unit in the world and it runs the biggest organ-transplant programme in Europe.

The sight of the hospital evokes another memory bite from behind: 'When I was a nurse on the wards at the QE, I used to look out of the window at the university clock on night shifts and wish the time away.' This is exactly what my wife, herself a former nursing sister at the QE, says.

BOURNVILLE AND BEYOND

At the top of **Selly Oak** high street we reach a major junction. Away to the left lies the enchanting oasis of calm that is **Bournville Village**, home to the Cadbury factory and the Bournville Village Trust. If you have time, it is worth a detour. The bus that heads up there is the number 11 Outer Circle – it is an extraordinary bus route, one that orbits the entire city of Birmingham. Hop on an Outer Circle bus at Selly Oak and just over two hours later, you'll be back where you started.

But here on the 144, we merely skirt the edge of Bournville Village Trust Estate, before climbing into the busy suburb of Northfield. This is mock-Tudor territory, but the woman behind me has more than architecture on her mind. 'That's where you went boozing in the war; you liked to get boozed up you did,' is her take on her husband's relationship with Northfield.

There is a sense of getting out of the city, but Birmingham is deceptive. It's a fast run downhill to **Longbridge** – not to reach sylvan glades and misty meadows, but rather to discover the forsaken heart of the Midlands motor industry. Aha, no surprise that the voice from behind has a thought on Longbridge's complex industrial legacy: 'I wonder what they'll do with the Orstin? That used to be the picture house over there.'

FAREWELL TO BRUMMAGEM

The A38 turns right at this point and it's only a short run to the edge of the Birmingham conurbation. There are glimpses left to the **Lickey Hills,** where the tram terminus used to be, disgorging Brummies in their thousands for a taste of the countryside on their day off work. Slow progress along Rubery high street affords more glimpses of the Lickeys in close-up. As we rejoin the bypass,

THE GHOSTS OF THE CAR INDUSTRY

The **British Leyland** operation at **Longbridge** used to be a striking feature (no pun intended) of the British motor industry. The assembly lines that paused neither for breath nor sleep (except of course when silenced by the rallying cry 'all out, all out') delivered hundreds of vehicles every day; that image still lives with this Birmingham boy. Before British Leyland it was the **Austin works**, and most locals still refer to the entire site as 'the Austin' (actually, 'the Orstin' in Brummagem dialect). But the motor industry here is gone now, save for a modest production operation in a corner of one of the old units. The 144 bisects a vast site where once many thousands of Brummies clocked on and off daily. Now billboards foretell a **glorious new age**. 'A New Heart for Longbridge,' they proclaim. It is already taking form. What say the spirits and shades of assembly-line technicians and union-shop stewards of this vision I wonder? The Longbridge stage of the journey is an opportunity to reflect on the old and the new, the lost and the foretold.

the bus races out of Birmingham and we have our first fleeting glimpse of the glorious Malvern Hills in the distance.

Thus, less than an hour out of Birmingham, we reach **Bromsgrove**. The town's A E Housman connections are worthy of research and, if ever you find yourself this way again, do visit the unusual and impressive **Avoncroft Museum of Historic Buildings** (☎ 01527 831363; www.avoncroft.org.uk; open 10.30–17.00 Apr–Oct, but not on Mon exc Jul & Aug; otherwise only on weekends). Bromsgrove is roughly the halfway point on your journey and if you're ready for lunch, alight at the bus station and head to the right, along the pedestrianised high street, to the *Maekong Thai* restaurant (12 Worcester Rd; ☎ 01527 578888). I reckon it's the best food in town.

The A38 out of town first climbs steadily then begins to drop away as a Worcestershire vista unfolds. Look out for a small traffic island, where just right of centre is a delightful image that you won't have time to photograph, sadly. It's the escarpment of the **Malvern Hills** as a backdrop to the huge Droitwich transmitter, which will tug at the heartstrings of wireless devotees from days of yore. A mile further on, to the right, is Webb's Garden Centre, a feature in these parts for generations. The family has been trading on this spot since the middle of the 19th century. If the prospect of Thai food didn't grab you, stop here for a snack.

The small town of **Droitwich Spa** is soon reached – once famed for its brine baths opened in the 1880s, natural brine having first been mined and exported by the Romans – but look first for

GHELUVELT

Gheluvelt takes its name from the **village in Flanders** where in 1914 one of the early set-piece battles of World War I took place. Some 190 men of the local Worcester Regiment were killed or wounded. Many of those injured were later to be housed in this part of town. Gheluvelt is a fine example of a **municipal park**.

the curiosity of the Chateau Impney hotel on the left, just before you enter the town. The pace quickens after Droitwich, but keep glancing front and left for further glimpses of the Malvern Hills.

ARRIVING IN WORCESTER

At Perdiswell we cross the **Worcester** city boundary, and after a gentle downhill stretch through rows of attractive Victorian villas on either side, the road reaches a traffic light junction with a toll house to the right. This marks the start of the final mile of our journey to the bus station, and it will be time well spent to alight here and view the architectural treasures that await on foot.

The key sight in this part of town is **Gheluvelt Memorial Park** (see box opposite). You can wander into town through St George's Square, full of charming Regency and early Victoriana. A few hundred yards further on is the imposing **Shire Hall**, latterly refurbished to house the city's Crown and County Courts. Immediately following is the lovely Victorian Art Gallery and Museum ('the Victoria Institute'), while ahead lies the beautiful ironmongery of the railway bridge at Foregate Street Station, immediately preceded on the right by the Odeon cinema, one of Oscar Deutsch's Art Deco finest. The bus station is to be found soon after the railway bridge and down to the right, at Crowngate.

If you have time to tarry, make your way to Friar Street to visit the delightful Tudor house (☎ 01905 612309), or take a look at the National Trust's medieval **Greyfriars' House and Garden** (☎ 01905 23571). There are cafés and eateries aplenty nearby. And do return. Many treasures await in this lovely county town. But what a contrast to Birmingham. We have swapped commercial muscle for a gentler, softer England. ∎

ABOUT THE AUTHOR

NIGEL ROBERTS lives on the 144 bus route. He works on sustainable development projects with communities in Belarus blighted by the Chernobyl catastrophe. He is author of *Belarus*, published by Bradt Travel Guides.

A FAMILY TALE

One name which has been a recurrent thread in the development of bus transport in the **East Midlands** is Barton. Thomas Barton was first and foremost an engineer and an early pioneer of oil-fired engines. But clearly he and his family saw the potential of public transport. The **Bartons** offered a pony-and-trap service along the seafront at Mablethorpe, but by 1897 had upgraded to a motorised service carrying 11 passengers. This was one of Britain's first bus services not to have horses doing the work upfront.

A similar service was launched in **Weston-super-Mare** in 1899. The choice of location for these early bus services shows that travel in a motor bus was in the early days marketed as recreation rather than as a necessity. The bus was novel and exciting. It was a treat associated with being on holiday at a seaside resort such as **Mablethorpe** or Weston-super-Mare.

Thomas Barton's Weston experience was not entirely positive. Many of the men with great influence in the affairs of Weston had vested interests in the horse trade. The Barton family's enthusiasm for motorised wagonettes ruffled local feathers. Before long, their licence was revoked and the family returned to Lincolnshire.

In 1908, Thomas Barton and his son **set off to London** on the Midland Railway, intent on buying a new vehicle. Travelling south from Leicester, the two men chatted with the only other occupant in their carriage who was a director of a company that had just started making charabancs. A deal was done on the train, and the Bartons did not even proceed to London. They alighted at Luton and returned to the East Midlands, making plans along the way. The following weekend they **launched their bus service** from Long Eaton to Nottingham. The route still runs today.

The Bartons were ever innovative. When fuel was short during World War I, Thomas Barton devised a creative alternative of storing town gas in a balloon above the bus. Drivers were advised to avoid low bridges. The Barton family bucked convention in other ways. In summer 1913, Thomas's daughter Kate took to the wheel of a vehicle and, at age 20, became Britain's **first female bus driver**. 'Girl as Chauffeur of Omnibus: Sisters as Conductors,' reported the *Daily Mirror*. The centenary of this moment of social progress passed with too little remark. ∎

A Tale of Two Doctors
PROSE AND POISON

Richard Lakin

29 Stafford

Service no. 825 | Journey time 75mins

OS Landranger 127, 128. Every 30mins Mon–Sat, hourly on Sun.
Operator: Arriva.

Lichfield

Our journey begins in Gaol Square, close to HM Prison Stafford – as it is known these days – where the murderous **Doctor William Palmer** met his end in June 1856. Thirty thousand people crammed the streets to watch him hanged that day, but on a chill winter morning I'm almost alone in Gaol Square. I am stamping my feet to keep a little warmth as I wait for the bus number 825.

My hometown of **Stafford** doesn't shout about its heritage. It is perhaps a little shy of its better-known neighbours Chester and Shrewsbury, but there are interesting discoveries to be made. King Charles I and Prince Rupert stayed in the Ancient High House,

---

STAFFORD

The **Ancient High House** is free to visit and open 10.00–16.00 Tue–Sat. The **Shire Hall Gallery** and historic courtroom where the replica death mask of Dr Palmer is on display are free to visit and open 09.30–17.00 Mon–Sat and 10.00–16.00 on Sun. For sustenance before the bus ride try the **Soup Kitchen**. It dates from the 16th century and is tucked away in Church Lane close to Stafford town centre (☎ 01785 254775; open 09.00–17.00 Mon–Sat).

---

a wonderful Elizabethan timber-framed building towering above Greengate Street.

In the **Shire Hall** a replica death mask of Dr Palmer can be seen and the former Crown Court and its treasures remain as a reminder to the poor souls sentenced to death – or transported for life for offences as pitiful as stealing a loaf of bread. One of Stafford's former MPs was the playwright Sheridan. A blue plaque stands above the entrance of his former house, but a greater literary figure awaits us on our journey through the unsung landscapes of the Trent Valley to Lichfield.

ACROSS CANNOCK CHASE

We leave Stafford behind and the floodplain glints in the winter sun as we make the steady climb up Radford Bank. The breaks between the houses widen as we pass tennis courts, villas and Victorian cottages hemmed in by hawthorn and privet.

At **Milford Common** mountain bikers and runners go through their stretches, heels to bums and knees to chest. For years the Common and surrounding Cannock Chase provided welcome escape for a few short hours for factory workers and labourers who spent their lives grafting in the local industries of shoemaking and mining. A few precious hours were stolen on the fairground rides or sprawled on picnic blankets. The **Little Fawn café** (☎ 01785 664439) on Milford Common wins no prizes for its architecture,

---

SHUGBOROUGH

Many visitors are drawn to the **beautiful gardens** and, in particular, eight monuments of national historic importance from the enormous neo-classical arch on the hilly Shugborough skyline to the delightful Chinese House. Among the eight is the **Shepherd's Monument** built in 1748 and rumoured to have links to the Holy Grail story (☎ 0845 4598900; open 11.00–17.00 Wed–Mon from mid-March till mid-October; admission free).

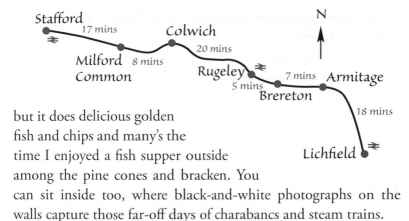

but it does delicious golden
fish and chips and many's the
time I enjoyed a fish supper outside
among the pine cones and bracken. You
can sit inside too, where black-and-white photographs on the
walls capture those far-off days of charabancs and steam trains.

Another curiosity is the Wimpy shack – once a familiar sight
on British high streets – tucked away, but busily flipping and
frying, beside the Barley Mow pub. We pause at the gates of the
Shugborough Estate, once home to the celebrated photographer
Lord Lichfield (see box opposite), before passing through hills and
valleys blanketed in copper bracken and swathed in mist.

Cannock Chase is a wild, open space within easy reach of
millions, so perhaps it is inevitable it has attracted more than its
share of stories. Thousands of soldiers trained here before going off
to the trenches of the Great War and a military cemetery is tucked
away amid the trees. There are lost mine shafts and abandoned
quarries and even tales of UFOs.

We pull up tight to the kerb and an estate worker in green
overalls steps out, cupping his hands and lighting a roll-up. The
doors stutter as they slam shut, wafting in the sweet cool air of the
forest before the drift of tobacco reaches us. We cross the bloated
River Trent on a cobbled bridge so tight the bus can barely pass,
but hardly a soul gets on or off in the villages of Colwich and
Little Haywood.

COAL COUNTRY

Next stop is the former mining town of **Rugeley**, dominated by
the four cooling towers of its riverside power station. An estate

of new orange-brick houses has sprung up close to the bypass. A sign says, 'Yes, 95% mortgages are back' as if it's the news we've all been praying for. We leave the main road and cut through an estate of grey pebble-dash houses, picking up chatty pensioners looking forward to perms and all-day breakfasts. I crane my head for the accents: Scots, Scots, Black Country and Geordie. The pits in south Staffordshire drew plenty of miners from the north.

Rugeley's most infamous son, the previously mentioned William Palmer, trained as a doctor but his real love was for horse racing and womanising. He was accused of as many as fifteen murders by poisoning, but only convicted of one murder, that of John Parsons Cook, whose grave can be found along with the Palmer vault in the town's **St Augustine's Churchyard**. It is a short walk from the house the doctor grew up in and the pubs he frequented. The talk from my fellow passengers today is of troublesome feet and aching joints. Perhaps they should be grateful Palmer can no longer practise in their parish.

We stop in Coalpit Lane in **Brereton** and driver Mark says a few words to Reg and Albert who are getting off here. The two men confide that they are heading off for their full English. We drive on and pass through Armitage – a name familiar to anyone who has ever drank too much (or perhaps met with Dr Palmer) and stared at the porcelain in a bathroom.

Arriving in Lichfield

Soon the three spires of the magnificent **Lichfield Cathedral** appear, towering over the rooftops ahead. The bus empties and I head for the cathedral, which was dedicated shortly after the death of St Chad in AD700.

The St Chad Gospels are a wonderful sight and the stained Herkenrode Glass in the Lady Chapel is stunningly beautiful, but, perhaps sensing scandal, my roving reporter's eye is drawn to the figure of Bishop de Langton. Once treasurer to Edward I the bishop spent five years in prison for adultery, misappropriation

For further information on Lichfield Cathedral's treasures, history and stories visit www.lichfield-cathedral.org. Admission is free, but donations are encouraged. The **Doctor Johnson Birthplace Museum** in Breadmarket Street is open every day of the week and admission is free (☎ 01543 264973; open 10.30–16.30 Apr–Sep, 11.00–15.30 Oct–Mar).

Chapters Restaurant, beside Lichfield Cathedral, has a 13th-century walled garden which is a delight in the summer (☎ 01543 306125; open daily 09.00–17.00 Apr–Oct and an hour less Nov–Mar). Also visit the **Tudor of Lichfield** tea rooms in Bore Street (☎ 01543 263951) for a delicious selection of cakes and chocolates in a wonderful building dating back to 1510. The tea rooms are just a stone's throw from the Samuel Johnson Birthplace Museum.

and murder (and several other offences so bad I had to look the words up). He even had to visit the Pope twice to seek redress.

The need for a dictionary takes us neatly onto another doctor. The **Samuel Johnson Birthplace Museum** is a great way to spend a diverting hour or so. I explore the basement kitchen where the nine-year-old Samuel read *Hamlet* and the bookshop where he worked for his father. It took Doctor Johnson ten years to complete his dictionary, a process he described with characteristic wit as 'a harmless drudge.' A copy can be viewed in the attic of the house and, yes, upon inspection it is clear the last reader has used it to look up a rude word.

The city is proud of its most famous son and **Samuel Johnson** frequently returned home. 'Every man has a lurking wish to appear considerable in his native place,' he said. The two Staffordshire doctors are remembered for very different reasons, but Johnson's fame is rightly far greater. Better to be a poet than a poisoner. ■

ABOUT THE AUTHOR | **RICHARD LAKIN** trained as a reporter in Staffordshire. In 2009 he won the *Daily Telegraph's* 'Just Back' annual travel writing prize for his essay The Great British Seaside. Follow Richard on Twitter @Lakinwords.

Across the Cotswolds
A Dream of England

Edward James

Cheltenham

Service no. 853 | Journey time 1hr 45mins

OS Landranger 163, 164. Thrice daily Mon–Fri, 4 services on Sat, one on Sun.
Operator: Swanbrook.

Oxford

I grew up in a working-class family in South London and we never strayed far from the metropolis. Yet even then I knew the grey stone cottages of the Cotswolds; I knew them from birthday cards, calendars, chocolate boxes and the lead illustration in the article on 'England' in my encyclopedia. Likewise I knew the **dreaming spires of Oxford** long before I became a student there. The Cotswolds and Oxford may not be typical of England, but they are everybody's dream of England, in England itself and across the world.

So come live the dream with me and join me on a ride from Cheltenham to Oxford on the number 853 Swanbrook bus.

GATEWAY TO THE COTSWOLDS

Some journeys on this route start further west in Gloucester, but the classic 853 route is the main section that runs east from **Cheltenham**, so let's hop aboard here. It is a route that cuts across a swathe of Cotswold countryside that is ill-served by railways and is largely bypassed by modern motorways.

Much as I love buses I have yet to find a beautiful bus station. Cheltenham's Royal Well bus station stands alongside the town's grandest building, a fine white Regency terrace, now the council offices, but alas all we see from Royal Well is the back view of drainpipes and backyards. In compensation there is a glimpse of the Gothic granite of **Cheltenham Ladies College**. 19th-century Cheltenham was a spa town and an educational centre, hence its motto 'salubritas et eruditio.' Today it specialises in gambling (the racecourse) and electronic spying (GCHQ). Any suggestions for a new motto?

A small crowd is waiting for the bus, mostly young people. Despite its reputation as a retirement centre, Cheltenham actually has a younger age structure than most English towns. A party of Korean students are making a first visit to Oxford. They have been in England only three weeks. One of them sits next to me and she delights in every mile. I meet her again on the return journey and she shows me her photos – 'they'll love these in Seoul!' She too is living the dream.

At first, Cheltenham looks less than perfectly elegant as we weave through the one-way system in the city centre, but once we strike **London Road** we find ourselves cruising past the white stucco Regency terraces with their black wrought-iron balconies which are the Cheltenham trademark. Cheltenham was once best known as a retirement centre for former Indian Army officers and colonial civil servants. Several of its finest **Regency terraces** were built by the East India Company for its pensioners.

This is not the route to Cheltenham followed by George III and the Duke of Wellington when they came to take the waters at the newly opened spa. They arrived from Cirencester over Leckhampton Hill (pity the poor coach horses!). We take the road Thomas Telford laid out in the 1820s, going almost due east. The modern A40

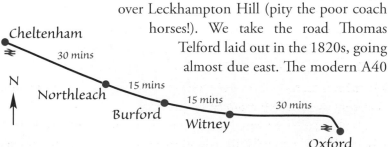

Cheltenham
30 mins
N
Northleach   15 mins
Burford   15 mins
Witney   30 mins
Oxford

mainly follows Telford's route, but the present alignment bypasses the villages through which Telford's coaches once galloped. Our bus will take the old way, down the village high streets.

The Cotswolds wrap close around Cheltenham on three sides, so we are soon into a steep climb through thick woods, passing the only lake on our journey. This is **Dowdeswell Reservoir**, the source of Cheltenham's water, built to tame the River Chelt which has flooded the town on several occasions. The hill we are climbing is the scarp face of the Cotswolds, a giant ruckle in the blanket of sedimentary rock covering southern England and a distant ripple from the orogeny that created the Alps. Once we reach the crest we break out onto a broad upland with views which seem to stretch for ever. Before long we are looking down to the left into the broad, shallow valley of the **Windrush** on its unhurried way to join the Thames.

THE HIGH COTSWOLDS

Our first village is **Andoversford** and then comes Northleach, which the locals insist is a town not a village; a good part of the local website is devoted to explaining that villages just grow but towns are planned. As we enter, we pass the 18th-century prison (see box top right) and then proceed down the high street to draw

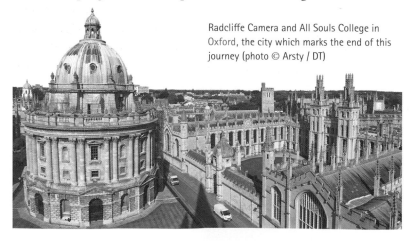

Radcliffe Camera and All Souls College in Oxford, the city which marks the end of this journey (photo © Arsty / DT)

up in the marketplace. The grey stone buildings with their stone-tile roofs look too good to be true, like a purpose-built medieval town, as indeed it is. After all, Northleach was designed by the Abbot of Gloucester in the 13th century. The garden fences still follow the boundaries of the plots he laid out for his tenants.

We go back onto the modern A40 and this time, rather disappointingly, we keep to the main road and don't go through the centre of **Burford**, although there is a brief view down the high street from the roundabout. It's the natural midway stop on this journey. Burford's steeply sloping high street is the stuff of picture postcards and certainly fuels dreamy images of quaint charm.

Next comes **Witney** and this time there is no bypassing; we halt right up beside the market hall, in the midst of a busy street market. The town was long famous for its blankets, which were popular with the Native North Americans in the days of the fur trade. The last blanket mill closed in 2002 but Witney remains a thriving town with good shops and tea rooms. It is popular nowadays with those who cannot afford Oxford house prices.

East from Witney, the traffic on the A40 very noticeably increases in speed, and drivers jostle more keenly for road space. Signs for the M40 motorway suggest we are getting closer to an England that is less relaxed. But look away from the main highway over the water meadows that surround the River Windrush and the **River Evenlode** and there is still plenty of space for dreams.

OXFORD

Nobody can 'do' Oxford in a day, let alone an afternoon, so you must be extremely selective. I recommend a tour of the incomparable **Bodleian Library** (30 and 60-min tours daily, extended tours of 90-min Wed & Sat). It is only a short walk from the bus stop and if you arrive on the 12.30 bus take care to book your afternoon tour before you have lunch (try my old 'local', the nearby **King's Arms** owned by Wadham College).

For the best view of the 'dreaming spires' climb up to the cupola on top of the **Sheldonian Theatre**, the hall where all Oxford graduates receive their degrees. And if you've seen all the colleges, try the prison, which is now a museum, a shopping centre and a luxury hotel (yes, you can sleep in one of the former cells). It was once a Norman castle and the motte still looms over the highway, giving another Oxford panorama. For a myriad further ideas call at the **visitor centre** in Broad Street.

OXFORD REVEALED

And now here we are, gliding through the genteel suburbs of north Oxford to end our journey outside Balliol College, right beside the **Martyrs' Memorial**, where Archbishop Cranmer was burnt at the stake in the reign of Bloody Mary ('we will light such a candle'). Everything – colleges, libraries, theatres, shops and parks – is just a short walk away.

As the sun dips, I am back for the homeward run. Kevin, the driver, welcomes me back on board. He has driven this route for three years and says he is rostered on the **Oxford** run four times this week. 'I never tire of it, it's a wonderful journey,' he says with a smile. 'It's nice at any time of year, but make sure you come back and do it again in mid-summer.' That's a piece of advice I'll certainly follow. ■

ABOUT THE AUTHOR | **EDWARD JAMES** is a former pension-scheme adviser to the governments of Kyrgyzstan and Albania. He lives in Cheltenham.

EAST ANGLIA & THE FENS

I n Journey 35 in this section of the book, Laurence Mitchell remarks that Lowestoft was once a town for seafarers but that they have long gone. The landlubbers who now populate England's easternmost town surely no longer go down to the harbour to make their escape. We have a Polish friend who works in Lowestoft and she tells us that nowadays anyone who tires of Lowestoft life makes for the bus station. 'I'm not sure I'd really stay in Lowestoft were it not for the X1,' confides Marika.

It must be said that we actually quite like Lowestoft, but we can also see the appeal of the X1. It is an extraordinary bus route. Here is a local bus that threads its way from Lowestoft to Peterborough, a journey of about 115 miles. It is up there in the premier league of long-haul locals.

If you have a bus pass, you could probably save a packet on heating bills by just spending hours every day trundling through East Anglia on an X1. Whether it would be the most comfortable retirement is another matter, for some of the Gemini double-deckers that work the X1 have now clocked up well over half a million miles. There is talk of new buses being introduced on the route in early 2014.

An end-to-end outing on the X1 runs to over three and a half hours. Marika tells us that the timetable suggests the possibility of a wee stop at King's Lynn bus station. 'All depends on whether the bus gets is on time,' she states.

Apart from the possible strain that the X1 might impose on the average bladder, we do wonder if this marathon route across East Anglia and the Fens is quite the best introduction to the region. Better, perhaps, to sample the five routes that we present here in

Bus-Pass Britain Rides Again. Among this handful of journeys is one that is unusual in relying upon a guided busway. This novel technology does not entirely dispense with a driver, but it does allow him or her to sit back, relax a little and even take their hands off the wheel. Now that's something we'd not want to see on the X1 – or indeed on any other route in this book!

Urban and Rural

A striking aspect of this region is the evident disconnect between the principal cities and their rural hinterland. Norwich, Cambridge and Peterborough are all progressive go-ahead places. Yet venture beyond the boundaries of those cities, and you will quite quickly find yourself immersed in quite another world.

This contrast is beautifully captured in Anna Blair's Fenland journey from Chatteris to Cambridge (Journey 32 in this section). When Anna first suggested the route, her idea was a journey from March to Cambridge, but that route was recently axed. Therein lies a lesson. This part of England has been sorely afflicted by reductions in rural bus services in 2012 and 2013. The cuts have particularly affected evening and Sunday services.

Yet while some services are being trimmed or cut completely, we note that elsewhere in the region operators compete for business on trunk routes. In late 2012, Anglian Bus introduced a new express service from Yarmouth to Norwich, competing head-to-head with First's X1 service which also links the two towns on its long journey across the region. With First offering X1 buses every 15 minutes on that leg, we do wonder if free capacity might not be better deployed on otherwise underserved routes. ▪

MORE FAVOURITE JOURNEYS

The following routes from this region were included in *Bus-Pass Britain* (2011): Cromer to King's Lynn and Diss to Beccles.

Through the Heart of Norfolk

Laurence Mitchell

King's Lynn

Service no. 1/11 | Journey time 1hr 45mins

OS Landranger 132, 144. Eight journeys Mon–Fri, four on Sat, no Sun service.
Operator: Konectbus.

East Dereham

This route in west Norfolk is actually two services combined, as the number 1 service from King's Lynn takes five minutes off in Watton to morph into the number 11 before continuing to East Dereham – same bus, same driver, different number. This is not the fastest way between the two end points – for that you would want the X1 Peterborough to Lowestoft service – but this less direct route provides a more rural ride. Along the way, it nicely captures the feel of **local landscapes**.

LEAVING LYNN BEHIND

At King's Lynn – just plain 'Lynn' if you're local – take time to look around the **King's Lynn Museum** (☎ 01553 775001; www.museums.norfolk.gov.uk; open 10.00–17.00 Tue–Sat; admission free Oct–Mar), which is conveniently located right next to the bus station. The star of the show here is the **Seahenge exhibition**, which focuses on the mysterious Bronze Age wooden henge discovered nearby at Holme-next-the-Sea in 1998. Locals worried that the 4,000-year-old timbers would be spirited away to London but, with a creditable concern for local sensibilities, most of them were brought to Lynn for display.

A quick survey of my travelling companions as we leave the bus station suggests that I am probably the only one who does not yet have a bus pass. Our bus edges through the traffic, passing **Greyfriars Tower** which is all that remains of a former Franciscan monastery. Some like to refer to this as the 'leaning tower of Lynn' for obvious reasons, although most locals simply remark that it looks 'a bit on the huh.' Next it's along London Road and past Southgate, a surviving fragment of a fortified town wall.

Leaving Lynn's **historic centre** behind, we are soon in an unprepossessing zone of industrial estates, car showrooms and 'drive-thru' fast food emporia but quickly leave this behind to manoeuvre round the town's enormous Hardwick roundabout before joining the eastbound A47.

Almost immediately we are in open country and the winter-bleached arable fields that line the road have rooks assembling in them, the imminent nesting season clearly on their minds. Many of the houses we pass by are made of **Norfolk carstone**, a gingerbread-like local sandstone that provides one of the main building materials in this corner of the county. The churches on the first part of this bus journey are constructed of it too – at Middleton and also at East Winch, where we pass a spanking-new housing estate built on land that not long ago would have been

THE VANCOUVER CONNECTION

With a long-standing maritime tradition, **King's Lynn's South Quay** has launched many a ship. It is from this same quay that **Captain George Vancouver**, a local man born in King's Lynn, embarked to explore Canada's Pacific northwest and subsequently give his name to a large island and prominent city in British Columbia (as well as a shopping centre in his home town). There is a golden statue of him atop the Parliament Building in Vancouver's state capital, Victoria, while an altogether more modest statue of the seafarer clutching a sea chart and sporting a tricorne hat stands in front of the **Customs House** at King's Lynn's Purfleet Dock.

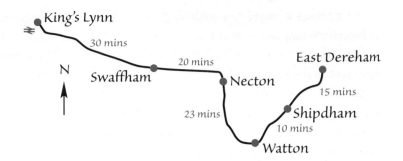

pushing up sugar beet. A little further on there are glimpses of water through birch trees as we cross the valley of the **River Nar** and then we leave the trunk highway to stop in Swaffham.

SWAFFHAM TO WAYLAND

Swaffham has a **compact centre** gathered around a square where pride of place goes to the butter cross, which has a neoclassical dome topped by the grain goddess Ceres. This seems wholly appropriate in such an arable region, as does the large Italianate brick **Cornhall** that faces opposite, although the latter has now been taken over by a well-known national coffee chain and orders for cappuccinos and skinny lattes have long since replaced heated conversation about wheat prices. Swaffham is wholesomely attractive but far from twee: across the road, a Chinese restaurant called East Garden displays a large banner that shouts, 'Eat as much as you like – EVERY DAY.' If a similar banner were put on show in more fashionable Norfolk towns like Holt the restaurateurs would probably find themselves tarred and feathered and driven out of town. Such is Swaffham's effortless authenticity that the town was chosen as one of the locations for filming Stephen Fry's *Kingdom* but the real-life Norfolk accents that echo around the **Pedlar's Hall Café** where I stop for a cuppa are altogether more convincing than those heard in the TV drama.

I catch the next bus out of town to pick up where I left off. Soon we're back on the A47 under the huge rotating turbine blade of the **Ecotech Centre** as we head east along the dual carriageway to **Necton** where we turn off south.

We are entering the wide open landscape of central Norfolk now and there are long views to the south as we approach Ashill. Ashill turns out to be much more of a proper village, centred on a large green, and after this we pass through **Saham Toney**, which has a primary school built almost entirely of flint as is the church next door. The village sign declares this to be 'a Wayland village,' part of the same historic Hundred that includes Ashill and Watton where we are heading. But the name Wayland has other connotations in most people's minds around these parts: **Wayland Wood**, just south of Watton, is a tract of ancient woodland that is said to have inspired the *Babes in the Wood* legend, while nearby Wayland Prison was home to both Jeffrey Archer and Reggie Kray for a while (but not at the same time).

HEADING FOR THE CENTRE

Watton is surprisingly busy, but not in a good way, its high street shuddering under what seems to be a non-stop procession of lorries thundering along it. No wonder the town is twinned with the asthmatic-sounding German town of Weeze. Watton is probably best known for its clock tower, which was built to house a fire warning bell after part of the town was destroyed by fire in the 17th century. The clock itself though is nowhere to be seen and a hand-written sign informs that it has been 'removed for restoration.'

The few minutes that Konectbus 1 takes to change into the number 11 is sufficient to catch the spirit of Watton. Then we hit the road again, now bound for East Dereham. We follow a twisting road for several miles before reaching **Shipdham**.

Just before we enter the village we pass a sign that advertises 'horse muck 30p' – a bargain for allotment holders like me but somehow I doubt that the driver would be keen on making an unofficial stop.

THE MID-NORFOLK RAILWAY

For Norfolk bus travellers broad-minded enough to consider another mode of transport, the **Mid-Norfolk Railway** (☎ 01362 690633; www. mnr.org.uk) between East Dereham and Wymondham (pronounced 'Windum') provides a highly enjoyable appendage to the Konectbus 1/11 journey. The **volunteer-run MNR** was established in 1995 when it bought and restored 17.5 miles of previously disused track between the two market towns. Its long-term aim is to continue the route as far as Fakenham. **Diesel trains** run most days between April and October.

Shipdham lies at the heart of the county, the dead centre of Norfolk. Large for a village, its **high street** is nearly two miles long end-to-end. But despite its length, it appears to possess just one single working pub at its western extremity, which means a long walk for a pint for villagers from the 'wrong' end of the street. The church, halfway along and visible from some distance, has a strange decorative cake-stand-like structure perched aloft its tower that makes it look a bit Russian Orthodox but in truth this is probably all that can be said to be notable about the village.

Central Norfolk, a low plateau with little to break the horizon other than pylons and isolated farmsteads, is a comparatively austere landscape compared with that lying further west, and it comes almost as a relief to arrive in the cosy market town of **East Dereham**. Compared to the territory we have just passed through this seems a veritable metropolis, with a marketplace, a host of good cafés, banks, pubs – and even a cinema. Indeed, High Street, which leads off the marketplace, might even be said to have something of an urban buzz about it. If this were not enough, there's a double-decker bus ready and waiting that promises a 'Norwich fast service' for those for whom even the bright lights of East Dereham seem a little dim. ■

ABOUT THE AUTHOR | **LAURENCE MITCHELL** is author of *Slow Norfolk and Suffolk*, published by Bradt Travel Guides in 2010. He has also written Bradt guides to both Serbia and Kyrgyzstan.

THE MEDIEVAL AND POSTMODERN FENS

Anna Blair

Chatteris 🚌

Service no. 9 | Journey time 90mins

OS Landranger 143, 154. Nine services daily Mon–Sat, no Sun journeys.
Operator: Stagecoach.

Cambridge ◀

The question of the best mode of transport for exploring the **Cambridgeshire Fens** has been much discussed. John Betjeman wrote that seeing St Wendreda's Church in March justified 'cycling forty miles in a head wind.'

On a Saturday in March each year, a bold group of walkers set off from March to walk via Chatteris to Cambridge. They do this for the sole purpose that their hike might be dubbed the March March march. Punts and canoes surely have their place in Fenland transport and then there is the rare Fenland town that still has train services.

Chatteris is not so blessed. Cast back half a century and diesel trains dashed from Chatteris to Cambridge in 45 minutes. The

---

CHATTERIS

Chatteris is a town whose butchers and bus services, chandlers and cake shops have been particularly celebrated by the **Indie band** Half Man Half Biscuit. The band has done its bit to put Chatteris on the map, commending this **small Fenland community** for its low crime rate. But Stagecoach don't take risks and so the bus to Cambridge starts outside the police station.

---

rail route from Cambridge closed in 1967. Today the number 9 bus from Chatteris to Cambridge takes 90 minutes. If one lives in Cambridge – and perhaps even if one doesn't – it's an important journey to make, connecting a town that tends to think internationally with the landscape it actually sits beside, and making the **histories and myths** of the Fens tangible.

Boarding the number 9 in Chatteris, it is immediately obvious that this bus isn't built for sightseeing. It's a single-decker with disappointingly dirty windows. My fellow passengers are bored teenagers. But we are joined along the way by a couple of older travellers, one of whom climbs aboard carrying an old desktop computer.

These passengers rarely smile, speak or show interest in the landscape. This is not the Cotswolds, and these are not tourists. But one knows where one's going on the 9, and there's something beautiful about that: the road lies out before you as if the **flat country** were Borges' map – the map that is the size of the world and yet not the world itself.

In the middle distance is a paddock crowded with hundreds of **swans**, more than I've ever before seen together. I imagine the birds plotting, sharing secrets in this rural field before heading out to conquer Britain, their headquarters a secret linking all swans together.

Across Fenland drains

We soon cross the **Hundred Foot Drain**, a highlight of the trip. It's beneath us almost instantly, a mirror interrupted by skeletal trees. It appears as if nature has stolen and drowned the landscape, asserting itself where people dared to build houses. In actuality this waterway, like other Fenland soaks, is nature harnessed; water's aggression has been channelled here so that the countryside itself can be habitable.

The tiny settlement of **Mepal** sits beside the Drain, dwarfed by the water. We continue along Mepal Road, raised a few metres higher than the surrounding land. These elevated roads have Roman origins, originally built up to allow for flooded fields.

We first see Ely Cathedral from **Sutton-in-the-Isle**, usually known simply as Sutton. The small hill offers beautiful views across the countryside, which can be glimpsed from the bus in the gaps between houses. There's a striking 14th-century church at the village's highest point and, like Chatteris, Sutton was mentioned in the Domesday Book of 1086.

Ely isn't far from Sutton. We enter the town, passing a large Burger King as we turn into smaller medieval streets. In some ways, this bus ride strips beauty from the Fens: they become 21st-century reality, not medieval myth.

In other ways, though, I'm reminded of how much truth there is to Cambridgeshire's medieval myth, how visible it is even when wrapped in postmodernism's less proud constructions. **Ely Cathedral** is a highlight of this bus ride as it is a highlight of this country, and Stagecoach acknowledge this crescendo with a 15-minute wait while we change drivers.

It's best, anyway, to dismount at Ely and explore. Originally named for its eel fishing, Ely is filled with antique shops, faux-independent candy shops aimed at tourists and birds circling around the cathedral. Further from the bus route, there is the **River Great Ouse**, where men walk dogs even in winter and Cambridge University's top rowing teams practise every morning.

ELY CATHEDRAL

Ely Cathedral, begun in 1083, is one of England's best **Gothic** cathedrals. It's hard to miss, towering over the Fens, but it's possible to miss some of the surprises inside. On the upper level is the excellent **Stained Glass Museum** (☎ 01353 660347; www.stainedglassmuseum.com; open 10.30–17.00 Mon–Sat, 12.00–16.30 Sun), with information and examples drawn from across different periods. If you've the energy for climbing stairs, the cathedral also offers **tours** of the Lantern and West Towers, the latter offering magnificent views across Cambridgeshire.

The most beautiful mo-
ments on the 9 occur as the
bus moves slowly between
Ely Cathedral and the square
before slipping along a narrow street
lined with stone buildings. We stop at
Tesco only a minute later, and passengers
nod at one another as they settle into
their seats. After the first minute, though,
there's a return to silence, with only the
regular roar and squeak of the bus as
it accelerates and slows with traffic.

The flat landscape provides
space for thinking, and the steady
onward passage of the bus is comforting, ensuring thoughts are
always literally – if not figuratively – going somewhere.

Chatteris
11 mins
Mepal
30 mins
Ely
17 mins
Chittering
N
35 mins
Cambridge

CAMBRIDGE IN CONTEXT

The bus turns into a number of **industrial parks**, shiny and new
with no connection to the landscape. '2000 offices to let,' reads
one sign, and I wonder what Cambridgeshire will look like in the
future, if the damp puddles and fields will be gone completely.

As it is, the industrial parks feel like interruptions: this world
belongs to seagulls and cows herded along country paths. When
dark clouds speed in, one can feel the sky extending across to
Holland. There are no major mountains lying between the Fens
and Siberia and this, they say, is why it can be so cold in winter.

This stretch of the road puts **Cambridge in context**: a modern
centre with its own satellite villages, not a medieval escape from
London. These villages are often forlorn spots. We speed through
Chittering without slowing. The last such village on the road from
Ely is Milton, where the number 9 slips off the A10. Milton has
the dramatic aura of a pioneer town, the first settlement after the
stretch flatness of the Fens.

At first, it seems a dark caricature of a country village. The town's main landmark, another Tesco, is designed in a postmodern approximation of Tudor style; fans of quirky architecture will be amused by the triangular clock tower. Nearby, a pub advertises large screen televisions ahead of ales.

Nonetheless, the bucolic is just two blocks from the bus stop at **Milton Country Park**. Fishermen wait patiently on the jetty and swans snicker amongst the reeds. This ecosystem, too, is indebted to the modern era; the creation of these lakes was facilitated by the extraction of materials for mid-century roads.

Milton is divorced from **Cambridge** proper by the A14 highway, suburbia's moat. Wider than the grandest Fenland drain, this road is a means of containing modern forces, directing cars around rather than through Cambridge. Everything feels tamer across the highway, and all the exhaustion of the Fens hits me, a sense of disbelief in the landscapes I've passed; the world behind feels instantly distant.

We pass the Cambridge Business Park, many houses, a furniture shop and a large roundabout. We **cross the Cam**, where genteel swans peck at boathouses painted in college colours, and the bus slips down the road between Midsummer Common and Jesus Green.

In late 2012, a bus on this route crashed off Victoria Avenue and through the fence, leaving tire tracks and stunned passengers in the wake of its premature stop on **Jesus Green**. I want this to be always the end for this journey, bringing the wild loneliness of the hours across the Fens to a more dramatic halt than a simple turn around a corner and into the central bus station. It isn't today, though, and I step off the bus and into Cambridge, an adult Disneyland that feels like a mirage, utterly improbable after hours of England's outback. ∎

ABOUT THE AUTHOR | **ANNA BLAIR** is a graduate student at the University of Cambridge.

Look, No Hands!
On a Guided Busway

Brendan Fox

Cambridge

Service Busway B | Journey time 2hrs

OS Landranger 154, 153, 142. Hourly Mon–Sat, no Sun service.
Operator: Stagecoach.

Peterborough

You may be surprised to learn that a through bus from Cambridge to the county's second city, Peterborough, is a recent affair. The service started in 2012, but has echoes of an older route. I have happy memories of the two-hour run in the days when there was not only a driver but a conductor as well, who even had time to chat. But that route was axed in 2001, and its recent revival is a good reminder of how transport technology has evolved since the millennium.

The **Cambridgeshire Guided Busway** opened in 2011 and was an instant success with passengers. No surprise therefore that bosses at Stagecoach soon had Peterborough in their sights. They checked they had enough vehicles equipped with the special guide wheels needed for the busway and then extended some busway services beyond Huntingdon to Peterborough. Nowadays this weekdays-only service is branded as **Busway B**. The use of a letter rather than a number is a mark of how busway services are something different.

So what is a guided busway? Unless you're from Crawley, or remember the old schemes in Birmingham or Edinburgh, it is likely to be an alien concept. In fact the bus runs along a kind of track made up of concrete beams laid end to end. A lip on the beams makes contact with guide wheels on the sides of the vehicles, making the steering wheel redundant. There is one track for each direction of course, and it is narrower than a normal road. That gives us a clue as to why it was chosen for the route northwest from Cambridge. It is along a **former railway**, so the busway can be accommodated within the old railway structures.

CREATURE COMFORTS

Cambridge's modern but cramped **Drummer Street** bus station is not a place to linger. Fortunately, the special nature of the busway means that Stagecoach spared no expense when drawing up the specs for the buses to be used. Passengers are keen to climb aboard the Busway B for Peterborough. They sink into **luxury leather seats**, power up their laptops for the free Wi-Fi, chill out as the air-conditioning kicks in, and feel good about low emissions from the 100% biodiesel. This is no ordinary bus service!

We're soon away, crossing the River Cam and passing **Magdalene College**. We stick to ordinary roads for a while, but at Orchard Park on the outskirts of the city, we get our first glimpse of the busway. It soon becomes clear that this section is just a spur, as our modern double-decker turns onto the busway

HISTORIC HUNTINGDON

Marking the midpoint of the bus route, the compact **market town** of Huntingdon is a good place to break your journey, especially if you fancy a bite to eat. Choose the **George Hotel** (☎ 01480 432444) in George Street to discover its link with local celebrity Oliver Cromwell (a museum is nearby). Dick Turpin was by all accounts a regular here too. Another good option is the **Café du Gallery** (☎ 01480 412622), tucked away in Newtons Court just off the high street. Expect tasty no-nonsense food and a friendly welcome. Be sure to wander a little further down the high street to the **medieval stone bridge** over the River Great Ouse.

proper. Here the B joins its sister routes, predictably known as A and C, but as these are operated by single-deck vehicles the B is definitely the way to go. Those big Fenland skies are at their best when viewed from the top deck of the bus.

Peterborough

28 mins

Sawtry

27 mins

N

The dashed line shows the busway section

Huntingdon

28 mins

St Ives

16 mins

Oakington

20 mins

Cambridge

With the driver's hands hovering only lightly over the steering wheel as the vehicle accelerates to around 55mph (it feels faster), the twin ribbons of concrete snake incongruously through the Cambridgeshire **rural flatlands**. Like the former railway whose trackbed we have usurped, the busway slips between the villages as if scared to get too close to where people actually live. Suddenly the old **Oakington railway station** is upon us, its 1847 building looking distinctly out of place alongside the 21st-century phenomenon that is the busway. This railway closed in 1970.

Now, by way of contrast, we come to a stop that is very definitely post-railway. The Longstanton park-and-ride facility is modern in style. Here, as at other stops, the concrete track gives way to a wider stretch of tarmac, keeping the driver on his toes and allowing buses to overtake if necessary. By now you may have spotted some of the dozen busway **'brick walls'** by artist Jo Roberts. Using locally sourced handmade bricks, Jo has taken various words suggested by schoolchildren and local residents, using wooden blocks to impress them into the clay. The last of these proclaims 'Oliver Cromwell' as we approach the end of the busway at the quiet market town of St Ives. After passing through the town's diminutive bus station we are soon winding a circuitous path through the various housing estates of its larger neighbour, **Huntingdon**.

ONWARDS TO THE NORTH

If you continue beyond **Huntingdon**, you'll be on the quieter portion of route B. The busway now well behind us, we stick to a B-road that parallels the A1(M) motorway. But this is no ordinary B-road. It is the old Great North Road, so it is a chance to imagine that you are a Roman soldier on a long march to York, or perhaps Dick Turpin fleeing north on Black Bess. The only pity is that our bus does not dive off the main road to take in the village of Stilton on the far side of the new motorway, but it does grace Sawtry with a detour. It is a chance to see **Sawtry's handsome green**.

Busway B has the demeanour of an express, so it shuns Peterborough's sprawling suburbs, sticking instead to the 'Parkway' arterial roads. It means that arrival in the city centre comes all too quickly. After catching a glimpse of the fine **Thorpe Hall**, built in 1656, the bridge over the railway marks our arrival at the city's Queensgate bus station and the end of our journey. It is a place with perfect onward connections both by bus and by rail. But not a guided busway in sight. That innovation is a privilege reserved unto just two places in Britain: Cambridge and Crawley. ∎

ABOUT THE AUTHOR | **BRENDAN FOX** is editor of Thomas Cook's *European Rail Timetable*. When not seeking out Eastern European trams or old buses he maintains a website with bus times for Peterborough at www.pbt.org.uk.

BENDY OR BORIS?

The bus business has always been innovative. In an earlier Bus Stop in this book (see page 144), we saw how Thomas Henry Barton brought much ingenuity to bus operations in the late Victorian and Edwardian period. In the journey from Cambridge just described by Brendan Fox, we read how modern **guided busway technology** helps speed passengers on their way in comfort and safety.

Buses are so much a part of the fabric of our cities, so woven into the texture of everyday life, that meddling with buses is a sure way of **exciting public opinion**. Remember the outcry when bendy buses first appeared on the streets of London? Articulated buses had proved very successful in many cities across the world, but their arrival in London was judged by many of a more conservative disposition to herald the demise of civilised life in the capital.

Outraged citizens saw the **bendy buses**, introduced while Ken Livingstone was still Mayor of London, as part of a left-wing conspiracy to challenge the reign of the traditional double-decker on London streets. When one of the new buses had a minor fire (which was quickly extinguished), the incident fuelled the imagination of headline writers. 'Fire-breathing buses threaten the capital,' screamed one tabloid. Media images suggested scrums of tourists fleeing self-combusting buses. Londoners succumbed to waves of nostalgia about the Routemaster buses of yesteryear.

Bendy buses were the political downfall of **Ken Livingstone**. **Boris Johnson** seized the moment. In his bid to become mayor, Boris promised to ban Ken's chariots of fire from the streets of London. And that's just what he did. Not since the first decade of the last century, when motorised buses suddenly pushed aside horse-drawn vehicles, has a capital city so dramatically changed its policy on buses. The new **Boris bus programme** has brought back double-deckers, but with a new design that has echoes of the much-loved Routemaster. Sadly, the vehicles do not comply with the latest carbon-emission standards, but that's the price that Londoners must pay for a slice of political vanity.

The bendy buses were sold off cheap, many ending up on Malta's roads. Back in London, **residents and tourists** all seem to like the Boris bus. Politicians across the world look in awe at the prowess in building the entire Boris brand on the back of a bus. ∎

THE CAMBRIDGE CHARACTER

Dominie Walters

Cambridge city service

Service no. Uni4 | Journey time 25 to 30mins

OS Landranger 154. Every 20mins Mon–Fri, no weekend journeys.
Operator: Stagecoach.

This is one of the shortest bus routes in this book. Yet it packs heaps of character into a journey of only about five miles. The route is subsidised by the **University of Cambridge** as a pro-environmental initiative to keep traffic away from the core academic area of the city. But the university also has many buildings and facilities beyond that central area so the Uni 4 bus also links research labs to the west of the city and the Addenbrooke's University Hospital in the south. It is the only **cross-Cambridge bus route** which doesn't trouble itself with the congested roads around the bus station and the shopping centre. Instead, it goes purposefully through the historic heart of the city. In doing so, it accidentally provides a potted tourist route, along with a snapshot of the quirkiness of Cambridge life.

ROLL CALL: BILL GATES TO GILBERT SCOTT

The Uni 4 is a mobile **Tower of Babel**. Just sit back and listen to the variety of languages spoken. Catch a couple of star researchers chatting over their latest discovery in the lab and even the English will sound like a foreign tongue. So there's a varied soundscape and a mix of people to match. Watch this chap here, doing a fair impression of an **absent-minded genius**, or that young woman over there, her face buried in some learned journal.

Those are the happy stereotypes of uni life, but the route packs a few surprises too. It's not all ancient buildings by a river crowded with punts and spanned by fine stone bridges, the green spaces dotted with cattle and shaded by willows. Just four minutes into our run, we turn off Madingley Road into **J J Thomson Avenue**, a road named after an early Nobel Laureate in physics. Here you'll catch the most un-Cambridge-like view you could imagine: futuristic buildings housing research labs, all set in a windswept open campus. Many are named after famous figures in the worlds of science, technology and innovation. The founder of Microsoft, I note, wants to go down in posterity as William Gates rather than the more familiar Bill.

We slip past one lab after another, stopping here and there to pick up students, researchers and support staff. Before long we are cruising south down **Grange Road**. Now just look at that extraordinary building over the rooftops. We all call it 'the U L' – that's short for University Library. It's an ungraceful abbreviation for a building that from

The 'mathematical bridge' in Cambridge
(photo © Toneimage / DT)

some angles looks just like a power station. That's no surprise, perhaps, for the architect of the library was Giles Gilbert Scott who also drew up the plans for Bankside Power Station in London (which now houses the Tate Modern).

Keep looking left and, as you reach the bottom of West Road, we'll see the **Backs**, that famous stretch of green space opening out to distant views of King's College Chapel and Clare College. The bus turns right here, and travels a short way along the Backs before turning left into Silver Street. **Silver Street** is closed to normal traffic apart from buses, taxis and bikes, so enjoy the privilege as you pass down to cross the river. The view from the bridge is a treat: on your left is the 'mathematical bridge,' a wooden footbridge of great ingenuity (see picture on page 173), and on your right is the mill pond, usually teeming with punts trying to get in and out of the punt hire station. Two bustling pubs, the Anchor and the Mill, front onto the mill pond, and their customers spill outside in good weather and give the area a party feel.

You will be very tempted to get off when the bus has squeezed along the narrow end of Silver Street and turned right onto Trumpington Street. You are in the heart of **historic Cambridge**, and you may want to go back and linger on Silver Street bridge watching the cheerful muddle of punts, or stroll along King's Parade. Definitely make time for coffee and cake at Fitzbillies.

FITZBILLIES

Watch out for this **bakery shop** on your left as you leave Silver Street. Get off at the next stop (Trumpington Street) and walk back. Fitzbillies is a Cambridge institution, rescued from closure by the Guardian food writer Tim Hayward. Generations of undergraduates have spent more than they should on its famous **Chelsea buns**. It has a great **Art Deco shop front**, full of celebration cakes, and a restaurant to the side. The latter serves interesting lunches, including savoury tarts and pies from the bakery, soups and salads (☎ 01223 352500; café open daily from 10.00; dinner Thu–Sat from 18.00).

THE BOTANIC GARDENS

The Gardens are open daily from 10.00, apart from a break over Christmas and New Year (☎ 01223 336265). The gardens still serve their main purpose as a **collection of specimens**: they have carefully labelled beds of plants, some grand trees, and fabulous lofty **glasshouses** which house, among other things, the carnivores of the plant world (a favourite with children). But Cambridge residents just use the gardens for the chance to laze around, picnic, and enjoy the calm. There is a smart **new café** and a shop.

Our bus journey continues past the grand neoclassical columns of the entrance to the Fitzwilliam museum, and out on **Trumpington Road**, a wide street with tall terraces of Victorian houses on the left and the Leys School on your right. The bus stop at the corner of Bateman Street is the place to hop off for the city's famous Botanic Gardens (see box at top).

The last part of the journey reveals a very different Cambridge. You will pass large blocks of new flats, a sixth-form college, language schools and a leisure park with an ugly Travelodge facing the road. Finally you'll get to the **Addenbrooke's Hospital** complex, as big as a small town itself. The hospital takes its name from a Cambridge don who in 1719 left a modest sum to care for the poor of the city. He could hardly have imagined that a small foundation would grow into a world-class medical facility.

Now you will have seen the many faces of Cambridge – the brash and gleaming new research buildings, the mellow colleges and bridges, and the mundane architecture of daily life. With luck you will have seen a fair cross section of the busy people of Cambridge: academics, nurses, language students, and ordinary townsfolk. You will have seen the **Cambridge character.** ∎

ABOUT THE AUTHOR | **DOMINIE WALTERS** was a Cambridge undergraduate in the seventies, when women were a novelty at Clare College. She now divides her time between Cambridge and Dorset.

From End of the Pier
To Under the Pier

Laurence Mitchell

Great Yarmouth

Service no. 601 | Journey time 90mins

OS Landranger 134. Hourly Mon–Sat, no Sun service.
Operator: Anglian.

Southwold ◀

G reat Yarmouth is not the place on most outsiders' lips when they speak of Norfolk. But, there again, nor is it Lowestoft that instantly springs to mind when Suffolk is mentioned. This bus service along England's easternmost edge crosses the county boundary to link these two workaday towns before terminating in a place that is much more a poster girl for the East Anglia coast – Southwold, a genteel resort where it can sometimes seem as if the 1960s have yet to happen. Despite a few common denominators – the **North Sea, boats, beaches** and piers – it is difficult to imagine two more different places than Great Yarmouth and Southwold, which is not to disparage either town but merely to note the cultural contrast that exists between the two.

Daniel Defoe once described Yarmouth as 'infinitely superior to Norwich,' but he was writing in the early 18th century when the herring trade was booming. Great Yarmouth has prospered as both a thriving fishing port and busy seaside resort in the past but slowly fell into decline in the late-20th century. Holiday makers switched their allegiance to warmer and cheaper resorts abroad. Nevertheless, enough remain faithful for it to retain two piers – **Britannia and Wellington**, the former having one of England's few remaining end-of-the-pier theatres.

Leaving Yarmouth

My journey begins just outside **Market Gates** in Yarmouth, next to BHS, where I find that the driver has nipped away for a coffee. When he returns I buy an 'Anywhere' day ticket, which allows me to get off in Lowestoft before continuing on to Southwold.

'You can use that anywhere, you know, even on Konect buses in Norwich,' he informs me helpfully, speaking as if the Norfolk capital were as distant as Samarkand. 'But not on the Park and Ride,' he adds. 'Anywhere but the Park and Ride.'

In Yarmouth, Norwich really does seem quite distant – far more than just 20 miles along the A47. Whilst waiting for the bus I had taken a stroll around and, venturing down **King Street**, discovered an enclave where, as well as a disproportionate number of hairdressers, trade seemed to be primarily focused on butchers' shops, tattoo parlours, tanning studios and Chinese take-aways. Polish supermarkets and a brightly painted café complete the picture, the latter with wall-mounted televisions showing Portuguese TV channels – this, a far cry from the sunny shores of the Algarve. The truth is, there's **little gloss** in Yarmouth these days – just the everyday needs of a working-class town and the cultural fixes of recently arrived immigrant communities.

TIME AND TIDE MUSEUM

There is nowhere better for getting a feel of what **Great Yarmouth** was like in its fishing heyday than at the town's Time and Tide Museum in **Blackfriars Road** (☎ 01493 743930; open 10.00–16.00 Mon–Fri, 12.00–16.00 Sat & Sun). It is easily reached by taking a short walk south from the bus station along King Street and then following the signs. The museum, set in a former Victorian herring-curing works and still bearing its lingering aroma today, celebrates Great Yarmouth's **maritime heritage** and growth as a seaside resort, and has recreated row houses as well as newsreels and photographs of the herring trade.

Pulling away to drive past the Victorian town hall at the top of South Quay we cross the **River Yare** by way of Harbour Bridge and turn left to travel parallel to the quay through Southtown. An industrial area of builders' yards screens most of the views beyond but a couple of ships can be seen at the quay – a trawler from Aberdeen and a black-painted vessel called *Keret* from Saint Petersburg. A little further on, the **Britannia Monument** can be seen rising high above the half-empty factory plots, a 144-feet-high Doric column topped by six caryatids and a statue of Britannia who, counter-intuitively, gazes inland with her back to the sea.

SOUTH TO LOWESTOFT

Southtown morphs invisibly into **Gorleston-on-Sea**, where the main street has yet more hairdressers and tattooists. A handful of retired folk get on at the Gorleston High Street stop before we turn right to pass through a mock-Tudor enclave along **Middleton Road** *en route* to the A12. If the name Gorleston sounds unpleasantly medical then at least there is a large hospital as compensation, and the bus briefly detours into the vast car park of the James Paget Hospital. Although a few hardy souls are sitting in wheelchairs puffing away in the smoking shelter, there are no passengers to pick up today – so our detour has been in vain.

A minute later we plunge into **farmland**. The fields are dull and khaki coloured in late winter. After a mile or two more, we cross

---

LOWESTOFT NESS

Ness Point (www.ness-point.co.uk) in Lowestoft is the **easternmost point** in the United Kingdom at nearly 1°46' east of Greenwich. The site is home to a directional marker known as the **Euroscope** and also to 'Gulliver,' Britain's tallest **wind turbine**. A quick inspection of the distances on the Euroscope will inform that you stand 465 miles south of Dunnet Head, the British mainland's most northerly point, and 352 miles from the Lizard, the most southerly.

---

the county boundary and turn off the main road to stop at a huge Tesco hypermarket that, somewhat pretentiously, has its very own clock tower, an unnecessary affectation considering it is open 24 hours a day. We slip past a holiday village – rather forlorn out of season – and enter the bungalow territory of **Gunton**. The enormous wind turbine at Lowestoft Ness suddenly comes into view looming over the North Sea ahead. Despite its constant proximity, this is the first time the sea has been seen on the journey so far. Another reminder of the sea comes at the stop next to **Lowestoft bus station**, where an Edwardian Catholic church is dedicated to 'Our Lady Star of the Sea' – the Virgin Mary imagined as a guiding star for seafarers.

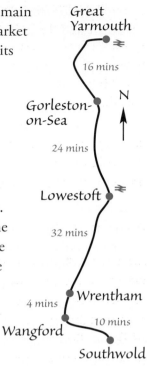

This church promotes itself as the most-easterly Catholic church in Great Britain, although pretty well everything in Lowestoft is the easternmost something or other.

Like Yarmouth, Lowestoft used to be very much a **town of seafarers**, once home to one of the largest fishing fleets in the country. Now the boats are virtually all gone but the gulls remain – muscle-bound herring gulls that swagger nonchalantly around town as if they own the place, which, in a way, they do. But, even without its fleet, Lowestoft is still worth an hour or two of anyone's time. If you take a walk to the ness you can delight in the knowledge that, temporarily at least, you are the easternmost person on British soil. Having bagged that windy extremity I take shelter in the **Poppies Tea Rooms**, which advertises 'breakfasts all day.' Given its heart-warming – and heart-stopping – generosity on the saturated-fat front, this establishment's large breakfast ('only £5.45, £5.95 after 10.30') would probably necessitate taking the first bus back to James Paget Hospital if it didn't stop you in your tracks there and then. Playing safe, I just plump for tea and a bun.

ALONG THE SUNRISE COAST

An hour later, I am back on the 601 southbound. This time the bus is a single-decker and surprisingly full. We go over the **swing bridge** and past a monument of a sou'wester-clad fisherman gazing seaward. Leaving Lowestoft, we stop at Pakefield's Tramway pub before reaching a retail estate at the edge of town where a beleaguered-looking woman gets off at the Morrisons stop, her six children in tow. The driver knows her by name and has been patient and understanding as throughout the journey she has done her best to get her charges, awkwardly distributed along the length of the bus, to behave and not annoy the other passengers. The kind driver even magically proffers tissues to wipe the toddler's nose at one point – a real credit to his profession.

We make a brief foray into **Kessingland** before returning to the A12 to pass through **Wrentham**, which might come close to most people's idea of a typical Suffolk village were it not for the main road thundering through it. The landscape has become more undulating now, with plenty of woodland and sheep in the

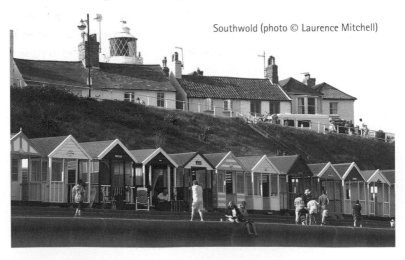
Southwold (photo © Laurence Mitchell)

SOUTHWOLD PIER

Southwold Pier (www.southwoldpier.com) is a good starting place to explore the town. The Southwold skyline is dominated by a lighthouse that mushrooms between the rooftops. To the south, the giant white golf ball of Sizewell B Power Station's dome can be seen in the distance. The pier is a family-run business (no entry charge). Apart from standard fare gift shops and cafés, the pier hosts the **Under the Pier Show**, an arcade of hilariously eccentric Heath Robinson-style machines created by **Tim Hunkin**. This includes delights such as 'whack a banker,' where you can wreak your revenge on the fat cats, 'my nuke', which allows you to load plutonium rods into your very own nuclear reactor, and 'pet or meat' where you get to decide the fate of an innocent lamb. Further along the pier is the infamous **Water Clock**, also by Hunkin, which chimes on the half-hour in an amusingly rude manner.

meadows – far more typical of the county as a whole. We leave the main road and wind down into **Wangford**, a pretty village with tidy cottages tightly bunched round a flint church. Then reed beds and marshes at the roadside signal the last stretch into Southwold.

Arriving at the western end of the town's high street, we pirouette around the King's Head before arcing north to arrive at the seafront right by the pier. From here it is but a short walk back into town. It's a cold day so I choose to head straight for a tea room but on any other occasion I might opt instead to visit the delightful **Sailors' Reading Room**, check out the wooden roof angels of St Edmund's Church or tour the Adnams Sole Bay brewery. Better still, I might even drink a pint of the selfsame ale at any one of the town's half a dozen or so pubs. With sufficient funds, the world is very much your oyster – or, rather, pan-fried sea bass – in **Southwold**, although you might struggle to find a decent tattoo parlour. ∎

ABOUT THE AUTHOR | **LAURENCE MITCHELL** is a Norwich-based writer. His blog *East of Elveden* celebrates the delights of the area described in the route (as well as spots even further east). Find out more about his work at www.laurencemitchell.com.

PENNINES & NORTH OF ENGLAND

T he Pennines and north of England offer some of the most varied bus experiences in Britain. Stand on the Wilmslow Road in Manchester on a busy weekday morning and you might well feel that here is bus heaven. A steady procession of buses slip by, using the Wilmslow Road bus corridor for their journey into town.

'Busiest bus corridor in Britain,' observed our Mancunian friend, as we watched in awe. Other cities may dispute the claim but, with seven bus operators competing on the bus corridor, you'll never wait long for the next bus. Frequency on the busiest section of the bus corridor tops 100 buses per hour at peak times.

That's one face of bus travel in this part of Britain. For another take on bus life in the north, head into the Pennines. The B6276 is an antidote to the Wilmslow Road bus corridor. It sweeps over bleak and windswept moorland on its way from the headwaters of the River Eden to the Tees Valley. The treeless Lune Forest is to the north, Stainmore Common to the south. And it was across this latter wilderness that we walked on a Wednesday morning in late October last year intent on getting the 572 bus to Barnard Castle. We missed the bus by a matter of moments. Close enough to the B6276 to see that it was a very handsome vehicle, one of antique style, bearing a Cumbria Classic Coaches logo.

Briefly, very briefly, we yearned for the Wilmslow Road bus corridor. Another bus in a minute perhaps?

A farmer driving an old Land Rover offered us a ride. 'I'll take you down to Middleton,' he said. 'We'll overtake the bus on the way,' he added. As indeed we did, and what a good thing that was for the next 572 was not scheduled until Easter. It's not Britain's least-frequent bus route (see page 85 for that), but the 572 is certainly a rare species. It's a one-way only service that operates on Wednesdays from Easter until the end of October.

Well, you'll not find the Wilmslow Road bus corridor nor the 572 to Teesdale in our medley of route in this section of *Bus-Pass Britain Rides Again*. But you will find eight journeys that capture the variety of bus travel in the region. We go to the Potteries region for an urban exploration. We have four journeys that lead us into national parks. And we pack in a surprise or two, with bus journeys through unpromising terrain that reveal just how interesting England's edgelands can be. We brave Billingham *en route* to prosaic Peterlee. We get an uncommon view of the M6 Thelwall Viaduct and check out the Manchester Ship Canal – once a major traffic artery. Indeed, in its heyday the canal was for ships what the Wilmslow Road is for buses today.

Holders of a concessionary bus pass for England can obviously roam at will across the region. But there are many regional bus passes that cover chunks of this region – and anyone can purchase those. For travels around the Peak District, for example, the 'Derbyshire Wayfarer' ticket (£11.10 for adults, £5.55 for children and 60+) allows unlimited rail and bus travel for a day over an area that extends well beyond Derbyshire's borders. Many individual bus companies offer great deals. An 'Explorer Northeast' ticket, which costs only £9.30 for a day, allows bus travel over a huge area that extends from North Yorkshire to Carlisle, Jedburgh and Berwick-upon-Tweed. ∎

MORE FAVOURITE JOURNEYS

The following journeys were included in *Bus-Pass Britain* (2011): the Honister Rambler circular route, the Hadrian's Wall bus service, Keswick to Windermere, Bowness to Glenridding, Penrith to Patterdale, Carlisle to Newcastle upon Tyne, Newcastle to Berwick-upon-Tweed, Buxton to Macclesfield, Hanley to Buxton, Matlock to Sheffield, Hyde to Oldham, Oldham to Ashton-under-Lyne, Leeds to Ripon, Bedale to Hawes, Whitby to Scarborough, Scarborough to York and Northallerton to Helmsley.

MILLS ALONG THE
DERWENT VALLEY

Helen Moat

36 Derby 🚐

Service no. 6.1 | Journey time 1hr 40mins
OS Landranger 128, 119. Hourly Mon–Sat, every two hours Sun.
Operator: Trent Barton Sixes.

Bakewell ◀

I am standing at Derby bus station, waiting to travel back
through time. This is the departure point for a journey that
takes in the **Derwent Valley mills** (a UNESCO World Heritage
Site) and continues to the picturesque Peak town of Bakewell.

My bus arrives and I climb aboard with city workers, shoppers
and other day trippers.

'Eeh up, m' ducks.'

'How ye bin?'

'Fair to middlin', aye.'

'Get on wi' thee.'

The flat **Derbyshire voices** bounce around the bus. The route
is well-used by locals and there is a lively atmosphere on the bus as
the travellers chatter and joke together.

The Sixes are a family of services run by Trent Barton. The
buses are clean and bright with large picture windows. 'Fancy a
road trip?' reads the advert for the company's 'Zigzag' ticket. It's a
pass that costs a fiver and gives unlimited bus travel across Trent
Barton land after the morning peak.

Soon we are leaving the leafy suburbs of Derby behind and
heading up the Derwent Valley on the A6. At first the landscape
is expansive, but slowly the hills close in. At **Milford** we catch

a glimpse of a water-powered cotton mill built by Jedediah Strutt. The Strutt family pop up here and there along this trip. We pass over a low-built stone bridge and continue, with the River Derwent now on our left, before long reaching **Belper**. At first sight it's a down-to-earth place but you see its mills soaring heavenward like industrial cathedrals. We find Jedediah here too. He built the North Mill which nowadays hosts a homely museum exhibiting a wide range of factory paraphernalia including spinning machinery.

Bakewell

23 mins

N

Matlock

8 mins

Cromford

7 mins

Wirksworth

22 mins

Belper

28 mins

Derby

Trent Barton like to tease their passengers. I am warming to the mill theme, but now we leave the Derwent Valley, detouring west through undulating farmland to serve **Wirksworth**. It's worth stopping off at this pretty market town popular with artists. Beyond Wirksworth the countryside begins to change. Here the land is higher, the hillsides steeper with rock faces rising dramatically from the valley. The bus driver, foot hard on the brake, inches down to the village of **Cromford**. The bus squeaks past impossibly narrow three-storied terraced homes with tiny, tiny windows.

Hidden treasures

The bus stops outside the market square beside the handsome Greyhound Hotel. If you look carefully, there's a narrow lane hidden away in the corner of the square that leads up to **Scarthin Books** (☎ 01629 823272). The bookshop sits opposite the village pond, home to mallards and a swan. This is a fine place to while away an hour or two. Scarthin's is an eccentric, higgledy-piggledy establishment composed of a series of connecting rooms that are filled with an odd assortment of objects and furniture (and books, of course). Need freshening up? The toilet has an ancient roll-top

THE WILLERSLEY CASTLE SAGA

Richard Arkwright, tiring of the gloomy Rock House next to Masson Mill, bought a large tract of land from Florence Nightingale's family and set out to build an elegant mansion, Willersley Castle, on the sunny side of the valley close to **Cromford Mill**. As luck would have it, the house burnt down as soon as it was completed and Arkwright had to wait a further two years for the house to be rebuilt. Fate was to conspire against him again as the unfortunate Arkwright died just before he was due to move in.

bath in it! Require refreshments? Uncover the secret organic café hidden behind a curved bookcase. But best of all are the weight-bent shelves of new and second-hand books. You need look no further if you want to learn more about the Derwent Valley mills.

Of all the mills on the trail, **Cromford Mill** is surely the most significant. It was the first successful water-powered cotton-spinning mill in the world. Built by Richard Arkwright (who started out in partnership with Strutt), Cromford Mill has been carefully restored and is an excellent example of industrial history.

TO MATLOCK AND BEYOND

Now back on the A6, the bus heads towards Matlock Bath. Not far out of Cromford is Arkwright's **Masson Mill**. It is mainly a shopping complex nowadays, but there's also a small **museum** in its bowels (☎ 01629 581001; open daily 10.00–1600 Mon–Sat, 11.00–16.00 Sun). Between the retail clothing, you'll find bobbins of all shapes and sizes, baskets of cotton and a clocking-in machine for the workers. A tour of the tucked-away museum will give you the chance to see the spinning machines at work.

Just across the road from Masson Mill is Arkwright's large, rambling house. An oppressive, towering presence, it was a constant reminder to Arkwright's employees that they were being watched, even when Arkwright was absent from the mill. And

Arkwright kept an eagle eye on his workers at all times, locking the factory gates precisely at six every morning. If a worker didn't make it in time, regardless of the reason, they lost a day's wages. Nonetheless, Arkwright's employees were fiercely loyal to him as he provided them with money, homes and a week's holiday (as long as they didn't leave the village). He also refused to employ children under the age of seven. But ultimately, Arkwright was a man of his times, a strict and fearsome autocrat.

The bus continues on through **Matlock Bath**. The Victorians called this part of the valley 'Little Switzerland' but Matlock Bath is more of a 'Little Blackpool' with its rows of souvenir shops, slot machines and fish-and-chip shops. It even has its own illuminations. Unlike Blackpool, there is, of course, no sea at Matlock Bath, but the promenade that runs alongside the river gives the landlocked town a seaside feel.

The bus now squeezes through the narrow valley with its soaring rocks and passes under the cable cars that rise up to the cave system on the **Heights of Abraham**. Soon the bus reaches the town of Matlock.

Cromford Mill (photo © Geoffrey Allerton / DT)

Slightly off the Derwent trail on the outskirts of Matlock is Lumsdale, a forgotten wooded gorge. Hidden off a narrow country lane and obscured by thick undergrowth, few venture here, yet it's a place of strange decaying beauty. The first mill was built here in the 1600s. By the height of the

Industrial Revolution, there were at least seven mills crammed into this narrow dale.

It's worth making your way out there to climb the **steep-sided ravine** (knees permitting) to the ruins of the old mills. If you close your eyes, you can almost smell the ground minerals, the crunched bone of animal, the chaff of the wheat and the woven cotton and imagine the millstone grinding and the voices of mill workers hanging in the heavy, dust-filled air. High above the dale, a waterfall spills a hundred feet. At the top, there is one surviving mill pond of three.

Back on the bus, we wind our way through **Darley Dale** and on to Rowsley. There's one last mill here: Caudwell, a flour mill with a riverside café, craft shop and museum. The bus now enters the **Peak District National Park**, fittingly signed with a millstone, then makes its way through woodland, dale and hill, past the stately home of Haddon Hall and on into the picture-postcard town of Bakewell. Here you can grab yourself a Bakewell tart and a coffee and reflect on the Derwent Valley mills that line the gateway to the beautiful Peak Park. It's a fine finishing point on a magnificent bus route rich in history. ∎

ABOUT THE
AUTHOR

HELEN MOAT is happiest when travelling and writing about her experiences. Her writing has been published in the *Guardian*, the *Daily Telegraph* and *Wanderlust* magazine.

A PEEK AT THE PEAKS
OFF TO MAM TOR

Ian M Packham

37 Sheffield 🚌

Service no. 272 | Journey time 50 to 70mins

OS Landranger 110. Hourly every day.
Operator: First South Yorkshire, TM Travel, Hulleys of Baslow.

Castleton ◀

I have a choice of three bus operators on this short route. There is something contrary about taking the off-white First South Yorkshire double-decker into the Peak District. It gives a definite sense of energetic Sheffield washing over the city boundary into a rural hinterland. I prefer the **double-deckers** for that very contrariness, though the other two companies playing the route, TM Travel and Hulleys, use single-deckers that are perhaps a little more luxurious, relaxed and friendly; country buses entering the city rather than a city bus in the country.

The **centre of Sheffield** lies just five miles from the border with Britain's first national park, and only 16 miles from my destination of Castleton. Yet every year the majority of the ten million plus visitors use their cars, creating increasing problems with congestion and pollution for the national park authority and Peak District inhabitants. It's unusual to see more than a handful of tourists on the 272. The bus is used primarily by residents of the scatter of **Derbyshire villages** that lie on the route.

The journey starts at Sheffield Transport Interchange, positioned between the train station and the city centre's galleries, winter garden and shopping district. This is the heart of Sheffield and one of the city's most diverse areas. Gallery-goers mingle with

HIGH, LOW, WHITE OR DARK PEAK?

The term White Peak comes from the colour of the area's limestone bedrock. The area is also called the Low Peak to distinguish it from the High Peak region of the national park. The High Peak area is formed from a **high moorland plateau** of dark stone. It is recognised as the highest and wildest part of the Peak District. In contrast to the White Peak, the limestone beneath the heather of the High Peak is covered by a cap of **millstone grit**, a coarse-grained sandstone. This ensures the soil above it is continuously wet through the winter months, creating a dark soil that gives the High Peak its alternative name of the **Dark Peak**.

after-school skateboarders; and busy shoppers with cloth-capped elderly gentlemen. The Interchange gives no sense of the feeling of freedom to come, the uninspiring glazed structures trapping the diesel fumes of waiting buses.

INTO SUBURBIA

From the heart of the city, the 272 tracks southwest towards the leafy, green parks and ancient woodlands that dot the commuter belt of suburban housing along **Ecclesall Road**. A key artery for the city's inhabitants, the road is an excellent area in which to get a sense of Sheffield's welcoming atmosphere. Despite being Britain's fifth-largest city, Sheffield is proud of its reputation as a friendly city and of having the highest proportion of trees to people of any city in Europe. I'm frequently told the city 'is the largest village in England' –it certainly feels like it.

My bus continues along Ecclesall Road for more than three miles. The change from side roads of suburban housing and narrow shop-fronts to larger industrial premises records my departure from the city centre.

The route kisses ancient woodlands before edging past **Dore**, one of the wealthiest suburbs of the city. Now part of Sheffield,

Dore was once a town of neighbouring Derbyshire. Before that, it was the boundary between Anglo-Saxon Northumbria and Mercia, and the site where Wessex's King Ecgbert became the first 'Overlord of all England' in AD829. Following a twist in the road to face west on passing Dore, a small cluster of fields becomes visible. The bus cuts a stolid figure between the farmland that separates the Sheffield conurbation from the wilds of the moorland.

The route continues with few true turns though the road it follows changes name several times, marking its progress from village to village. Now **Hathersage Road**, it loses its pavements to verdant verges and hedgerows outside settlements. The cream stones of Sheffield are swapped for the greens, browns, and purples of the Peak District.

The simplicity of the bus route allows me to examine the open landscapes that surround the vehicle. My seat on the top deck gives a unique, even unusual, perspective on rolling heathlands and the limestone outcrops of **Hope Valley**. It's a name that lingers in my thoughts like the aromas of a warm pint of ale washing over my tongue. On the road verge is a simple round stone on a rectangular plinth that marks our entry into the national park. Farms and woodland continue on the left, moorland of a mysterious almost sinister purple in the spring light to my right.

After the Fox House Inn in **Longshaw**, the bus follows the road's tight twists first right then left, passing over Padley Gorge. The farmland disappears, the untamed wilderness mixing with woods before the stone buildings of Hathersage come into view and the bus enters Derbyshire.

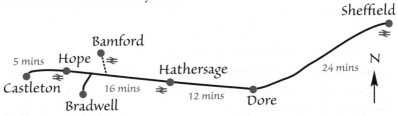

The dotted line indicates that the route is only used on certain journeys. Bradwell to Castleton takes 10 mins.

The route beyond **Hathersage** sees the fields return, their boundaries dotted with deciduous trees. The road straightens out as it continues its passage further westward, now paralleling the Hope Valley railway line. Crossing the Pennines to link Sheffield and Manchester, the line was completed in 1894.

Near Bamford railway station, the next stop along the Hope Valley line, the buses operated by Hulley's make a short detour from the main road, turning north to serve Bamford, a village of 1,400 residents. The village, less than a mile off the main road, is home to the Touchstone Sculpture Trail, created to commemorate the millennium. The five-mile trail is a good place to stretch stiffening legs. The modern monolithic sculptures were designed by local families and created by resident artist Jenny Mather. They depict the four elements of earth, wind, fire, and water, and are also combined in a fifth sculpture in the centre of **Bamford**.

FROM GREEN PASTURES TO WHITE QUARRIES

A second diversion, made by most buses on this route, takes us down to **Bradwell**, a village of stone-built cottages. It seems a traditional sort of place, but the view is not quite the rural idyll one might expect. A cement factory and adjoining quarry give a bold splash of grey-white, offsetting the rich green of surrounding farmland.

The cement factory at Bradwell is a foretaste of what is to come. Hope has an even larger cement works, a strange cuboid structure beside an even taller, slender round smokestack. Mercifully, this eyesore is largely hidden from the village, which has a fine location at the point where **Peakshole Water** joins the River Noe.

It is just a few minutes to the final stop. Castleton is an easy village to navigate. **Peveril Castle** stands proudly on a vantage point to the south of the town centre; the four limestone show caverns of Treak Cliff, Blue John, Peak, and Speedwell are all a short walk to the west. It was in these caves that minerals like semi-precious Blue John used to be mined.

THE CASTLE THAT NAMED A TOWN

The English Heritage-owned **Peveril Castle** right in the heart of Castleton is an excellent place to get to grips with the history of the High Peak (☎ 01433 620613; open daily 10.00–16.00 Apr–Oct, call for other times). With a keep occupying the southern corner dating back to 1176 and the reign of Henry II, the ruined castle has a great position overlooking the town from a steep hillside. Already recorded in the Domesday Book, the roughly **triangular Norman fortress** has sheer drops on all but one side. A breathy winding path leads up the remaining side, giving superb views across **Hope Valley**. It's possible to enter several rooms in the keep, including a Norman-era toilet.

Mam Tor threatens the village with shade to the northwest, a great rounded mound looking like a benign green boil on the skin of the earth. It is threatened in return by the sheer number of visitors that wrestle with its steep flanks each high season in the High Peak.

At 1,696 feet, **Mam Tor** is the spiritual focus not only of Castleton, but of my whole journey on the 272 from Sheffield. For much of the route I have followed Hope Valley, which ends in the shadow of Mam Tor. The source of Peakshole Water lies below the hill too, before running beside cottages and paths so narrow it is difficult to pass the postman and his large red shoulder bag.

Mam Tor's summit provides views of the castle, and the cement works at Hope. For me the contrasting vertical structures, old and new, demonstrate the enduring struggle we have in this crowded country between maintaining our open spaces and providing the jobs and materials we need for our cities. It's this very clash between the countryside around **Castleton** and the city of Sheffield that the 272 helps to highlight. ∎

ABOUT THE AUTHOR | **IAN M PACKHAM** is a scientist, adventurer and speaker. He enjoys off-beat, off-season travel, preferably by public transport, and is developing a career in writing.

HEADING UP HANLEY
A POTTERIES RIDE

William Jones

Newcastle-under-Lyme

Service no. 26 | Journey time 55 to 70mins

OS Landranger 118. Every 20mins Mon–Sat, hourly on Sun.
Operator: First Potteries.

Hanley ◄

You can get from Newcastle-under-Lyme to Hanley easily on a direct bus. But if, like me, you enjoy nosing around old industrial areas, take service 26 instead. It describes a 12-mile horseshoe, visiting four of the six **towns of the Potteries** – a post-industrial landscape that whilst not always inspiring still provides glimpses of a proud civic and manufacturing past. Listen to the locals chatting as you ride along; you get the impression they all know each other!

Newcastle-under-Lyme has a different character to other places on this route. It has the air of a market town. The wide high street is dominated by the handsome Guildhall and a market is indeed still held here six days a week. The pottery industry never really developed here and the town has distanced itself from its more industrial neighbours to the east.

When six Potteries towns came together to form the city of Stoke-on-Trent early in the last century, Newcastle kept its distance from the upstart agglomeration and has keenly preserved its identity ever since. Fine **seasonal floral displays** enhance the market-town feel. As soon as the bus leaves Newcastle though, things begin to change as we pass the terraced streets of Hartshill and descend towards the Trent Valley and Stoke itself.

Names are complicated here. Stoke has given its name to the conurbation, but when locals speak of the 'city centre' they mean Hanley, the undoubted commercial centre of the federation. I hear two students chatting as we roll downhill into Stoke. 'It's all take-aways and abandoned stuff here,' claims one. Her friend concurs: 'Yeah, Stoke is such a dump.' This does not bode well.

We can sense the decline here; Spode, one of the great pottery companies, was based right in the centre of town but the factory is now closed and empty behind padlocked gates. Discount furniture stores and charity shops seem to dominate, but look around – Stoke has a fine town hall, whilst opposite is **Stoke Minster**, not quite in the same league as York but worth a visit. Along London Road stands the unusual old library building with its big round windows and mosaic of Shakespeare, whilst close by is the Portmeirion Factory, still very much in business.

BLASTS FROM THE PAST

Below the junction with the A500 is the **River Trent**, squeezed between concrete retaining walls and looking disappointingly small. We reach Fenton, perhaps the most diminished of the

STOKE MINSTER

In 2005, this fine church of **St Peter ad Vincula** was designated Minster in recognition of its spiritual role in the city. Built in 1826–30 it is very much a church of the **Industrial Revolution**. There are memorials inside to those great potters, Wedgwood and Spode and their families. Examine the fascinating diamond-shaped memorial tiles of local families and individuals. The Czech cross was donated by the wife of **Sir Stanley Matthews** whose funeral took place here. In the churchyard are the remains of an older church, overlooking the tomb of Josiah Wedgwood himself (☎ 01782 747785; 12.30–13.30 Tue, 09.30–15.00 Wed, 12.00–15.00 Thu–Sat; but if the ladies who look after the church are around they will let you in!).

six towns. At first it seems to have no centre, but a short walk leads to a square overlooked by the massive brick Christ Church. Here are a distinctive group of civic buildings including the town hall, courts and library, all eerily disused. I need a coffee but the Bonaparte bistro has met its Waterloo and is boarded up. Nearby is a piece of public art: a shiny metal spike with the motto 'Fenton – onward and upward' but somehow it does not convince. But wait – here we get our first sight of that Potteries icon: the bottle oven. Three **fine kilns** still stand in a factory yard in Fountain Street. Try to imagine living in an area which once had over 2,000 of them laying down a smoky pall across the surrounding streets.

We trundle along King Street towards Longton passing a series of car washes and repair yards, discount furniture shops and take-aways, squeezed in amongst rows of terraced housing. In the midst of this is the elegantly restored **Foley Terrace**, unfortunately looking straight out onto a garage forecourt. We pass the empty building that until recently housed factory shops for Wedgwood and Royal Doulton before reaching Longton.

Longton still has enough older, interesting buildings to give an idea of what a Potteries town might have looked like in the past. Return to the traffic lights and survey the scene. Behind the imposing iron railway bridge is the towering Crown Hotel whilst facing them is the fine frontage of the town hall. Immediately behind that is the Victorian gem of **Longton Indoor Market** (held 09.00–17.00 on Wed, Fri & Sat). Built in 1862 with a French Renaissance-style towered entrance, interesting shop fronts fill the arches either side.

Inside are over 70 stalls run by independent traders. The **Lamplight Café** is a good place to eavesdrop on the lively chatter of Stokies. By contrast the adjacent Bennett Precinct with its seventies architecture and peeling paint is unattractive. But it contains one little treasure – a tiled mural celebrating the legendary Spitfire and its creator, Reginald Mitchell, a local boy held in great esteem in these parts. Head uphill to the Gladstone Pottery Museum with its magnificent bottle ovens ; this is *the* place to find out about the pottery industry. Return via parallel Sutherland Road with its striking 19th-century factories, all disused but thankfully now listed buildings – although it is not easy to see how they might be used again in the future.

FLORENCE AND BEYOND

After Longton the bus is busier; it has become a parking zone for pushchairs as young mums manoeuvre their charges in the limited space, infants eyeing each other curiously once parked. A lady negotiates her way past the congestion, cheerfully greeting

Bottle kilns at Longton (photo © William Jones)

several other passengers. She is soon ensconced next to a friend regaling her (and the rear of the bus generally) with details of her recent

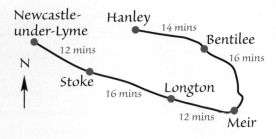

trip to her son's. ('I'm not so keen on his wife though...').

At the roundabout in Florence (alas no Ponte Vecchio or Duomo here, just a petrol station and chip shop) we head towards the A50. But this mini motorway has truncated our road, forcing our bus to limp slowly up a surprisingly steep hill in a housing estate, our driver skilfully avoiding parked cars and the bus coming down in the opposite direction. In Meir, the library has evocative pictures showing an inter-war suburb with Art Deco buildings and virtually traffic-free roads. But time has moved on; only one side of the junction retains the 1930s shopping parade, a huge NHS building, a shop-and-flats block and a KFC having replaced the other period pieces.

From Meir to Hanley is mainly residential through Weston Coyney and **Bentilee**. Again, local friendships seem strong. 'Alright duck, where you off?' is a typical greeting. 'Just goin' up Hanley, duck!' a common reply. Around here everyone is 'duck' or 'duckie' – be they friends or strangers. Indeed, we have to go uphill to arrive in Hanley, the commercial heart of the Potteries today. We finish on a positive note in the shiny new bus station, the first part of a bigger regeneration of this side of town. The joys of **Hanley** await – planners in the past have not been kind to the townscape, but the Potteries Museum is worth a visit for the extensive collection of ceramics and a real Spitfire to honour that man Mitchell. ∎

ABOUT THE AUTHOR | **WILLIAM JONES** is a retired teacher who enjoys exploring Britain by train and by bus – even though he does not yet have a bus pass!

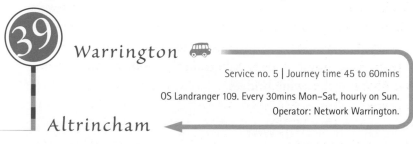

Of Canals and Railways
Off to Manchester

James McCollom

39 Warrington 🚗

Service no. 5 | Journey time 45 to 60mins

OS Landranger 109. Every 30mins Mon–Sat, hourly on Sun.
Operator: Network Warrington.

Altrincham ←

Towns built on hills seem strange to me. I suppose it's a result of growing up in the Mersey Valley, a wide, flat river valley with few distinguishing landmarks. Despite the predominance of farms and mosses between the two cities of Manchester and Liverpool, the area has a long history as a focal point for communications: from the Roman and medieval times, through the canals and railways of the **Industrial Age**, to the motorway age and beyond. This bus route travels between the old industrial town of Warrington and prosperous Altrincham, which nowadays is part of Greater Manchester. Despite my aversion to gradients, this is one of the more undulating routes in the area, for part of the journey running astride the north **Cheshire sandstone ridge**.

Heading out from Warrington's modern bus interchange, the bus travels south over the River Mersey at Bridge Foot, historically the lowest bridging point of the river and just shy of the tidal limit. There's a steep incline over the former railway line to Timperley (which we'll encounter again), then down past the town's bus depot on the left. Network Warrington is one of only a handful of remaining municipal bus companies in Britain. Today a limited company, but still owned by the council, its red-and-cream vehicles have been a familiar sight in **Warrington** for 110 years.

Along wide tree-lined Wilderspool Causeway, the bus is often full and standing as far as Priestley College, where students disembark. The heart of the former Greenall Whitley Land comes and goes: whilst the fine brewery buildings opposite still stand, they are now converted to flats and offices, and the distillery 'vere zey made ze Vladivar vodka' burnt down years ago. Even the brewery's flagship pub, the Saracen's Head, is now run by Manchester-based brewers.

Onwards across the **Manchester Ship Canal** — known as the 'Big Ditch' when it was constructed by navvies as a way of getting ocean-going ships to Salford in the 1890s — we pass over one of the town's swing bridges.

UNDER THE MOTORWAY

Stockton Heath is the first of the villages we pass through on our journey, though it isn't much of a village these days: it's the local centre for the affluent southern suburbs of Warrington and prone to traffic. Was it ever thus, when a citizen from the nearby Roman settlement had to pop into Deva for a new toga? The bus turns left at Victoria Square, with its popular bars and restaurants, and out into leafy suburbs.

Passing under a tall stone bridge – the former Timperley railway, now part of the **Trans Pennine Trail** footpath between Liverpool and Hull – the bus comes out at Latchford Locks on the ship canal. Whilst Stockton Heath bustled, Thelwall is an altogether sleepier place, where Morris Men might still ply their trade outside the Pickering Arms pub. Another quirk is the Thelwall Ferry, a rowing boat across the ship canal that operates in the 'rush hour' and at lunchtime. Horses' heads peek out of stables just before **Thelwall Viaduct** comes into view. Often mentioned on travel bulletins, these twin structures carry the

N

Warrington

10 mins

18 mins

Stockton
Heath

Lymm

15 mins

Dunham

Altrincham

10 mins

AROUND LYMM VILLAGE

The **Lymm Heritage Trail** takes in the main points of interest. It is a three-mile signposted walk taking in the canal, Lymm Dam and the old mill in Slitten Gorge. **Market day** is Thursday and takes place on the car park next to the canal between 10.00 and 16.00. Lymm has various **pubs and eateries**. My favourites include the Coffee House (14 Eagle Brow; ☎ 01925 551797; open daily), Elmas (2 Pepper Street; ☎ 01925 756049; open 16.30–23.00 Mon–Thu, 11.30–23.30 Fri–Sun) for Mediterranean-style food, and the Spread Eagle (47 Eagle Brow; ☎ 01925 757467) for a pint and a warm fire.

main north-south M6 motorway 93 feet above the ship canal. The number 5 is very much a route of bridges, as shortly afterwards the Bridgewater Canal is crossed via a humpback bridge.

Completed in 1776 and one of the pioneering canals of the Industrial Age, the boats on the Bridgewater Canal are so much smaller than those on the Manchester Ship Canal. Whilst originally built to transport coal, most traffic these days consists of pleasure-seeking narrowboats.

TO THE FRINGES OF MANCHESTER

Lymm is the next stop, a quaint little village with an increasing number of housing developments around the edge. The heart of the village is tucked into in a sandstone ravine. Our bus edges carefully down narrow Rectory Lane, stone walls on either side and a canopy of trees, to reach Lymm's centre – where there are the cross and village stocks that are key ingredients in modern conceptions of 'quaintness.'

Lymm was where my childhood journeys would end, whilst the double-decker would heave out of the village over the humpback canal bridge to turn round at **Warburton**. This would be a nondescript hamlet but for a few things: a surviving twelve-pence toll for cars on the bridge across the ship canal; a lovable

OUT AND ABOUT IN DUNHAM MASSEY

Dunham Massey (☎ 0161 941 1025; park open daily till dusk; house and mill closed Thu & Fri; last entry to house and gardens 16.00) is one of the National Trust's best-known properties in the region, featuring a Georgian mansion, well-manicured gardens, a working waterwheel and 190 acres of deer park. Access to the park is free, but a fee is charged to view the house and gardens. **Pubs serving food** in the vicinity include the Axe and Cleaver (☎ 0161 928 3391; open daily 11.30–23.00) near the church in Dunham Town, and the Swan With Two Nicks (☎ 0161 928 2914) in Little Bollington, accessed over the River Bollin by footbridge.

muddle of a grade-one listed former church; and an episode of the archaeology show *Time Team* that was curiously short on artefacts. More recent notoriety comes in the shape of a proposed new high-speed rail route. Trains could cross the ship canal at 185mph in the future. Will this prove controversial, or simply the next chapter in an area where so many modes of transport have blazed a trail?

We wind through country lanes past small clumps of housing, the occasional sharp corner and oncoming traffic, but rarely stop for custom amidst the hedgerows. For the last time, the route passes above the Trans Pennine Trail and then below the **Bridgewater Canal**. In years gone by, the underbridge clearance was so tight that only single-deck buses with specially contoured roofs would fit. Today's structure however dates from the seventies and is a nondescript concrete trough. Immediately on the right lies the Dunham Massey estate, hidden away behind a substantial red-brick wall, which the road follows as we head towards our final destination. **Altrincham** is unexceptional, but we end our run at the Interchange, a place where a transport mode from yesterday, the urban tram, has made a happy renaissance. Manchester is now just a dozen stops away on frequent Metrolink trams. ∎

ABOUT THE
AUTHOR

JAMES McCOLLOM is a web developer and commuter by trade, occasional blogger and enthusiast by choice. In 2009 he travelled the length of Britain by bus over six days.

The Pride of the Dales
Yorkshire Beckons

Sheila Scraton

40 Ilkley

Service no. 74 | Journey time 50mins

OS Landranger 104, 98. Every 2hrs Mon–Sat, no service on Sun.
Operator: Pride of the Dales.

Grassington

Having lived for most of my life to the west of the Pennines, I'm a recent convert to the **White Rose county** of Yorkshire where I now live in Wharfedale. Living here has helped me appreciate the beauty of green hills, dales and rugged moors as well as the sea, sand dunes and distant mountains of Snowdonia, which had previously been the focus for my outdoor adventures.

The **Yorkshire Dales** provide plenty of excitement and great scenery on their trails, rivers and crags for those looking for outdoor challenges, but they are also known for their friendly tea shops, cafés and pubs that make visiting the area so special. Most but not all the dales are named after their rivers. You'll search in vain on maps for any River Wensley. But there is most certainly a River Wharfe, and that is the river which has gently eroded Yorkshire geology to create one of the county's most beautiful dales.

LEAVING ILKLA MOOR BAHT 'AT

The journey starts in **Ilkley** – easily accessible by train or bus from both Leeds and Bradford. It's worth spending a short time in this lovely spa town before boarding the bus. Ilkley is surrounded by unspoilt scenery with Ilkley Moor rising above it and the Cow and Calf rocks (the playground for many local and visiting rock climbers) visible on the skyline. There are plenty of attractions, not least the healing waters of the **White Wells** and the famous Betty's Café tea rooms but don't dawdle for too long as there are many more sights to enjoy along the route. I make sure I get a seat on the right of the bus and in the back three rows, as these seats are slightly higher giving great views.

Our small, single-decker bus pulls out and on a cold winter's morning there are just half a dozen locals, plus dog, sitting chatting. I ask the driver whether the bus ever gets full. 'Try coming after the spring bank holiday in May, love, every bus is full of visitors off into the Dales.' Today there is plenty of space and, as we leave Ilkley, I get the first views of the fast-flowing **River Wharfe** over to the right, before we turn off the main road into Addingham, a picturesque sort of place that once boasted five textile mills. All long gone.

Beyond **Addingham**, industrial heritage gives way to ancient ruins and the spectacular Bolton Abbey estate, the land and property of the Duke of Devonshire. This area has been the inspiration for poets and artists such as William Wordsworth and J M W Turner. Glance out of the window and it's easy to see why: a lovely medley of green hills, fields, streams, waterfalls and trees. The

A WALK ALONG THE WHARFE

It's well worth getting off the bus at **Bolton Abbey** and taking some time to explore the priory and take a walk along the river. The paths are beautifully maintained and provide great walking through mixed woodland. There are **marked nature trails** surrounded by carpets of wild flowers, especially bluebells in the spring. Usually it's possible to catch a glimpse of a variety of birds including treecreepers, nuthatch and Great spotted woodpeckers. Drop into the **café** just along from the priory for home-baked cakes or ice cream or continue with your walk to the Strid, where you can head back up to the main road to pick up the next bus as it passes.

road becomes narrower and more winding and I begin to appreciate the driving skills of our driver as he negotiates narrow bends, carefully passing tractors and delivery vans as they come towards us. As we pass the Devonshire Arms Hotel I get my first glimpse of the 12th-century priory, **Bolton Abbey**, once the home of Augustinian monks. Although now in ruins, the old priory makes a stunning picture alongside the River Wharfe, with the craggy and wooded backdrop of **Simon's Seat**, the hillside rising behind it. Here, it's possible to leave the bus to explore the priory, or take a stroll along the riverside path.

Grassington

13 mins

N

Burnsall

5 mins

Appletreewick

17 mins

Bolton Abbey

15 mins

Ilkley

THERE'S NOTHING LIKE A DALES VILLAGE

The road from Bolton Abbey becomes even narrower and it's hard to imagine how the bus gets through the constricted archway (originally carrying water across to the abbey) which provides quite a challenge even for cars. We are definitely at the size limit and our driver judges it perfectly with about an inch to spare! Just past the Strid car park with its excellent tea room and gift shop, the Dusty Bluebells (☎ 01756 710431), the next spectacular view comes into sight. It's hard to know at this point whether to turn and look back towards Bolton Abbey or look ahead at the ruins of the 15th-century **Barden Tower**. Either way, I can't help but marvel at these ancient buildings and the people that lived in them over the centuries.

From here on towards Grassington, it's the villages that take my attention. We cross the River Wharfe at **Barden Bridge**, yet again a major feat for our driver who has to reverse and line the bus up before perfectly manoeuvring it across the bridge. The road now follows the river on its other bank towards the lovely village of **Appletreewick** (pronounced 'Aptrick' by the locals). We are in limestone country and the fields and limestone walls create a distinctive pattern on the hillsides.

The bus stops outside the **Craven Arms**, a traditional Yorkshire Inn. This is a popular pub for walkers and it seems for some regular bus passengers who catch the bus each week at lunchtime from Ilkley, returning several hours later, well satisfied with good food and local brew.

Leaving Appletreewick the bus continues to negotiate the narrowing road until it once more crosses the Wharfe on an ancient, five-arched packhorse bridge that leads into Burnsall. This is another pretty Yorkshire village with stone cottages, hanging flower baskets, tea rooms, the Red Lion pub and the 12th-century St Wilfrid's Church. In the summer it's a popular spot, especially the green fields leading down to the river, which become busy with families, picnickers and anglers fishing for trout.

The bus continues having picked up more locals in **Burnsall**. I catch a glimpse of a buzzard hunting across the dale and wonder

CAFÉS AND PUBS ALONG THE WAY

The **Yorkshire Dales** are known for their cafés and pubs serving local specialities. In Ilkley, you can feast on a 'fat rascal' (a Yorkshire cake very like a scone) at Betty's tea rooms, have home-made cakes or Yorkshire ice cream at the Cavendish Pavilion or Dusty Bluebells along the Wharfe by **Bolton Abbey** or try any of the numerous cafés in Burnsall and Grassington. Along the route, you can visit the Fleece at Addingham, the Red Lion at Burnsall or the New Inn or the Craven Arms at Appletreewick. All are excellent but for a real traditional pub with log fires, gas lamps, stone-flagged floors, oak beams, good food and cask local and real ales, the **Craven Arms** (☎ 01756 720270; open daily from 11.30 with a lunch break on Mon & Tue between 15.00–18.00) is hard to beat.

whether the red kites have made it this far up Wharfedale yet. Before reaching the T-junction, where we turn right for Threshfield and the final run into Grassington, I spot the right turn down to **Linton Falls**. Although I can't quite see the river at this point, I know Linton Falls are well worth seeing as the water cascades through channels of soft limestone. It makes for a spectacular display especially after heavy rain. I stay on the bus as I know that I can walk down to the falls from the other side once we reach our destination.

As we cross the Wharfe for the final time we go up the hill and into **Grassington**. It's quite a change to see a busy town after such a tranquil journey, with people in their outdoor gear and walking boots and others who look more local going about their daily business. The bus drives into the lovely cobbled square and most people get off to choose somewhere for lunch or do their shopping.

I stay on board as the bus continues for one more stop to the **National Park Centre** (www.yorkshiredales.org.uk) just a few minutes away. This is worth a visit to sample the café, shop or the interpretive displays about local industry, farming and tourism. However, I'm heading off down the path at the back of the car park to see the Linton Falls. ∎

ABOUT THE AUTHOR | **SHEILA SCRATON** has discovered the history and scenic beauty of the Yorkshire Dales since moving there and walking regularly in the area.

SUNDAY OUTINGS

There has been a quiet revolution in bus transport in some areas of the Pennines and northern England in recent years. Seasonal networks of **special bus services** have allowed visitors to access some of the most outstanding landscapes of the region. We feature just such a route in the next essay in this book. Colin Speakman, the author of that route, manages the social enterprise that runs some of the summer-Sunday bus services in the **Yorkshire Dales**. With 40 volunteers, Colin's team provides affordable public transport to some of the remotest communities in the region.

But cuts in public spending across Britain threaten such initiatives. Encouraging residents of the cities of northern Britain to visit the five **national parks** in the region makes total sense. And getting those visitors to make pro-environmental choices when it comes to transport is good for our national parks. So initiatives like **DalesBus** (serving the Yorkshire Dales National Park) and **Moorsbus** (providing Sunday services to and around the North York Moors National Park) benefit both townfolk and those who live within the national parks.

Moorsbus services have been progressively scaled back over the last four years. In its heyday, the Moorsbus network operated on up to 90 days each year (including daily services during the school summer holidays). In 2009, Moorsbus carried 74,000 passengers. Total passenger numbers in 2013 are unlikely to top 12,000 – no surprise perhaps as the network operates only on about three dozen days in 2013. Once city dwellers become accustomed to driving into the North York Moors National Park, that habit sticks. **Funding** for Moorsbus teeters on the brink, and Colin Speakman talks of a similarly perilous situation in the Yorkshire Dales National Park. 'We provide bus services to remote areas that are of no interest to commercial operators,' he argues.

Of course in the national parks of the Pennines and North, there are some **commercial operators** who show ingenuity and initiative. In summer 2013, for example, Arriva operated Sunday service 714 from Gateshead and Newcastle to Kielder Water in the heart of Northumberland National Park. And Stagecoach run the remarkable Honister Rambler service in the Lake District, a route which tackles some formidable gradients. ∎

Crossing the Buttertubs
NORTHERN DALESMAN

Colin Speakman

Lancaster

Service no. 832/831/830 | Journey time 3hrs 10mins

OS Landranger 97, 98, 92, 99. Once on Sun and bank hols (seasonal).
Operator: Dalesbus.

Richmond

T he Northern Dalesman is a different kind of bus service. It runs not because of the wishes of a local council or a national park, nor even a bus or coach operator. It is, rather, a genuine community initiative, created because a group of individuals who love the Dales felt so passionately about the loss of many Sunday bus services to and within the **Yorkshire Dales National Park**, they set up their own not-for-profit social enterprise, the Dales & Bowland Community Interest Company.

Over the last six years, this company has taken responsibility for the funding, management and promotion of the Sunday and bank holiday network serving the national park. This network is now firmly branded **DalesBus** (www.dalesbus.org), and there are comprehensive rover tickets and excellent connections with train and other bus services, designed *by* users *for* users.

The jewel in the crown of the DalesBus network is the Northern Dalesman. This is a route that operates every Sunday and public holiday from early May to mid-October. It crosses the **Pennines** to link the historic county town of Lancaster with the market town of Richmond, along the way taking in some fabulous mountain and moorland scenery. The greater part of the route lies within the boundaries of the Yorkshire Dales National Park.

Keld
8 mins
Thwaite
Reeth
Richmond
25 mins
N
20 mins
25 mins
↑
Hawes
25 mins

This **three-hour journey** is really a one-off. Perhaps no other regular scheduled bus service in England allows the traveller to enjoy such a remarkable range of landscapes. More's the pity – it runs little more than two dozen times each year. But those with an appetite for bus timetables will find year-round services that cover some parts of the same route. But not all: this is the only bus route that takes in the spectacular **Buttertubs Pass** – the 'up and over' mountain road that links Wensleydale with Swaledale.

Ribblehead
15 mins
Ingleton
50 mins
Lancaster

The bus leaves Lancaster numbered 832, morphing at Ingleton into the 831 and then at Hawes into the 830. But passengers making the entire journey can stay on the same bus throughout.

INTO THE DALES

Sunday morning, at an hour when most folk are either at church or asleep, there's an eager gaggle of outdoor types waiting for the run into the Dales. The first part of the journey is happily undemanding, as we follow a pleasant-enough route along the Lune Valley, picking up more passengers in villages along the way.

Ingleton is the first real visitor destination. The village with its winding main street is dominated by a great railway viaduct, long bereft of any trains, crossing the narrow gorge of the River Greta. Beyond **Ingleton**, the mood of the landscape changes, becoming strikingly dramatic. We slip past White Scar Caves – one of the finest show caverns in the north, rich in stalactites and stalagmites – with the B6255 road climbing between two of Yorkshire's mighty **Three Peaks**. The great flat-topped summit to our right, above some of the most impressive limestone pavements in the British Isles, is Ingleborough. To our left is the long, whaleback shape of Whernside, the highest of the Three Peaks, and reached via an impressive ridge walk from Ingleton.

At Chapel-le-Dale with the Old Hill Inn (☎ 01524 241256), a popular walkers' pub, we cross the route of the Three Peaks Walk. Soon the great 24-arch stone **viaduct of Ribblehead** comes into sight. Once under the viaduct, the Northern Dalesman turns up the bumpy drive to Ribblehead Station (which has a small visitor centre) to await the arrival of the train.

For may people this is the easiest and best way of experiencing the Northern Dalesman, by taking the celebrated Settle and Carlisle rail route. Through trains from Leeds connect conveniently with the bus. Most of those who climb aboard here have rucksacks or walking poles (or both). This is real integrated transport – something that Britain could and should do so much better.

Once past the Station Inn the bus begins the climb out of Ribblesdale up to Newby Head, through an area of wild and desolate countryside crossed by the new **Pennine Bridleway**. We breach the watershed between the Ribble and the Ure, then drop gently through Widdale into Upper Wensleydale, and the little market town of Hawes.

THE WATERFALL TRAIL

Ingleton's lovely **waterfall walk** starts a quarter of a mile below the village (admission £5 as the paths and estate are private), then follows a series of carefully engineered footpaths and footbridges up the valley of the River Twiss past the swirling white waters of Pecca Falls to majestic **Thornton Force**, returning along the valley of the Doe past Beazley and Snow Falls. Not only are the waterfalls spectacular, but the trail is one of the most fascinating geological walks in England, with ancient Silurian and Cambrian rocks superbly exposed underneath the dominant **Carboniferous limestone**.

SWALEDALE

For many people Swaledale is the most beautiful of the entire Yorkshire Dales: green, intimate, and beguilingly lovely. This is a valley famous for its **drystone walls** and **scattered barns**. The latter recall a sustainable farming practice followed between the 17th and 20th centuries, storing hay above the cattle for insulation during the winter months to provide both warmth and sustenance. Sadly it was very labour intensive, which has meant that the barns, walls and wonderful, herb and flower-rich meadows, are now very much at risk. Thanks to various **conservation projects**, many of these iconic features of this delicate rural landscape are now being preserved.

Hawes is a town with character. Its busy main street boasts a Tuesday market – sadly not the day the Northern Dalesman calls. As well as the usual choice of cafés, pubs and shops, there are many other reasons to visit the town – the Hawes Creamery, five minutes' walk from the centre. It is here that the famous Wensleydale cheese is made, so memorably promoted by Wallace and Gromit. Visitors can watch the cheesemakers at work. You can connect at Hawes into Journey 35 in Bradt's last book on British bus routes (*Bus-Pass Britain*, published in 2011).

The Northern Dalesman calls at the old railway station which is now the **Dales Countryside Museum** and National Park Centre – if you are making the entire run from Lancaster to Richmond, you'll cherish this chance of a toilet stop. There is still a stationary tank engine and coach behind the station buildings as an evocative reminder of the town's railway heritage. But now our bus takes to terrain where no railway has ever ventured.

UP AND OVER

The Northern Dalesman heads north out of town, crossing the **River Ure** over an ancient stone bridge before heading up to the hamlet of Simonstone. To the left, a paved path crosses the fields towards Hardraw, where England's highest waterfall, behind the Green Dragon Inn, thrusts down a rocky ravine.

Now comes a real test of driving skills and engineering. The gradient on the narrow mountain road suddenly gets noticeably steeper. Low gears are needed. The engine growls and rumbles. Pity the poor cyclists who in July 2014 will tackle these formidable gradients in the opening stage of the Tour de France.

We quickly emerge from tame country hemmed in by white stone walls into the more expansive landscape of **Abbotside Common**. Here the line of the road is marked by posts which in times of snowfall are sometimes the only indication of where the route lies. The bus, now well laden with passengers, climbs nearly 1,000 feet to the summit of the pass. At 1,726 feet this is one of the highest roads in the Pennines.

The views are breathtaking. To our left is the massive whaleback of **Great Shunnor Fell**, one of the highest points of the Pennine Way. Away to our right is Lovely Seat. 'Last time I was up there, it was anything but lovely,' quips a voice from the back of the bus. 'So darn windy, I lost my hat.' But his voice is drowned out by the many expressions of surprise at the scenery around. Over the top, we see the celebrated butter tubs that give the pass its name. These are water-carved potholes and limestone columns said to look

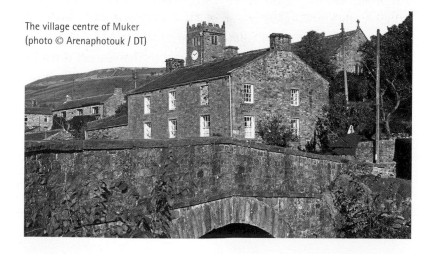

The village centre of Muker
(photo © Arenaphotouk / DT)

like wooden tubs. Then on down around quite terrifying bends, with views along the whole length of Swaledale. It is the contrasts that make these landscapes. Here we are atop a wild moor, but Swaledale below seems like a green paradise.

Down in the dale, we serve a medley of Swaledale villages. We stop in Thwaite (birthplace of the famous wildlife photographers Richard and Cherry Kearton) then head up to the hamlet of Keld. It is on both the Pennine Way and Coast to Coast Path, so the starting point for some very special walks in Swaledale. The bus reverses in the lane that leads up to Tan Hill Inn (☎ 0133 628246), England's highest pub, before returning to Thwaite and continuing along the narrow road down the dale, often squeezing over bridges and passing cars or tractors with only inches to spare.

The next village, **Muker**, with coffee shops, the Farmers Arms and the Swaledale Woollen Shop, is the starting point for many walks over Kisdon or up Swinner Gill. Then follows Gunnerside, a village with many remnants of the great lead-mining industry of the dales. Next are the linear villages of Low Row, Featham and Healaugh, bringing us to Reeth, with its huge village green. This is the unofficial capital of Swaledale, with a lively tourist office and a good museum on Swaledale life (☎ 01748 884118).

From **Reeth** the dale is less dramatic, but equally impressive. The road curves through Fremington to Grinton, then on through thickly wooded countryside, below Marrick – with its medieval priory (now an outdoor centre) – and Marske, before finally crossing the River Swale to ascend to the market town of Richmond, dominated by its Norman Castle on a high cliff above the river, its huge marketplace and unique Georgian Theatre.

For most people **Richmond** is the natural terminus of the Northern Dalesman. It's hardly a conurbation, so most travellers will continue northeast on the Arriva bus to Darlington. ■

ABOUT THE AUTHOR | **COLIN SPEAKMAN** is a writer and environmentalist from Ilkley, West Yorkshire. He is Chairman of the Yorkshire Dales Society, campaigning to protect the Dales and to promote its green travel networks.

INTO THE PENNINES
ALSTON AND BEYOND

Carol Purves

Carlisle

Service no. 680 | Journey time 75mins

OS Landranger 85, 86. Once daily from Carlisle, thrice from Brampton Mon–Sat, no service on Sun. Operator: Telford's Coaches.

Nenthead

In 2014, the family-run company of Telford's Coaches will celebrate its fiftieth anniversary. No doubt there will be some festive frolics at the company's base at the delightfully named Tweedon Brae in Newcastleton in Scotland. But villagers in a swathe of rural communities across the border in northern England will surely also give thanks to the Telford's team. For this company, more known for its luxury and executive coach-charter business, also provides **lifeline bus services** to many remote villages. In the hills and valleys of northeast Cumbria, as indeed in parts of neighbouring Northumberland, Telford's is a familiar bus operator – just as indeed the company's vehicles are a regular sight on the byways of southern Scotland.

FROM SCHOOL BUS TO SERVICE BUS

A weekday morning, sunny and clear, and this is a chance to see two of Telford's best in **Brampton Market Square**. They are gearing up for action. The 185 is heading east to Haltwhistle and the 680 will boldly strike southeast into the hills, bound for Alston and beyond. 'Watch out,' says the driver as I climb aboard the 680. 'This bus has more germs than any other,' he adds with a smile. 'I'm just off a school run. Look at the mess the children have left.'

Well, those earlier travellers have indeed left evidence of their presence, but a bit of litter doesn't bother me and I settle down for the ride. It's uphill all the way as we head out of Brampton. We stop at the level crossing at **Milton**, waiting for a Newcastle-bound train to speed by. 'Happens every day,' says the driver who is clearly a creature of habit – surely a virtue for a bus driver.

Heading east now, our route parallels an old railway line built to serve quarries and collieries in these hills. We stop here and there in small villages with evocative names: Hallbankgate, Coalfell, Midgeholme, Halton Lea Gate and Slaggyford. Away to the south is **Bruthwaite Forest** (curiously devoid of trees) and Hartleyburn Common (whose open aspect is conspicuously interrupted by a modern plantation of conifers).

It's an odd mix, here and there some tame farmland but more often wild moorland. On one journey, the bus driver pointed out a grouse shooting party taking to the hills. Isolated shooting boxes on the surrounding fells are a reminder that the grouse season can

CARLISLE CONNECTIONS

The **timetable** for the Telford's Coaches 680 is remarkably complex for such a sparse service. The full route runs from Carlisle to Nenthead, but in truth only one bus each day makes the full journey. That's the lunchtime departure from Carlisle. But don't let that trouble you. There are plenty of buses on other routes from **Carlisle to Brampton**, generally running every half an hour. It is only a 20-min run from Carlisle over to Brampton. Take time to have a look around Brampton. As the local community website (www.brampton.co.uk) nicely puts it, this little town in the **Irthing Valley** is 'drenched in history.' The website further advises that Brampton is a Starbucks-free zone, but with a plethora of decent coffee shops around town, Starbucks are perhaps wise to have kept their distance. You can pick up information on Brampton in the library on the market square (☎ 016977 2189) or in the nearby tourist information centre (☎ 016977 3433) located in the historic **Moot Hall**.

be big business in these parts.

On another trip, made on a bitter winter day with a sharp wind, snow draped the hills and little wisps of spindrift danced over the road. Fortunately the local council's gritting trucks and snowploughs were busy keeping the roads clear. In such weather, the journey makes one reflect on the mobility that residents of urban Britain take for granted. There are times in winter when this area might be quite inaccessible – cut off by snow from the outside world.

Brampton
24 mins
Carlisle
20 mins
Lambley
5 mins
Knarsdale
12 mins
Alston
10 mins
Nenthead
N

SOUTH TYNEDALE

At **Lambley** we join South Tynedale, a valley that was once served by one of England's most beautiful branch railways. It was lucky to survive the Beeching cuts, but then succumbed in 1976. Yet there is a silver lining in this tale, for now the **old rail route** affords a dozen miles of glorious walking through Northumberland countryside.

From the bus, we see the old railway viaduct at Lambley, and then we cross under the **South Tyne Trail** at Knarsdale. If you are up for a walk, Lambley is a good place to hop off the bus to follow the South Tyne Trail northeast to Haltwhistle. Being an old railway line, it makes for perfectly graded easy walking. It is five miles to Haltwhistle, which has good train and bus services to both Newcastle and Carlisle. Or at Haltwhistle, you can connect onto the AD122 Hadrian's Wall bus route.

All roads in this area lead to **Alston** and soon our bus is nudging through a line of tractors and other farm vehicles into the middle of this small market town. We pause for a few minutes outside Henderson's Garage, which is clearly a little mecca for buses in the northern Pennines. It is a place for buses to meet. They stop and

ISAAC'S TEA TRAIL

Our route on the 680 bus from **Alston to Nenthead** broadly follows part of the Issac's Tea Trail. Don't expect lush plantations of Darjeeling. But there is a tea connection. **Isaac Holden** was a local miner who had a tough life. Illness and a downturn in the mining industry robbed him of his job, so he became an itinerant tea seller in the region. The long walks from village to village in the hills gave Isaac plenty of time to think, and his thoughts turned to religion. He became a **Methodist**, using whatever money he had to support the chapels of the dales. He is remembered with affection for his work with the poor and needy of the region. The **trail is marked** by green signs bearing an image of Issac.

chatter to each other, just as their drivers and passengers exchange a few words. Choose the right day and you can even get a direct bus from Henderson's to Keswick or Newcastle upon Tyne (but do check those timetables carefully, for both those connections are summer-only services).

Alston is a likeable town. Many of the late 17th and 18th-century buildings are full of character with their stone-slab roofs and walls of local creamy-grey stone. The frequent outside stone staircases indicate that the inhabitants once lived upstairs with the cattle below, providing early central heating as well as protection from the **Border Reivers** – the raiders who held sway along the Anglo-Scottish border from the late 13th to the beginning of the 17th century.

If you are inclined to linger, there are two good pubs on Market Street, the Angel Inn (near the parish church) and the Crown Hotel. The **Blueberry Café** (☎ 01434 381928) and Cumbrian Pantry (☎ 01434 381406) are good for snacks. From Alston there are beautiful walks to Garrigill and **Ashgill Force**, and information about these walks can be obtained from the town hall at the bottom of Market Street, which also serves as a library as well as a tourist information centre.

PATHS OF DISSENT

Alston is not quite the end of our journey, and the final stretch is in many respects the most interesting. We leave town, following a ledge on the northern side of **Middle Fell**. The River Nent is way down below to the left. We follow the valley up to Nenthead, the last village before Killhope Summit (which marks the boundary with County Durham). **Nenthead**, so strangely remote, has a mood all of its own. It was a purpose-built industrial village, planted in the hills to attract miners. Commerce may have been at the heart of the venture but the Quaker owners of the mine built housing, a school, a reading room, public baths and a washroom for the miners. The houses were built from 1790 and in 1814 a village school was erected and then rebuilt in 1834. Miners were said to have spent so much time in the new library that the price of beer had to be reduced in the Miners Arms to attract customers. The Quaker sponsors of the project seemed not to mind that most of the inhabitants favoured **Methodism**.

So it may seem like the end of the world, but Nenthead was one of the first Pennine villages to have electric street lighting and the children of the village were well educated. The mine closed in 1961, and nowadays the village relies very much on hikers and cyclists who stop off in Nenthead.

If you are planning on returning to Brampton or Carlisle, you may get no more than a glimpse of Nenthead, for the bus leaves almost immediately for the return journey. So check there is a later bus back. There has been a **seasonal bus service** from Nenthead over the hill to Killhope and Stanhope – a true trans-Pennine adventure branded the 'Roof of England' route. As this book goes to press, it is not yet certain if this route will run in 2014. For bus travellers, Nenthead may really be the end of the road. ∎

ABOUT THE AUTHOR | **CAROL PURVES** is a freelance writer. She lives in Carlisle and loves exploring her home region – whether by bus, on foot, or even occasionally in a car.

Coals to Newcastle
Tyne Tees Express

Brian Robson

 Middlesbrough

Service no. X9 | Journey time 80mins

OS Landranger 93, 88. Hourly Mon–Sat, no service on Sun.
Operator: Go North East.

Newcastle upon Tyne

Years ago, 'Tyne Tees' was the name of our local commercial TV station. Friendly faces with local accents brought us news, weather and even birthday greetings from their studios in Newcastle. Nowadays, the brand has been swept away in favour of a stronger national identity for ITV, and that little bit of local colour is no more. Sad, perhaps, but the name lives on – not least as the Tyne-Tees moniker is still applied to the fleet of buses which ply the express route between Middlesbrough and Newcastle.

Bridging the Tees

The plum-coloured **Tyne Tees Express** double-decker which awaits me at Middlesbrough's central bus station leaves me in no doubt that I've found the right departure stand. 'Newcastle Middlesbrough – every 30 minutes' scream the slogans on the side, also advising that our bus is equipped with Wi-Fi internet and electric sockets. This is a thoroughly modern bus route.

So I'm upstairs for the view as, on the stroke of the hour, we pull away on the run north to Newcastle. Middlesbrough is red-brick country, but the view is more than just Victorian terraces. There's a glimpse of the **Tees Transporter Bridge** to the east. An ingenious solution to the challenge of crossing the Tees whilst not affecting navigation on the busy river, the Transporter is a rare breed of bridge. Motorists drive gingerly onto a gondola suspended by cables from a blue ironwork super-structure, and are hauled across the river in just 90 seconds. Sadly, our bus takes the less exotic but more practical option of the modern **Tees Flyover**, which does have the advantage of offering us further views of the Transporter.

We are not long on our way when we stop at **Billingham**. It's due for regeneration – one of those modern planning euphemisms – so I want to pay a visit to the town's shopping centre before renewal work begins.

Billingham's town centre was built as part of a planned expansion of the area in the 1950s. It was intended to provide facilities for the growing workforce at the nearby ICI plant. An unusual circular tower block which resembles Birmingham's more famous Rotunda dominates the skyline.

As Billingham's chemical works have declined, so too has the town centre. The deserted precinct reminds me of town centres in the former eastern bloc. There's a sculpture – entitled 'family group' – which would surely have been at home in Belgrade or Bratislava thirty years ago, the shirtless father bending to lift his son aloft. All that's missing is a 'workers of the world unite' inscription.

The art gallery is forlorn, a hastily printed sign announcing Stockton Council's decision to close it permanently. I'm beginning to wonder where everyone is, so I walk further into the precinct where posters outside the **Forum Theatre** proclaim that the Grand Opera of Belarus is appearing soon. Perhaps the X9 has delivered me into an alternative socialist universe? The Forum is pretty dead but a lone member of staff in the foyer tells me that Billingham is more a spot for sport than **Belarusian opera**. She suggests I take a look at the nearby leisure centre.

Here, indeed, there is life aplenty with a gym, swimming pool and ice rink. Youthful shrieks fill the air, and the café is packed with anxious-looking parents waiting for children to emerge from the rink, hopefully with limbs intact.

I settle down with a tankard-sized cup of tea and read about how that upcoming regeneration will transform Billingham life, whiling away time before the next X9 arrives to whisk me onwards.

WIND AND WEAR

Once on board, the bus rejoins the A19 dual carriageway at Wynyard, and we cruise northwards. **Windmills** fill the air, with some particularly huge turbines to the east as signs welcome us to **County Durham**. It's not just windmills of the modern variety, either. Soon we pass a pub called the Windmill, and to the left emerges its namesake – a slender red-brick windmill of the traditional variety, its sails sadly no more. Clearly the winds which are buffeting our tall double-decker as it makes its way north have been put to productive use for many years.

Signs by the A19 invite us to 'locate, invest, succeed' in Peterlee. On cue, our bus sweeps into the town, built to provide homes for the **Bevin Boys** who had toiled in the Durham coalfields during and after World War II. My top-deck seat affords views over terraces of hexahedron houses, most of which have had their cube-like quality destroyed by the addition of a pitched roof.

They owe their design to abstract artist **Victor Pasmore**. East Durham's new Jerusalem attracted the finest creative minds, and Pasmore was enlisted to provide a 'synthesis of architecture, painting and sculpture' in the town's Sunny Blunts estate.

Pasmore's efforts proved controversial. One complaint – perhaps apocryphal – is that his penchant for floor-to-ceiling windows left no room for curtain rails, much to the disgust of

East Durham housewives, some of whom are perhaps on our bus now, taking a jaunt to Newcastle for its shops and market. At the time the *Northern Echo* wrote that the houses were 'brave and imaginative in their general design' but 'wretched and shabby in their details and practical execution.' A fair assessment.

Now bereft of the mines it was built to serve, **Peterlee** is experiencing hard times, but lying halfway along the route, it makes a useful stop to stretch your legs. The bus station has limited facilities, but toilets are available in the Asda supermarket and the Five Quarter pub offers good-value food (Hailsham Place; ☎ 0191 578 5880; open 08.00–23.00 Mon–Sun).

Moving on from Peterlee, we catch glimpses of the North Sea, but as we enter Sunderland, further windmills give way to a more unexpected sight – what appears to be a Greek temple set atop a steep hill. Penshaw Monument is a folly, modelled on the Temple of Hephaestus in Athens. Erected in 1844 in memory of the Earl of Durham, the monument's Doric columns are now in the care of the National Trust.

Soon, we're crossing the third of the Northeast's major rivers, the **Wear**. You may glimpse to your right a concrete barge which marks the site of the proposed New Sunderland Bridge. When constructed this will be the tallest bridge in England, and – in a

PASMORE'S PAVILION

Pasmore's houses weren't his only contribution to **Peterlee**. Even more infamous is his **Apollo Pavilion**. Slabs of concrete float above a lake, an anonymous monument which Pasmore intended to 'lift the activity and psychology of an urban housing community onto a universal plane.' It didn't work out as he intended. So despised was Pasmore's structure, that in the 1980s local residents invited the Territorial Army to blow it up as an exercise. Fortunately it was saved this ignominious end, and has enjoyed a **reappraisal** in recent years. The Pavillion has been restored, and now enjoys listed status. Find out more at www.apollopavilion.info.

region where local rivalries matter – give the Wear a crossing to rival Middlesbrough's Transporter or Newcastle's Tyne Bridge.

For now, though, Sunderland's most famous sight remains **Penshaw Monument**, and the city's most famous export the Nissan car. A cluster of ten more windmills tower above the ugly Nissan plant. The dirty chemical and coal industries of the Northeast's past are giving way to the clean electric cars of Europe's most productive car factory. The 'Leaf', as the latest model is known, is now reckoned to be the best-selling all-electric vehicle ever.

Across the Tyne

Heading into the Tyneside conurbation, the X9 halts briefly at Heworth metro station, one of 60 stations on the UK's first modern light-rail system. Box-like yellow **metro trains** have shuttled around Tyne and Wear for over 30 years now, with the drivers' plea to 'stand clear of the doors please' being as much part of Geordie life as the London tube's more famous instruction to 'mind the gap.'

Next stop is **Gateshead**, where many of my fellow passengers rush to alight for buses to the Metro Centre – Europe's largest shopping centre, built on the site of a former ash dump. Hit by the success of the Metro Centre, Gateshead's town centre is currently in transition – an ugly 1960s shopping complex is being

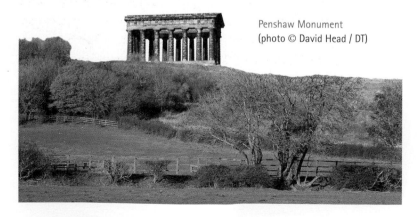

Penshaw Monument
(photo © David Head / DT)

A VERY SOCIAL SERVICE

With free Wi-Fi on board, it's no surprise that the X9 figures in **social media**. It even has its own Twitter hashtag: **#TyneTeesXpress**. And regular X9 users meet not just on the bus but in a dedicated Facebook group. That's where I first ran across **Colin Dunn** who often uses early morning buses to Newcastle. He explained: 'We're a close-knit family on the X9. Some of us have been getting this bus for 20 years, and we make the hour-long journey more interesting by talking, doing crosswords and having quizzes.' Colin is now the group's self-appointed communications tsar and was keen to share the group's exploits with me. 'Hey, I must tell you about my fiftieth **birthday party**. I decided I didn't want a party at work, but I did want a party with my friends from the bus. We all get on well with the very friendly drivers, so I invited them too. The bus company made a special cake for me, the drivers got me a bottle of very nice whisky and we had a great night. For me, it was surreal!'

replaced by an ugly modern complex. At least the 1960s version was graced by the Owen Luder car park made famous in the film *Get Carter* – its raw concrete now a thing of the past as one form of progress is replaced by another.

Crossing the River Tyne into **Newcastle**, the 'blinking eye' Millennium Bridge arcs into the sky and the shell-like Sage Gateshead music and arts venue shimmers in the sun. On the Quayside beneath the **Tyne Bridge**, lawyers and art lovers mingle, distinguishable from each other by the degree of purpose with which they walk. When our bus terminates, some of the passengers sitting alongside me will take the walk down what Betjeman described as the 'descending, subtle curve' of Gray Street to join those already in the courts, coffee shops and barristers' chambers. From chemicals and coal mines to electric cars and contemporary art, my journey through England's Northeast has concluded. ∎

ABOUT THE AUTHOR | **BRIAN ROBSON** lives in Sunderland. He has driven along the A19 more times than he'd care to remember, but prefers the journey by bus – especially when accompanied by his son Barney.

SCOTLAND

When **Laurence Sterne** first set foot on French soil, he was impressed with what he found. In *A Sentimental Journey through France and Italy* (1768) he remarked how some matters are better ordered in countries beyond England. The English bus traveller venturing north of the border into Scotland might be similarly impressed.

Of course, an English concessionary bus pass finds little recognition in Scotland – but there are exceptions. Travel on the afternoon bus from Newcastle upon Tyne to Jedburgh (service 131 operated by Munro's) and the driver will gladly accept an English bus pass for a journey right through to Jedburgh. It's one of those oddball exceptions – and conversely holders of a **Scottish National Entitlement Card** (NEC) can ride the 131 from Jedburgh down to Newcastle. The NEC can also be used for other cross-border journeys, eg: to Berwick-upon-Tweed and Carlisle.

Residents of England nearing retirement age can only look with envy across the border where their Scottish counterparts can get a free NEC on their sixtieth birthday. And the Scottish NEC is in many respects far better than the English pass. The distinction between local bus services and long-distance coach services in Scotland is less cut and dried than south of the border. The Scottish NEC can be used on many express and limited-stop bus services in Scotland. There is a **remarkable network** of such routes within Scotland. That benefits not just NEC holders of course. It is possible to make long hops in Scotland in a manner that comes as a great surprise to visitors from England. Thus the thirteen-hour journey from **Carlisle to Thurso** requires just two changes of bus – in Edinburgh and Inverness. None of those three legs break any records. If you are chasing records, look to the 915 Citylink service from Glasgow to the Isle of Skye which gets a mention on page 247 in this book. You can check out that route and other Citylink services at www.citylink.co.uk.

Traveline Scotland (www.travelinescotland.com) is a great resource for planning journeys by bus across Scotland. It has a comprehensive library of timetables for all Scottish bus services. There you'll find the times of buses that vary with the tides on Barra, and details of the rare expeditions to wild Rannoch made by Broons Buses and Taxis. The latter journey through the Highlands featured in the prequel to this volume.

A TARTAN MEDLEY

In this volume too, we have some journeys that venture to the **very extremities** of Scotland's bus network. Four of the seven Scottish routes that we present here are on **islands** – compensating for the fact that in the last book we focused fair and square on the mainland. Of the three mainland routes, one is on the Cowal Peninsula, a little fragment of the mainland that has much of the character of an island. We also include two **long hops** on the mainland – each has a travel time of about three hours, marking these two routes out as among the longest in this book.

Remember, though, that **Scottish cities** have many interesting local bus routes for which we simply had no space in this book. In late 2013 and on into 2014 many Glasgow city services are getting their biggest shake-up for years. One service that won't be included on Glasgow's new bus map is Stagecoach's idea for an 'amfibus', designed to link Braehead and Clydebank on opposite sides of the Clyde. Had it come to pass, the bus would have paddled over the Clyde between Renfrew and Yoker. ■

MORE FAVOURITE JOURNEYS

The following Scottish routes were included in *Bus-Pass Britain* (2011): Berwick-upon-Tweed to Galashiels, Dunoon to Portavadie, Glasgow to Campbeltown, Pitlochry to Rannoch Moor and Inverness to Thurso.

By Bus with the Bard
A Burns Encounter

Richard West

Dumfries

Service no. 102 | Journey time 3hrs

OS Landranger 84, 78, 72, 65, 66. Thrice daily Mon–Sat, once on Sun.
Operator: Stagecoach.

Edinburgh

This is a journey that can start and end with Burns. In and around **Dumfries** he lived, drank, farmed (with mixed results) and at nearby Brow Well tried to cure his final illness by immersion in icy waters. Of the monuments to him in Dumfries itself, the most appealing must be the **Globe Inn** (☎ 01387 252335; open daily from 10.00), his regular howff. It is a cosy, welcoming pub where the literary connection is recognised but not overdone. Dumfries plays the Burns card, but not overwhelmingly so and still feels like a working town with a pretty high street – a little scarred by the effect of recession and competition from out-of-town supermarkets.

Scotland's Southern Uplands

Waiting for the bus at Whitesands, you can contemplate the fine river frontage, the sweep of the **River Nith** and the crumbling stone steps down to the racing weir. It is sad that the pedestrian-friendly development hereabouts is for now rather let down by riverside buildings that await renovation.

Once clear of the town, the bus makes steady progress along the A76, the main route towards Kilmarnock. Hollywood is the first village, but you will be lucky indeed to spot any stars hereabouts. Ellisland Farm, where Burns tried his hand at agriculture, is a little further along the way.

Auldgirth and **Closeburn** both still boast eating options (a picturesque inn and a functional snack bar respectively), village stores and working rural post offices, but alas no longer railway stations. The station at the small town of Thornhill is also long gone, but, if you are minded to do the journey in stages, this elegant spot with its broad high street, unspoilt townscape and selection of eateries makes a good first stopping-off point.

Thus far, the countryside has been hilly and wooded, but at **Carronbridge** the bus turns off onto a narrowing road and suddenly the hills close in. The climb to Dalveen Pass has begun. Under a graceful railway viaduct, round a bend, and bulky mountains immediately loom in front. The trees fall away and the route ahead appears barred by the great bulk of the **Lowther Hills** and its outliers. Now we have all the scenic grandeur of the Highlands transposed into the Southern Uplands of Scotland. Yet despite the sense of remoteness, there are still working sheep

BUS WARS

The journey described in this essay is one of a family of bus services linking Dumfries with Edinburgh. There are **additional journeys**, numbered 100 or 101 (and even a weekly 199) which follow different routes, all serving the small town of Moffat along the way.

These services have been the subject of **mighty tussles** between operators over the last year, with the various councils that subsidise them piling into the fray. For many years, **MacEwans Coaches** ran the routes, winning local approval for their service. In November 2012, the contract for the service was suddenly awarded to Stagecoach, the change being effected with just a very few days notice. Recriminations, threats of legal action and an inquiry followed. As this volume goes to press, there is talk of another **change of operator** in late 2013 or early 2014 – with the possibility that, on many journeys on Route 102, a change of bus may be necessary in Biggar.

Edinburgh ⇌
20 mins
Morningside
24 mins

N

Penicuik
15 mins
18 mins   West
Biggar   Linton
26 mins
Abington
18 mins
Elvanfoot
23 mins
Thornhill
25 mins
⇌
Dumfries

farms, and the route is long established, as part of the valley once carried a Roman road. The scattered settlement of Elvanfoot, announced by its tiny kirk and large cemetery, is a slightly surreal spot, sitting in an upland mountain bowl that is traversed by the M74 motorway and the main-line railway from London to Glasgow. The 102 sticks firmly to the old road – although the notion of a local bus in the Scottish hills slipping onto a motorway is an engaging one. The next stop is **Crawford**. A handful of mock-Tudor houses seem to have migrated here from suburban Surrey. The long-derelict Post Horn Hotel, surely a pit stop in the days when a drive from Glasgow to London was much slower and more adventurous than today, is well past renovation.

At **Abington** we make a bizarre detour into the M74 service area, amid a sea of trucks and the inevitable strong smell of burgers. Soon we are back in more rural surroundings, following the valley of the infant Clyde. At Roberton a church on a rocky bluff marks the site of a much more ancient place of settlement. At Lamington 'Sunday fishing' is forbidden in the river and at Coulter, a huge banner across the front of the attractive Mill Inn assures potential customers that 'There's no horse in our haggis!'

Biggar is the first community of any size since we left Dumfries. The town has an air of prosperity, its long central square well tended and lined with a wide range of independent shops. It is also home to a puppet theatre and a gasworks museum, an oddball combination of tourist attractions surely not replicated anywhere in Britain. Burns is not far away, for hereabouts lived one Archibald Prentice, a well-to-do farmer and significant subscriber to Burns' 'Edinburgh Edition.' Now the bus turns away from the Clyde and runs through sheep country once more at the foot of the Pentland Hills.

Approaching Edinburgh

You can soon begin to sense the commuter pull of Edinburgh. **West Linton** is a very pretty, if slightly over-egged, conservation village of the sort that often appeals to middle-class commuters. But then, just as you think it's all going to be an increasingly suburban landscape into Edinburgh, the bus makes a sharp turn down an improbably narrow road and diverts via Penicuik to reveal an altogether different face of what is now Midlothian.

You are suddenly in **ex-mining country**; the Shottstown Miners Welfare Club proves it, even if coal is no longer extracted hereabouts. The houses are more modest, and although Penicuik is still a lot more vibrant than many ex-mining towns, there are the inevitable empty shops. The local building material is a warm, gold stone which lifts the atmosphere, even on a dreich day.

Shortly afterwards, as the bus drops towards **Edinburgh**, you see on the right the first views across the city, and in good weather the Firth of Forth and the hills of Fife beyond. Although the long-distance view is grand, the initial approach to the city close-up is less inspiring. The bus picks its way across the city bypass, past a derelict '60s roadhouse but, after the elegant sweep of Braidlaw Park, is suddenly in a world of upmarket urban bustle.

The citizens of Morningside can clearly sustain a wide range of independent retail services. You may soon lose count of the number of interior design shops, delicatessens, complementary therapy practitioners, coffee shops and wine bars that line the route. Morningside gradually merges into Bruntsfield, a more bohemian student district. The same warm sandstone tenements; the shops are still varied, but geared to more modest pockets.

After the homey suburbs and on passing the **Usher Hall**, a sharp right turn at the end of Princes Street brings you suddenly to the pure theatre that is tourist Edinburgh. You are immersed in the landscape of a million tourist photos. Nothing here needs much introduction; Princes Street Gardens, the castle, the former North British Hotel, Arthur's Seat and the Old Town ranging up the hill across the railway tracks.

But the link with **Burns is not forgotten**. He came to live in the city in 1786, and was, for a time, feted by wealthy Edinburgh society. Although the novelty value of the Bard later wore off for the Edinburgh glitterati, he himself foresaw this. He did not allow this relatively short-lived social and intellectual whirlwind to change the underlying principles of his work. Today, walking tours will show you the numerous addresses that figured in the poet's all-too-brief period of fame.

Most folk will get off in **Princes Street**, and this may be just as well since the very end of the trip is rather an anticlimax as the bus picks its way to the cavernous St Andrew's Square bus station.

So there you have route 102. Warm urban streetscapes, verdant valleys, an upland vastness, from Roman history to all the paraphernalia of 21st-century communications. From workaday towns with lost industry to urban chic and tourist superstar city. Not bad for three hours and under a tenner! ■

ABOUT THE AUTHOR | **RICHARD WEST** is a retired civil servant looking forward to getting his bus pass soon and re-visiting bus routes like the 102.

Jewel in the Clyde
The Isle of Arran

Helen Hughes

45 Brodick

Service no. 324 | Journey time 80mins

OS Landranger 69. Six journeys Mon–Sat, four on Sun.
Operator: Stagecoach.

Blackwaterfoot

As the CalMac ferry from Ardrossan steams into **Brodick Bay,** you will see the buses waiting by the pier – if you can tear your eyes away from the hills. Few terminals can be in such a picturesque setting. The older houses are traditional red sandstone, there is a castle hiding among the trees across the bay, and just north of the village is Arran's highest peak, Goat Fell (2,866 feet). The visitor information centre (☎ 01770 303774) is also at the pier. It's best to get on the bus at once as it can be very busy in summer and the bus may well be full when it sets off. Sit on the right for the sea view, on the left for the hills.

For first-time visitors to the **Isle of Arran**, the 324 bus gives a fine introduction to a fragment of Scotland that has always punched far above its weight. Along the way we visit Glen Chalmadale, then skirt the shores of lovely Kilbrannan Sound with enticing views across to the Mull of Kintyre. Our destination is Blackwaterfoot, a village that by the direct road (called 'the String') is less than a dozen miles from where we start at Brodick Pier. But it is worth making this great loop around the northern half of Arran.

So we are off, leaving Brodick and already we realise this island is **packed with history**. Just after the golf course, look out for our first standing stone on the right. The island is littered with these which date back 4,000 years to the Bronze Age, a reminder that people have been coming here for ages. Shortly after the **Arran Heritage Museum** (☎ 01770 302636; open daily 10.30–16.30 late March till late October; www.arranmuseum.co.uk), the route diverges from the direct road over to Blackwaterfoot. Viewed from the top of Goat Fell, you'd see why that latter is called the String. Our route is briefly lined with beech trees and with luck you might see a red squirrel. Their grey cousins have never made it across the water so the reds are relatively flourishing.

HEADING FOR THE HILLS

Once past the castle, the road plays hide-and-seek with the shore, where sometimes seals bask on the rocks. Approaching the pretty village of **Corrie**, in clear weather there is a good view of the hills with Glen Sannox and its dramatic peaks. The glen was once home to a barytes mine and the track provides a pleasant walk. As the road turns inland and climbs up Glen Chalmadale, the line of hills on the left is broken by the jagged gap of the 'Witch's Step'. On the right are the old peat banks, once an important source of fuel for the islanders.

Then we drop down to **Lochranza** and pick up the coast again. There's a useful ferry link from Lochranza over to Kintyre. Lochranza is home to a distillery that makes Arran's celebrated single malt whisky (☎ 01770 830264; open daily 10.00–17.30

BRODICK CASTLE

Brodick castle, built in 19th-century baronial style, is invisible from the bus. Ask to be dropped off at the gates. There are **landscaped gardens** (especially lovely in spring when the rhododendrons are flowering), waterfalls, ten miles of woodland trails and a **Bavarian summer house**. Ranger services, a shop and a tea room are also available (phone ☎ 0844 493 2152 for opening times of the castle).

Mar–Oct, 11.00–16.00 Mon–Sat Nov–Feb). A less appealing aspect of the village is that it is starved of sunlight, kept in the shadows by the surrounding hills.

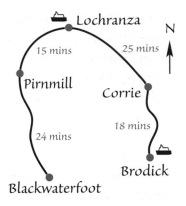

Arran seems so very Scottish but the demography is actually quite dynamic. Young folk from the island move away to the mainland to look for work and affordable housing. And migrants come in. Nowadays, the bus driver on this journey is as likely to be Tadeusz as Tam.

Past the end of Lochranza lies the lonely grave of John McLean, dated 1854. A cholera victim, the sailor was refused burial in Lochranza or Catacol in case the disease spread. In the end, he was buried between the two communities.

The next bead in the string of coastal villages is **Catacol** where we pass the Twelve Apostles, a picturesque row of 19th-century cottages built for tenant farmers who were cleared from the glen to make way for sheep. Sad to think their descendants can no longer make a living here either.

The bus bumps over a set of switchbacks, another result of Arran's **remarkable geology** where the rocks have been folded over on themselves. Unless you have a cast-iron stomach, I wouldn't sit at the back of the bus – the Arran road surfaces in general leave something to be desired. For the bus drivers, it's part of the fun. 'I love the job,' said one. 'The roads can be challenging. Not exactly single track, but still narrow. We get a lot of tour buses and camper vans on the island in summer. Meeting those can be interesting!'

We rattle into **Pirnmill**, once the home of bobbin makers for the weaving trade, another long-gone source of income on the island. The hill at Whitefarland takes the bus away from the shore up to a view across to Carradale on Kintyre. Then, from the bottom of Imachar Brae, it's a flat run by the sea to **Machrie**, which is more a scattering of farms and cottages than a village. There are numerous ancient sites in this area, once home to Bronze Age communities. The most spectacular circles on **Machrie Moor** were excavated in the 1970s and are about a mile from the road. It is an easy walk and you can get off the bus at the start of the track.

The last three miles run through pleasant farmland, mainly populated by sheep. The hedgerows in spring are bright with gorse and honeysuckle. The final view is, I think, the best of them all: across the silken **Kilbrannan Sound** to the Mull of Kintyre, Sanda Island and, on a clear day, the thin flat line of the Antrim coast. The bus draws to a halt by the harbour in **Blackwaterfoot**.

You can enjoy local produce for lunch at the Kinloch Hotel (☎ 01770 860444) and watch grey seals on the rocks at low tide. Alternatively, if you do want to stretch your legs and have stout footwear, it's a brisk half-hour walk to the **King's Caves**. Here, Robert the Bruce is said to have seen the spider whose repeated attempts to complete her web inspired Robert to try once more to defeat his foes. Pictish symbols are carved at the back of the main cave (take a torch). In spring, there are nesting fulmars and black guillemots on the cliffs. You'll see oystercatchers on the rocks and gannets diving out at sea. There is plenty of time for a walk to the caves and a picnic lunch before heading back to the bus. ■

ABOUT THE AUTHOR | **HELEN HUGHES**, originally from Yorkshire, now lives in Glasgow. She has been going to Arran since before she was born.

COWAL IN CONTEXT

Jackie Scott-Mandeville

46 Dunoon

Service no. 484 | Journey time 80mins

OS Landranger 63, 56. Twice daily Mon–Sat, no service on Sun.
Operator: West Coast Motors.

Carrick Castle

I retired to Argyll's Cowal Peninsula in 2007. My bus pass is handy for exploring this part of the Highlands which is like Scotland in miniature. Cowal featured in *Bus-Pass Britain* (in 2011) with a journey that tracked west from Dunoon to Loch Fyne. This route, which starts by heading north from Dunoon, gives a very different perspective on **Cowal's varied landscapes**. We take in mountains, glens and sea lochs.

Dunoon, the only town on Cowal, enjoyed its heyday in the early 20th century when Glaswegians would take day trips and holidays 'doon the watter' to this hillside resort on the Clyde Estuary. The red-tiled domes of the Edwardian bandstand and pier pavilion are near the bus and ferry terminal.

The mid-morning 484 bus trundles along the A885, joins the A815 at the suburb of Sandbank, and passes Holy Loch, an estuarial inlet and the site of a submarine base during World War II (and a US Navy base from 1961–92). Gulls wheel overhead and striking black-and-white oystercatchers, with their red legs and beaks, potter about the mudflats. Ahead, mountains loom above forest, and, after the junction with the A880, there are lovely picnic and walking spots such as Puck's Glen and **Benmore Botanic Garden** (☎ 01369 706261; open daily Mar–Oct).

BENMORE TO ST CATHERINES

A narrow rock cleft defines the entrance to the glen of **Loch Eck**, a deep, freshwater, glacial lake formed after the Ice Age in a trough scoured out by ice two million years ago. Wind-ruffled or glittering in sunlight, the loch reflects the mood of the weather above. Ben More guards the waters below. Sometimes the loch's surface is so still that the mountains above are perfectly mirrored. Loch Eck is the only loch other than Loch Lomond to host the powan, a freshwater whitefish. The road runs the loch's length for seven miles, scenic vistas at every turn, passing two inns, the Coylet and the Whistlefield, both old drovers inns and comfortable watering holes in which to relax in front of the fire on a winter's day with a pint of Fyne Ale or enjoy a summer lunch overlooking the loch.

Leaving Loch Eck behind, the bus passes through Glenbranter plantation forest before reaching the village of **Strachur** – the name means 'valley of the heron' – where it stops in the old centre by the Clachan Bar (☎ 01369 860500) and a restored smiddy, a blacksmith's forge still operating into the mid-1950s, open to visitors on summer afternoons. Strachur has an enviably pretty position on the shore of **Loch Fyne**. It is the longest sea loch in

DUNOON CONNECTIONS

Getting to Dunoon to start this journey is easy. There are **regular ferries** across the Clyde from Gourock (itself less than an hour by train from the heart of Glasgow). Or hop on **McGill's 907 bus** at Buchanan Street bus station in **Glasgow**. This service uses the vehicle ferry from McInroy's Point to Hunter's Quay – thus allowing you to ride from the capital of the Clyde to the capital of Cowal without having to leave the comfort of your seat on the bus. These through journeys to Dunoon with McGill's run nine times daily Monday to Saturday, with half a dozen runs on a Sunday. Once on **Cowal** you'll find the mood on local buses is more relaxed and convivial than on the other side of the Clyde. Unless the bus is ferrying children to and from school, there's always a good choice of empty seats on any route.

Scotland and famous for its oysters, salmon, and halibut. Blue or grey, the waters of Loch Fyne are always impressive, with tapestries of forest and fields colouring the Argyll hillsides on the opposite shore. Circling **Strachur Bay** we pass the famous Creggans Inn, once owned by the diplomat and soldier Sir Fitzroy Maclean (a suggested model for James Bond).

As we leave Strachur I glimpse, through the patchy woodland, a heron fishing on the shore line and a couple of fishing boats heading north up Loch Fyne. Then the road opens out again at **St Catherines** where the Old Ferry Inn, now derelict, is a reminder of the days when the ferry to Inveraray (ceased 1963) linked the old pilgrim and cattle routes across loch and glen.

The bus leaves the A815 at the summit of the hill above St Catherines, looking across Loch Fyne to Dunderave Castle, nonchalant Highland cattle chewing hay in the muddy field by the junction. It then turns right onto **Hell's Glen**, a steep single-track road through the Arrochar Alps.

Slowly up round sharp bends through a short stretch of moorland, we then pass through bottle-green Sitka spruce forest dominated by alpine mountain grandeur – Cruach nam Mult, Stob an Eas – then follow a ravine, cross a small stone bridge, descend a 1 in 5 incline towards

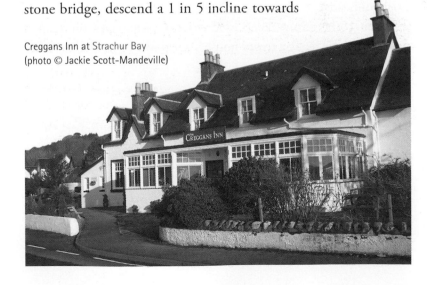

Creggans Inn at Strachur Bay
(photo © Jackie Scott-Mandeville)

Loch Goil, cut along a precipitous slope, and follow hairpin bends down into the valley. The occasional buzzard soars overhead, but beyond that there is little sign of life. This is barren and desolate country. Into Glen Goil I admire the valley's U-shape, cut by a glacier millennia ago. Woodland changes to green fields; a straggle of houses appear, and the bus crosses the River Goil to arrive in Lochgoilhead village, turning into a car park at the head of Loch Goil. All is quiet: a man walks his collies and a couple of ladies chat by the post office/shop, taking for granted the breathtaking view of the sea loch stretching several miles southwards.

LOCHGOILHEAD AND CARRICK CASTLE

Defying the remote location, the **Drimsynie Estate**, with its castellated hotel, chalets and static caravans is the next stop along the west shore. The route continues past the Ardroy Outdoor Education Centre and the five-star Lodge on Loch Goil with a tree house built into an ancient cedar. This busy holiday area contrasts with the deserted landscape further down the road, emphasised by Loch Goil's steep, fjord-like, forested cliffs brooding either side. The road finally peters out at Carrick Castle, four miles from Lochgoilhead.

The 15th-century keep of **Carrick Castle**, stark on a small promontory, is really a tower house, its forbidding aspect presently

A TRINITY OF INNS

Good spots to take a break on this route include the **Whistlefield Inn** on Loch Eck, situated in both Argyll Forest Park and Loch Lomond & Trossachs National Park (☎ 01369 860440; bar open daily in spring & summer from 12.30, from 17.00 Mon–Fri/12.30 Sat & Sun in winter). Don't miss the award-winning **Creggans Inn** in Strachur Bay, overlooking Loch Fyne (☎ 01369 860279) or the **Shore House Inn** in Lochgoilhead, a 19th-century manse with a new restaurant and terrace (☎ 01301 703340; open 12.00–23.00 Wed–Sun).

compromised by restoration work and a modern addition atop the tower, indicating the owner is in residence. Current occupation of such an isolated and ancient fastness seems paradoxical, but in summer this apparently deserted hamlet is full of activity especially with the **local boat club** in full swing. By the bus/car park an oddly grand, turreted, sandstone building looks out of place.

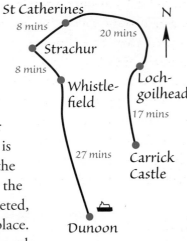

Suddenly a couple appear from the shoreline track who start an animated conversation with the erstwhile rather quiet bus driver, and they inform me that the edifice was originally intended as a hotel, never finished, and later converted into apartments. Despite the feeling of being at the end of the world, this is obviously a thriving little community, uncaring about the distance from shops, pubs, and other urban niceties, enjoying, as the couple explain, the escape from the 'rat race.'

Off to Dunoon to see her daughter and do some shopping, Jane turns out to be a chatty soul. She and Jock enliven the return journey. Back in **Hell's Glen** she points out where ruined stone cottages sit by a mountain stream, remnants of a pre-forest settlement. At the junction with the A815 she tells us about a 'gypsy ring' in a Highland cattle field where travellers used to get married. The sun has come out turning Loch Fyne and Loch Eck royal blue as we absorb the beauty of the loch and mountain scenery, now with a southerly aspect, and arrive cheerfully **back in Dunoon** in time for a late lunch. ∎

ABOUT THE AUTHOR | **JACKIE SCOTT–MANDEVILLE** is a retired university administrator who now enjoys the quiet life in a hamlet above Loch Fyne.

Dundee

Service no. 973 | Journey time 3hrs 35mins

OS Landranger 54, 53, 52, 51, 50, 49. Once daily, late May to early Oct only.
Operator: Scottish Citylink.

Oban

Sometimes, unfairly I feel, referred to in guidebooks as Scotland's 'Cinderella city,' **Dundee** has of late rediscovered an optimism that befits a city with a splendid estuarial waterfront and a beautiful hinterland. Of the 'three Js' that used to be the city's trademarks, the jute industry has long gone, but is recalled in the city's Jute Museum – housed in a former jute mill called Verdant Works. Jam too is no longer made and as for journalism, D C Thomson still publish their varied range of magazines and comics and the *Dundee Courier* in the city. But even that's threatened.

But there is much more here; the **Discovery Centre** recalling the days of Arctic exploration and whaling; Dundee Law, a volcanic plug right in the city commanding amazing views; and a **revamped waterfront**, transformed from the docks of old into a fine pedestrian space soon to be graced with a bold new structure housing a Scottish 'branch' of the Victoria & Albert Museum.

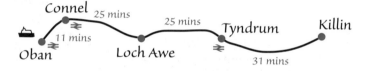

But the enduring image of Dundee for most folk must be the bridges; the road bridge which at high tide seems almost to sit on the surface of the river and, more famously, the railway bridge, which tragically fell down in a great storm in 1879 with the loss of 75 lives. The disaster was, of course, immortalised by the Bard of Dundee **William McGonagall**, whose doggerel made him famous in a way that would have made Robbie Burns wince.

RECLINING FROM COAST TO COAST

So, with Dundee having so much to offer, it might be with reluctance that one boards the Scottish Citylink coach that once daily during late spring and summer rolls right across Scotland to the west coast. There is a hybrid character to this **seasonal route**. The vehicle is a step up from a regular local bus. It has reclining seats and a loo. But for much of the route, this runs as a regular hail-and-ride service. You can wave down the coach in villages and on country roads that hug the side of Scottish lochs. Holders of a Scottish bus pass (here called a National Entitlement Card) can hop on and ride for free.

West from Dundee the 973 passes through the **Carse of Gowrie**, where the traditional soft fruit growing industry has, of late, undergone a spectacular revival. Modern techniques allow growing that is no longer tied to the passing seasons and have led to the landscape filling with polytunnels. Most of the produce is processed into jams, flavourings and drinks, but it is still good to see a traditional industry faring well in these hard times.

There is history here too. To the north amid the modest summits of the Sidlaw Hills lies Dunsinane, of Macbeth fame, an

ancient fortified site referenced by **Shakespeare** in his historically inaccurate play about a Scottish king who was actually, for his time, a progressive reformer and talented administrator. With the Tay to our left and passing the palatial home of one of the leading figures of the Scottish bus industry, Ann Gloag, to the right, the bus rounds Kinnoull Hill and arrives in Perth.

Perth is dubbed 'the fair city.' She never had the industrial heritage of Dundee, so her riverfront needs no regeneration, made up as it is of elegant Georgian frontages, public open spaces and purpose-built promenades. Surprisingly, the city boasts a small port at the limit of navigation. On certain dates in high summer, round-trip cruises operate from Newport, opposite Dundee, up to Perth – an excellent way of learning about the lesser-known history of the river, such as the tramways that used to service the salmon fisheries and the lost medieval port near Newburgh.

A self-consciously touristy city serving a wealthy hinterland, Perth offers varied cultural attractions including the unusual Ferguson Gallery housed in the old waterworks. The sadly diminished railway station recalls the days when trains converged here from seven directions; now just three routes remain, and the sandstone Station Hotel looks a little unloved.

Beyond Perth the traffic thins somewhat and the A85 road follows the broad valley of the tiny Pow Water past **Huntingtower Castle**. At Methven, rather unexpectedly, we spot a small War Graves Commission cemetery on the right. Crieff has an archetypical small Scottish townscape, with fine middle-class stone villas, a sloping square, a super-abundance of eating places, a well kept public park and a backdrop of mountains.

If you wish to tackle the 973 in sections – for it's a longish run – **Crieff** makes a good overnight stop. As in most small Scottish towns, there is no shortage of B&B signs in Crieff. Just ten minutes beyond the town, we pause at Comrie, which claims, a little improbably, to be the earthquake capital of Scotland. It lies directly above the fault line at the southern edge of the Highlands. Beyond here, the valley narrows significantly. Brown, green or purple hillsides (depending on the season) press in on the road and magnificent **Loch Earn** comes suddenly into view.

There are few other buses on this section of the route. Most of the students, shoppers and other local travellers have alighted, and one senses a change in the mood on board. These are people travelling for fun rather than out of necessity. There are tourists bound for the west coast and the Hebrides, and many backpackers and walkers. Fortunately the coach has ample luggage space to accommodate all those heavy rucksacks.

The village of **St Fillans** bears testament to changing holiday tastes; the substantial Victorian hotel lies sadly derelict, whereas local B&Bs look newly renovated and exude prosperity. The road is now right beside the water. The railway that once traced this route, closed even before Dr Beeching wielded his infamous axe, is lost on the forested hillside.

From Lochearnhead the route climbs up Glen Ogle, scene of the landslip which prematurely closed the direct rail route from Stirling to Oban in the 1960s. Crossing the narrow watershed at the head of the glen, we drop down once more into the Tay Valley, here decidedly upland in character and far removed from the tortuous, silvery and languid-looking river that we left at Perth.

A short detour from the main road brings us to the village of **Killin** at the west end of Loch Tay. This is another good choice for an overnight stop, particularly as Killin is home to the impressive Falls of Dochart, more a set of rapids than a waterfall, but none the less striking for that. The village has a well-developed tourist infrastructure, but for lunch or an overnight stay, the Falls of Dochart Inn makes a good choice.

Crianlarich is a road and rail junction. Nearly all travellers from the south to Fort William, Oban and beyond pass through here, and the atmosphere of this and the next village, Tyndrum, reflects this. Beyond the filling stations and the mildly American roadhouse atmosphere of the Green Welly Stop, **Tyndrum** does offer another example of a traditional Scottish industry making a comeback, with the recent resumption of gold mining in the hills hereabouts. A dozen passengers alight in Tyndrum. Not prospectors for gold, it seems, but travellers connecting onto the 915 to the Isle of Skye that pulls up behind us.

Westwards towards **Dalmally**, the next section is unremittingly bleak, a desolate valley overseen by bulky, rounded peaks with little habitation. The approach of the wooded shores of Loch Awe and the remains of Kilchurn Castle signal a return to more homely landscapes, at least for a time. Dating from the mid-15th century, the castle repays the short if often muddy walk needed to reach it, and Historic Scotland provides its customarily thorough information displays. Railway and road are soon hemmed in once again beside a branch of Loch Awe. Both train and bus give access

McCaig's Folly, Oban (photo © Deborah Hewitt /DT)

to the 'Hollow Mountain,' an unlikely but interesting tourist experience centred on a 1960s hydro-electric plant built inside **Ben Cruachan** (☎ 01866 822618; www.visitcruachan.co.uk).

After Taynuilt, Loch Etive brings the first taste of sea air from the west coast with advertisements for sea cruises. The remains of Bonawe Iron Foundry, also in the care of Historic Scotland, provide a reminder than this now much gentler, wooded landscape has an industrial past too, albeit one that has left very few traces.

At **Connel Ferry**, the loch narrows and the turbulent waters of the Falls of Lora swirl underneath the former joint road/rail bridge towards Ballachulish. Predictably, only the road remains, but you can still take a bus from here to Fort William. Connel is a good spot to linger and the homely Rowans B&B a comfortable place to stay (☎ 01631 710105).

And so to Oban, with **McCaig's Folly** dominating the skyline, countless B&Bs and an atmosphere which blends those of the traditional seaside, a working market town and an entrepôt for the islands. The seascape hereabouts offers a constant tableau of movement, from the frequent shuttling of the tiny Kerrera ferry and the larger boats to Mull, to the periodic arrival of ferries from the distant Outer Hebrides. ∎

ABOUT THE AUTHOR | **RICHARD WEST** is a retired civil servant and a keen reader of *hidden europe* magazine. He lives in Kelso and likes seeking out under-publicised journeys by train, bus and ship.

SHELTERED SPACES

Ah, the bus stop. No-one really *wants* to be at the bus stop. But in a busy Britain, the **bus stop** has some redeeming qualities. It rates as one of the few remaining public spaces where people just stand still. It is a place to observe detail, a chance to **share a smile** or a woe and an opportunity to attend to the passing minutes.

Bus stops deserve a better press – though Marilyn Monroe gave the humble bus stop a boost in popular culture with the 1956 film *Bus Stop*. Of course, just as there are various grades of hotels, so there are several categories of bus stops. In our book, any self-respecting bus stop aspiring to a star rating needs a **bus shelter**. The name of the latter has always struck us as extraordinary for a structure that is designed to shelter humans rather than buses.

In fact, we have spent years giving **star ratings** to bus shelters. We have travelled from one end of Britain to the other in search of the finest examples of the species. Brighton deserves a visit for all sorts of reasons. Some go for the beach, others to visit the celebrated Royal Pavilion. We go for the **Art Deco bus shelters** (definitely three-star attractions). Hilary Bradt, who wrote the foreword to this volume, tells us that there is a wooden bus shelter in Uffculme in Devon that was once the village butcher's shop. That's a two-star bus shelter for its novelty value.

For the **finest bus shelter** in Britain, you have to head a long way north. On the island of Unst in the Shetlands is the only bus shelter in the land ever to have received the ultimate accolade: our five-star rating. The landscape of **Unst** is pretty desolate and forlorn, but the bus shelter on the A968 east of Baltasound (at Grid Reference HP637096) is truly a sight to behold. It has an armchair, vases of flowers and many other creature comforts. Each year, a new theme is introduced. So in 2012, for example, the bus shelter was decked out in fine style to mark the Queen's Diamond Jubilee. Missing the bus in Unst becomes a matter for rejoicing when one can relax in such salubrious surroundings.

The Unst bus shelter is a marvellous community initiative, mirrored in London by the **edible bus stop** initiative. It started with one bus stop in Stockwell, but has expanded into a series of guerrilla gardening initiatives along the 322 bus route from Clapham Common to Crystal Palace. ■

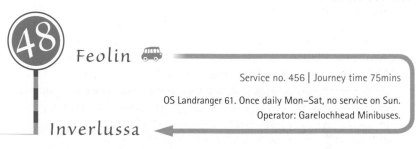

THE 456 TO INVERLUSSA
A JURA JOURNEY

David Hoult

48 Feolin 🚐

Service no. 456 | Journey time 75mins

OS Landranger 61. Once daily Mon–Sat, no service on Sun.
Operator: Garelochhead Minibuses.

Inverlussa

S eparating the Inner Hebridean islands of Islay and Jura is the
Sound of Islay, a narrow stretch of sea which is notable for
its powerful tides. Just after three every afternoon the MV *Eilean
Dhiura* whisks passengers across from Port Askaig on Islay to
Feolin Ferry on Jura, where a **white minibus** is waiting by the
concrete slipway. This is the 456 to Inverlussa. The journey will
take us some 25 miles along a single-track road, making a ten-
minute stop *en route* at Jura's main settlement of Craighouse.

Of our four fellow passengers, two are island residents,
heading for home with bags of shopping from Islay's capital,
Bowmore. The other two are American visitors, Betty and Jean
from Slippery Rock, Pennsylvania. We pile our luggage on board,
Mike the driver starts the engine and our journey gets under way.

CRAIGHOUSE: CAPITAL OF JURA

From **Feolin Ferry** the road clings to the shore, and Mike tells us
to look out for otters, which can sometimes be seen playing on
the rocks here. Soon the road slants inland and climbs steadily,
before descending after five deserted miles to the first sign of
habitation. This is **Jura House**, ancient seat of the Campbells

of Jura, who dominated the island for three hundred years until they sold the house in 1938. Three empty miles later, a road sign welcomes careful drivers to **Craighouse**, and we arrive at Jura's only village. Betty and Jean have booked in at the hotel, so Mike stops outside and helps them down with their luggage. Then a few metres further on we come to a halt outside the Jura Stores, and Mike disappears inside.

It is now becoming clear that the 456 is no ordinary bus. Mike emerges from the shop with boxes of groceries, a couple of newspapers, and a huge bag of dog meal, and these are all stacked on board. Betty and Jean rejoin the bus, having dropped off their bags at the hotel. We resume our northward journey.

Craighouse is a linear village, straggling for a mile along the shore northwards from the village centre. On the left there is a line of houses and cottages, with **Jura's whitewashed parish church** among them, and behind them in the distance stand the island's three famous peaks, the Paps of Jura (see box below).

To our right, the shore is lapped by the sheltered waters of **Small Isles Bay**. As we drive along, people we pass wave a greeting. Here and there we stop to allow Mike to make a delivery. If no-one answers the door, he walks in and leaves the newspaper or groceries inside – no-one locks their door on Jura. At the north end of the village we pass **Small Isles School**, the island's tiny primary school. Normally we would stop here to collect the school

THE PAPS OF JURA

The Paps of Jura are **three mountains** on the west side of the island. The highest point is 2,575 feet. They are steep-sided quartzite hills with distinctive conical shapes.

The word 'pap' is an **Old Norse** term for the female breast – despite the fact that Jura has three of them rather than two! They are very conspicuous, **dominating the island** landscape as well as the landscape of the surrounding area. They can be seen from the Mull of Kintyre and, on a clear day, from Skye and Northern Ireland.

THE ISLE OF JURA

Jura's population is small, but it is a large island. In a list of Scottish islands by size, it would come eighth, just behind Arran. But whilst Arran supports a population of over 5,000, Jura has barely 200. There is only one proper village, **Craighouse**, where you will find the island's only shop, the Jura Stores, a tea room, the bistro and restaurant the **Antlers** (☎ 01496 820142; bistro is open daily 08.00–17.00 and the restaurant from 18.30 – the latter requires advance booking), and the convivial **Jura Hotel** (☎ 01496 820243), which is the lively hub of island life. But the village is dominated by the Jura distillery; if people have heard of Jura at all, it is usually because of its delicate **single-malt whiskies**.

children, but today is a school holiday, so we cruise by without stopping.

Now the road is ours – there is no other traffic. After another mile or two we cross the Corran River by **Three Arch Bridge**, which was built in 1810 by the great Scottish civil engineer Thomas Telford. Next stop is at at the tiny hamlet of Lagg. Two hundred years ago this was an important place, with ferries to the mainland coming and going from Lagg pier – also built by Thomas Telford – but only a handful of people live here now.

Mike drops off his last box of groceries, and then the bus pulls noisily up **Lagg Brae** to enter an ugly expanse of tree stumps stretching for nearly three miles. Until recently this was Lagg Forest; the felling has left scars on the hillside, but there is compensation in that it opened up glorious views across the water to the Kintyre Peninsula and the Isle of Arran beyond.

After the forest, the road descends sharply to **Tarbert Bay** with its sandy beach. Mike

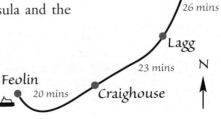

points out a white house, half-hidden by trees away to our right. 'See that house over there?' he says. 'It belongs to the prime minister's father-in-law.'

'Does he ever catch the bus?' asks Jean, but the noise of the engine drowns Mike's reply as he accelerates uphill for the last five miles of our journey, until we arrive at Ardlussa. Here is one of Jura's few road junctions: if you turn left, you can drive for three miles, and then walk another four miles on a track to Barnhill, the isolated house where **George Orwell** wrote *Nineteen Eighty-Four*.

TEA AT THE END OF THE WORLD

But we turn right, and head down to **Inverlussa**, surely one of the UK's most far-flung bus stops. The afternoon sun glints on the sea. The views across the **Sound of Mull** to the hills of Kintyre are splendid. A lone yacht is moored in the bay. There are a few stone cottages here, and next to the beach there is a trestle table with a hand-written sign announcing 'tea on the beach.'

On the table, an old biscuit tin contains a two-way radio, with instructions on how to order. However, we have cheated: we phoned ahead from the bus (Mike knew the number), and our tea and cake is already waiting on the table. We sit on the rocks for ten minutes, enjoying the tea, the lemon-drizzle cake and the utter peace of this remote spot.

Then it's time to go. We leave money in the honesty box, climb aboard the 456, and head back to **Craighouse**. It has been an amazing journey on this beautiful and virtually deserted island. There are young children living here at the north end of Jura, and the bus is needed to transport them to school in Craighouse. Without the children, it is hard to see how this bus service could possibly survive. So don't delay – go there while you still can! ∎

ABOUT THE AUTHOR | **DAVID HOULT** is a musician and island lover, who regrets that his English bus pass does not entitle him to free travel in Scotland.

SUAS GU DEAS
GOING 'UP SOUTH'

Rhona NicDhùghaill

49

Berneray

Service no. W17 | Journey time 2hrs 40mins to 3hrs

OS Landranger 18, 22, 31. Thrice daily Mon–Sat, no service on Sun.
Operator: Grenitote, Hebridean, DA Travel and others.

Eriskay ◀

O ur last two routes in this volume are set in the **Western Isles**,
the long sweep of islands which lie off the northwest coast
of Scotland. They form a beautiful breakwater against the wide
Atlantic and a final outpost of folklore, traditional culture and of
course the Gaelic language. The first of our duo of Outer Hebrides
excursions starts from Berneray (or Beàrnaraigh na Hearadh, to
distinguish it from its namesake at the far southern end of the
Outer Hebrides) and tracks south over seven islands – each linked
to the next by a causeway carrying a road.

Bus service W17 makes this marvellous journey. It is part
of the longer **Outer Hebrides spinal route** that involves several

---

HEBRIDEAN CO-OPERATION

No other journey in this book relies on such a **multiplicity of bus
operators**. The W17 section of the Outer Hebrides spinal route alone
depends upon the co-operation of nine different companies. This is a
another world from mainland Britain. Here bus companies co-operate
with each other rather than compete for the same business. On many
routes, you'll need to change buses along the way – sometimes more
than once. But it all **works seamlessly** with through fares and ticketing.

---

buses and two ferries. Schedules are perfectly co-ordinated so that, in summer at least, it is possible to leave the Butt of Lewis (at the northern end of the archipelago) early in the morning and arrive at Castlebay (on Barra, towards the southern end of the island chain) by evening. Taking some ten hours, this is one of Europe's most extraordinary journeys by public transport.

This essay covers one road segment of the entire overland route. We leave from **Berneray** and end in Eriskay. You can connect into this portion of the journey by ferries from the Scottish mainland and the Isle of Skye. Ferries from Uig on Skye land at Lochmaddy, while the boat from Oban (on the mainland) stops at Lochboisdale. Our bus stops at both piers.

A LITANY OF ISLANDS

I'm the only person waiting for the bus at the hostel in Berneray, the very start of the W17 route. The rustic thatched and whitewashed hostel, huddled low on the shore, nicely evokes a sense of isolation. From the deserted bus stop, I can hear the waves crashing on the white-gold beach and see the hills of Harris rising in the distance.

Right on time, a tired-looking, **white minibus** arrives, and I get on. This particular is unusual. The same vehicle runs right through to Eriskay slipway where it connects with the boat to Barra, the last inhabited island before rock is swallowed by sea.

LOCHMADDY

The little **port of Lochmaddy** warrants a stop. There is a hostel (Uist Outdoor Centre, ☎ 01876 500480) as well as a luxury hotel, Tigh Dearg (☎ 01876 500700). Somewhere in between is Redburn House (☎ 01876 500301), in the centre of the village, offering self-catering units or comfortable en-suite rooms.

Make time to visit the **Hut of Shadows**, just a couple of miles from the village. It is a low, small stone roundhouse with a turf roof that houses a rustic camera obscura. Ask for directions in Lochmaddy.

But this route is too good to rush, and many travellers will stop off for a few hours or even overnight at points along the way.

The driver chats easily while steering us down the single-track road to our first stop in Berneray village, where we pause to pick up two ladies bound for the shops in Lochmaddy. Soon after, a causeway takes us off Berneray and onto a desolate road over the North Uist moorland, before joining the main road. In around 20 minutes, we arrive in **Lochmaddy**, the largest settlement in North Uist.

A short walk from the pier is **Taigh Chearsabhagh**, a gallery and museum complex, which also houses a café, post office, and a Gaelic/English bookshop covering everything from poetry to history, horticulture to cookery, generally with a local flavour (☎ 01870 603970; open 10.00–16.00 Mon–Sat). After a bite to eat, while the weather's on my side, I spend an hour or two exploring the coastline at the edge of Lochmaddy, taking in the curious Hut of Shadows (see box opposite).

Back on the bus, across another causeway and the tidal island of Grimsay, we arrive in **Benbecula**. Something of a halfway house between North and South Uist, the island is also home to local council offices, a small airport, and an MOD centre, which give it a feeling of no-man's-land. In contrast, the school at Lionacleit is a hub of local activity, doubling as a leisure centre, cafeteria, library and museum, with almost all W17 journeys stopping here.

A short distance from **Lionacleit**, the low land dissolves once again into the clear sea lochs, and yet another causeway takes us on to South Uist. Like most of the Western Isles, the east coast here is home to numerous rocky inlets, while the west coast boasts lush machair and miles of golden beaches. South Uist also has mountains, and almost immediately the shapes of the largest,

Berneray
25 mins
Lochmaddy
20 mins
N
Grimsay
25 mins
Lionacleit
35 mins
Kildonan
15 mins
Lochboisdale
35 mins
Eriskay

Hecla and **A' Bheinn Mhòr** ('The Big Mountain', at 2,034 feet) are visible in the distance. I wonder if this is why the locals describe the journey down here as 'suas gu deas' – going 'up south'.

The bus rolls on, and we pass signs pointing westwards where the majority of the villages are, occasionally picking up or dropping off a passenger at a road end. In contrast, the craggy east side is barely inhabited. I ask the driver (once again, we are the only two people on the bus) if he's ever been walking there. 'Oh no,' he says. It turns out he is from Benbecula and a man more taken by windy two-dimensional landscapes. He's not used to hills.

UIST CURIOSITIES

There's a shower starting, so I decide to swap a stroll on the beach for a look round **Kildonan Museum**. The bus drops me off, and I head inside. The centre is open from April to October, seven days a week from 10.00 to 17.00, and houses archaeological displays, a collection of South Uist artefacts, and an archive room dedicated to the American folklorist Margaret Fay Shaw, who made the island her home. The museum café and craft shop also sell local produce, and whether you're in the mood for a bowl of soup or some handmade jewellery, there's lots to choose from.

Eriskay cemetery (photo © Rhona NicDhùghaill)

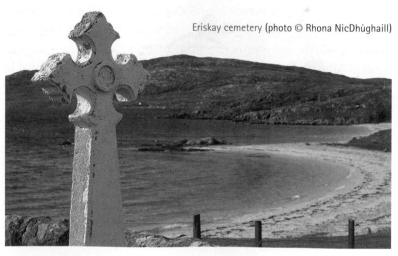

As I wait for the bus outside the museum, I chat to two young women who, like me, are heading for Eriskay. They're tourists, and have never been to the island before. 'You'll love it,' I tell them. 'It's small, but perfectly formed.' I also confess to being biased, as it's where my grandfather was born. Soon enough, the bus arrives, and we go on to Daliburgh and the port of **Lochboisdale**, before doubling back to the road south. In the falling light, the bleached grasses reach over and touch the ground beside them. From time to time, the tarmac sends out a spindly finger towards the coast and the townships of Baghasdal, Leth Meadhanach and Smercleit.

As we approach the bus stop at Gearraidh na Mònadh, my fellow travellers start peering through the window, exchanging puzzled looks. 'What's that?' they ask me, pointing. The distinctive local Catholic church, **Our Lady of Sorrows**, has caught their attention. It is a classic example of modernist (some might say brutalist) architecture. The contrast between the building and its surroundings is stark, a rare reminder that each decade has made its mark on these islands, however faintly. The tourists take a photo and the bus drives on, the church's flat face staring defiantly through the rear window after us. Glimpsing the white walls of the **Polochar Inn** ahead, we turn left and the road gets narrower still, its edges now gilded with sand.

Over the sea to Eriskay

As our route hugs the south coast of Uist, we look across to **Eriskay**, closer and smaller than Barra, its rugged appearance contrasting both with its diminutive size and with the uncanny azure lagoon in which it sits. We pass the old pier at **Ludag**, its grey concrete arm still outstretched to the sea, awaiting the embrace of the ferry long since discontinued. Soon, we're sailing across on the latter's replacement: a smooth and unromantic bridge and causeway. Today, the community of Eriskay relies on it, and in all weather it remains regular and dependable, as indifferent to our bus on its back as it is to the whales and dolphins that pass below it.

The W17's final destination is the **slipway** at the southwest of the island, but as I'm spending the night here, I get off in the island's only village. Like the whole island, it is compact, with the school, shop and pub all within shouting distance of each other. Those familiar with the story of *Whisky Galore* will be disappointed with today's Politician pub, which is a converted 1970s-style bungalow. But Eriskay delights in every other sense.

It's almost dark, so I head for the B&B, and think about how I'll spend the following day. A walk along **Prince's Beach** is a must, where visitors can read about Charles Edward Stuart who landed on the island and went on to lead the Jacobite rebellion of 1745. Then there's the small church of St Michael, sitting on a hill at the north end of the island. Its distinctive altar is based around the prow of a boat, reflecting Eriskay's fishing heritage, the remains of which can be seen at the natural harbour, Acarsaid.

I trudge on, suddenly tired, the day of island travelling catching up with me. Just as I get to the house, I hear a car horn. Sure enough, it's the W17 coming back from the slipway. Squinting into the setting sun, I give the driver a wave, before turning and closing the door on the salt air and sea. ∎

ABOUT THE AUTHOR | **RHONA NicDHÙGHAILL** is from Oban and lives in Glasgow. She teaches Gaelic to adults.

NEXT STOP ST KILDA
BY BUS ACROSS HARRIS

Fiona Rintoul

Tarbert 🚐

Service no. W12 | Journey time 45mins

OS Landranger 14, 13. Twice daily Mon–Fri (see box page 263), no service on Sat & Sun. Operator: K Maclennan.

Hushinish ←

The tiny beach-fringed settlement of Hushinish on the northwest shore of the **Isle of Harris** is quite literally at the end of the road. The winding single-track B887 peters out here, its final stretch subsumed by fine, silver sand. Stationed at one of Scotland's most westerly points, the four-house settlement has the feel of an outpost; across the sound is the now uninhabited island of Scarp. Climb up from Hushinish on a hillside path and on a clear day you'll be rewarded by a view of the abandoned island of **St Kilda** shimmering on the horizon.

Hushinish is separated from the main Tarbert to Stornoway road by a majestic landscape of rugged mountains and sodden bog, punctuated by teeming fishing lochs and tumbling, peat-reddened burns. Here the eagle soars, the stag bells – and the feisty **W12 minibus** bounces gamely past on weekdays. For Hushinish, though remote, is very accessible and the best way to go is by bus. Glance out the window as the W12 weaves round high-perched hairpin bends and you'll see why. The views south across **Loch a Siar** – turquoise on sunny days, a moodier teal when the heavens glower – are magnificent. It's hard to appreciate the glittering beaches of Taransay and South Harris if you're slumped exhausted over bicycle handlebars. Or positively dangerous if you are grasping a car steering wheel, white-knuckled after a near-death encounter with a kamikaze sheep on a Monégasque-style bend. Better to let a seasoned pro – used to transporting the island's children, post and supplies back and forth – take the strain.

The W12 bus is also ideal for **day walkers** who want to take on one of the many satisfying routes among the Harris hills that lie off the B887. A good source is *Walking on Harris and Lewis* by Richard Barrett (published by Cicerone Press). Do check bus timings before setting off, though.

ROADSIDE SURPRISES

The bus journey to Hushinish starts at the pier in **Tarbert**, Harris's main settlement. Reached from the Scottish mainland via the Isle of Skye and a 1hr 40-minutes ferry journey across the Minch, Tarbert itself may seem remote to mainland dwellers. There is, though, a certain familiarity to its neat **Victorian architecture**, small shopping street and two well-appointed hotels.

This feeling of familiarity persists when the W12 bus turns on to the main A859 road to Stornoway, the principal town on the

HILL WALK TO A STUNNING BEACH

For fit walkers, I recommend a day walk east over the hill from Hushinish to the pristine sands of **Mill Beach** (Tràigh Mheilen). The small, abandoned settlement on the **island of Scarp** is clearly visible from the mile-long beach. Some of the houses are now holiday homes. The beach is a great place for a swim, but don't be tempted to try to swim to Scarp. Powerful currents lie between you and the island.

From Mill Beach, you can make your way across country to **Glen Cravadale**, enjoying spectacular views of the Uig hills on Lewis to the north, and pick up a clear footpath by the north shore of **Loch a' Ghlinne**. The path rises steeply through the glen to a *bealach* (pass) at 712 feet, then descends to Loch Leòsaid where you can join the hydro-electric power station track road and descend to Amhuinnsuidhe for the W12 bus back to Tarbert.

Isle of Lewis. Yes, the views are breathtaking as you head along the coast from Tarbert to Ardhasaig and the steep, forbidding **hills of North Harris** come into view. But the A859 is a normal A-road. It is not until the W12 bus veers off the A859 onto the cliff-hugging switchback B887 at the foot of Clisham – the highest peak in the Outer Hebrides at 2,621 feet and part of the hill range that separates the 'islands' of Harris and Lewis (there's no water involved) – that the fun really begins.

Hushinish

Govig is not served by all journeys

N

10 mins

Amhuinnsuidhe

Govig

15 mins

Miavaig

20 mins

Tarbert

The bus winds first through the settlement of **Bunavoneader**, where you may be surprised to notice a towering chimney down by the shore. This is all that remains of a whaling station established in 1904 by a Norwegian company. The station was taken over in 1922 by Lord Leverhulme, then owner of Lewis and Harris, but his plans to expand the operation failed and it closed shortly after his death in 1925. It was revived briefly in 1950 to support a Norwegian whaler, closing definitively two years later.

As the W12 bus climbs out of Bunavoneader another surprise waits in ambush. Between the road and the shore, in the middle of a rocky bog, lies an artificial-grass tennis court. Coaching is to be had in Bunavoneader, and the court is 'available for hire every day of the year except Sundays,' according to a roadside sign – a toned-down version of a previous one that read 'no Sunday play.'

Harris and Lewis are traditional strongholds of the **Free Church of Scotland**, and the Sabbath is still observed here much more strictly than in the rest of Scotland. Elderly, black-clad ladies waiting at the roadside to be transported to church were once a feature of island Sundays, though they are dying out, and some relaxation – notably Sunday ferry sailings – has crept in.

From Bunavoneader, the B887 climbs vertiginously before twisting into a helter-skelter, gear-crunching descent to Loch

Miavaig. Sròn Scourst, a strikingly steep rock buttress, can be seen straight ahead.

EAGLE'S TERRITORY

At the head of **Loch Miavaig** is a path that leads to the North Harris Eagle Observatory, a timber building with a turf roof. Harris has one of the highest densities of breeding golden eagles in Europe with about 20 pairs resident on the island. White-tailed eagles are also regularly seen in Glen Miavaig, especially in winter, while moorland birds, such as the merlin, golden plover, greenshank, stonechat and wheatear, frequent the glen in summer.

From Miavaig, the road climbs again passing the red-painted **Cliasmol** primary school, which closed in 2008, then Cliasmol itself. As the road corkscrews back down to sea level, another surprise awaits: the white gates of **Amhuinnsuidhe castle**. You may laugh, or possibly cry, when the bus turns into the manicured castle grounds and the Scottish baronial pile, built in 1865 for the Earl of Dunmore, heaves into view. Nowhere do the architectural excesses of the aristocracy look more out of place than against the craggy backdrop of the Harris hills.

Beyond the castle is a small settlement which used to sport a post office shop, now sadly closed – thus runs the story of so many small communities in these islands. The only amenities along the B887 are at Hushinish itself, where there is a toilet block.

EATERIES

Take a **packed lunch** with you to Hushinish, as there are no shops or cafés. On the way back, you may wish to try the comfortable **Harris Hotel** (☎ 01859 502154). It offers excellent bar and restaurant meals (the latter in the season only) using local produce, as well as a wide choice of whiskies. The **Ardhasaig House** (☎ 01859 502500) also provides highly rated four-course evening meals featuring local produce. Advance reservation is required.

TRAVEL BRIEF

The W12 bus operates Monday to Friday during **school term** and on Tuesdays and Fridays only during **school holidays**. On those days it makes two or three round trips. However, convenient bus times facilitate a day trip. The morning bus leaves Tarbert at 07.50, arriving at Hushinish at 08.35. The return service leaves Hushinish at 17.00. An **additional service** at midday runs on Tuesdays and Fridays during school holidays. During term time that extra bus is timed for an early afternoon departure and then it runs only on request and not quite right through to Hushinish. It turns round in Govig. Call ☎ 01859 511253 to request a ride on this term-time extra service. At Tarbert, you can connect onto other island buses, including the **Outer Hebrides spinal route** to and from Stornoway.

Amhuinnsuidhe provides an excellent starting point for an ascent of hills such as Tiorga Mòr (2,228 feet) and Ullabhal. Get off the W12 bus just before the castle grounds at the track road leading to the hydro-electric power station in **Gleann Ulladail**. Very fit walkers may consider a backpacking expedition from Amhuinnsuidhe to Loch Reasort, possibly via Tiorga Mòr and Tiorga Beag. Alternatively, a path leads from the power station as far as Loch Uladail beneath the impressive buttress of Sròn Uladail – a manageable out-and-return route.

The W12 bus now heads along the final stretch, dipping and climbing extensively along the way. The road to **Hushinish** covers a majestic swathe of one of the most rugged landscapes in Europe, but journey's end is the jewel in the crown. With its lush machair grazing lands, sparkling waters and magnificent silver-sand beach, Hushinish, which has a permanent population of just four, is a breathtakingly beautiful spot. It's a place to pause and reflect on the web of bus journeys that criss-cross our islands. ∎

ABOUT THE AUTHOR | **FIONA RINTOUL** is a writer and translator. She lives in Glasgow.

Beyond Britain's Shores

Venturing by boat and bus to Ireland, France, Denmark and beyond

Dedicated slow travellers do not of course restrict themselves merely to buses, nor are their horizons limited to Great Britain. In this section, we give a few hints about journeys by ferry from Britain that connect conveniently into engaging bus services at the port of disembarkation. We mention just five bus services, connecting respectively with ferries from Britain that arrive in Saint-Malo, Calais, Esbjerg, Larne and Rosslare. We conclude with a glimpse at a wider world of bus travel. Yes, there are direct bus services from England to many countries.

There is something intensely satisfying about not going the way of the crowd. It is something that the editors of this book have made a lifelong mission. Imagine standing on the deck of a ferry as it edges into a continental port. Down on the car deck, families and truck drivers sit in their vehicles, eagerly waiting for the huge bow doors of the vessel to open, so revealing a first glimpse of France. Everyone is eager to hit the road. Satnavs are programmed and ready to gobble up the miles as vehicles speed south on the autoroute. When motorists are eventually given the green flag to drive off the ship, they'll hardly give a port a second glance.

French excursions

You have it far better up on the open deck. You are relaxed – that comes easily nowadays when the best cross-Channel ferries offer cruise-ship comforts. France has some superb local bus journeys that connect perfectly with ferries from Britain. Some of our favourite ferry crossings are the Western Channel routes. They are long enough to give a sense of being at sea. Brittany Ferries regularly sail overnight from Portsmouth to Saint-Malo, taking eleven hours for the journey. Condor Ferries offer daytime services from Poole to Saint-Malo via the Channel Islands. Both make fine journeys in their own right.

Saint-Malo has excellent onward bus connections. One route out of the French port trumps all others. It is the number 17 seasonal service from Saint-Malo to Pontorson in Normandy. In 2013, this summer route had thrice-daily services from Monday to Saturday and a single outing on Sundays. The journey takes in the lovely fishing port of Cancale, as famous today for its oysters as it was when Eugène Feyen painted the oyster-picking Cancalaises 150 years ago. Then the route hugs the beaches that fringe the Baie du Mont-Saint-Michel.

Of course, like all the bus routes mentioned in this section, you'll not be able to use a bus pass issued in Britain. But fares are cheap. The run right through to Pontorson takes 90 minutes and costs just €4. From Pontorson, it is an easy two-hour walk along the banks of the Couesnon to Mont-Saint-Michel. This is the perfect way to arrive at this tourist magnet on the Normandy coast.

CALAIS CONNECTIONS

Calais is surely the most prosaic and down-to-earth place on the French coast. The well-appointed boats of P&O Ferries will speed you over from Dover in just 90 minutes. Things have changed since William Turner painted the comings and goings at Calais pier in 1803. No longer is docking at Calais the hit-and-miss affair depicted by Turner.

The boats have long since been driven out of the centre of Calais, exiled to a desert of concrete and linkspans away from the town. It is a grim walk from the port of Calais into the middle of town (yes, we have done it!), but a shuttle bus awaits many arriving ferries.

Calais is a useful hub for bus travellers, and more interest was added to the local transport scene in June 2013 with the launch of a new *navette fluviale* service on the Calais canal, which cuts through the heart of the town. The futuristic vessel looks for all the world like a tram but is in fact a boat.

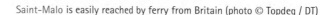
Saint-Malo is easily reached by ferry from Britain (photo © Topdeq / DT)

Pick of the out-of-town routes leaving Calais is the local bus service down the coast to Boulogne. It is a gem. We used it last year in crisp, clear winter weather when the hard frost shaped scenes of delicate beauty. The D940 coast road used by this local bus service is surprisingly hilly, particularly around Cap Gris-Nez. From time to time, there are glorious views across the Channel to the famous white cliffs on the Kent coast – which often look much closer than they really are. The route takes in beach communities like Wissant and Wimereux which were once popular holiday spots, much favoured by English visitors, but now strangely forgotten.

FROM ESSEX TO THE KATTEGAT

DFDS's overnight ferry crossing from Harwich to Esbjerg in Denmark is a journey worth making just for the voyage. For those who like long bus journeys, the lunchtime arrival in Esbjerg connects perfectly (except on Saturdays) with the number 980 bus, which runs right across Jutland to Frederikshavn. The service is styled the Thinggaard Express. By evening you'll be on the shore of the Kattegat, having along the way seen the quiet beauty of Jutland – a land of big skies and far horizons.

IRISH LINKS

Crossing from Britain to Ireland by ferry opens up many rewarding opportunities for onward bus travel. Stena Line operate from Fishguard in west Wales to Rosslare, where it is but a short walk from the ferry to the number 40 bus. This Bus Éireann route runs up to thrice daily, creating a ribbon across Ireland from Rosslare to Cork, Killarney and beyond. If you are there for the long haul, the journey to Tralee in County Kerry takes almost seven hours.

If your Irish horizons are more limited, and you just want a quick taste of the Emerald Isle, then the P&O Irish Sea services from Troon and Cairnryan (both in southwest Scotland) connect with the seasonal Ulsterbus service 252, which makes a wonderful tour of the coast of County Antrim. The journey from Larne via the Causeway Coast to Coleraine takes a shade under three hours. In 2013, this service ran twice daily from late March to late September (except that Sunday services had a more limited season, starting only in late June).

THE LONG HAUL

We have focused in this section on bus journeys beyond Britain that we judge to be especially enjoyable. There are of course many more such options, and some enthusiasts love nothing more than leaving Britain on a coach bound for some far-flung continental destination. In late 2012, there was talk of a direct coach link from Birmingham to Mirpur in Kashmir. It sounds a little improbable, but there is a sizeable Kashmiri population in Birmingham.

Brian Grigg, a contributor to this volume (see Journeys 6 and 9) has yet to hop on a bus from England to Kashmir, but he was first in line when iDBUS recently launched a direct coach service from London to Lyon in France. Brian paid just a tenner for the return ticket from London to Lyon and reports that for a good part of the outward journey, he was the sole passenger on board the bus. The route does however survive, with Eurolines also offering a direct service from London to Lyon in competition with iDBUS. Eurolines also has regular services from London to Berlin, Budapest, Paris, Prague, Vienna and many other cities across the continent. ■

MARKING TIME

The best places to find bus timetable information

Journeys beyond Britain's shores, like those described above, present special challenges in planning. Closer to home, anyone wanting to follow any or even all 50 journeys in this book has it much easier. Britain is blessed with a more comprehensive rural bus network than most of its European neighbours. Bus travellers in Britain also benefit from a high level of public transport information provision. Webwise travellers will generally find it very easy to access timetables. Those less inclined to access information on the internet may have to show a little more patience and ingenuity.

JOURNEY PLANNING WITH TRAVELINE

The obvious portal for travellers in England is *Traveline*, a service run by a consortium of transport operators and local authorities. You'll find their excellent website at www.traveline.info. Sister services covering Wales and Scotland are available at www.traveline-cymru.info and www.travelinescotland.com respectively. These websites allow you to plan local and longer journeys. We have found that, if you are planning a very long journey across Britain by local bus, then you'll have much better luck in securing sensible results by splitting your itinerary up into separate sections. You can call *Traveline* for timetable assistance for journeys throughout Britain at ☎ 0871 200 2233.

Moving to specific regions of Britain, you'll find for most areas other sources of travel planning and bus timetable information that may be vastly superior to *Traveline*. Individual bus companies often have their own websites and – at their best – they are excellent. But they usually reveal only details of their own services, and say not a word about the offerings of rival operators. So, for the last word on bus services in many parts of Britain, the best source of timetable information is often the county council or other local authority. Few offer interactive journey planners of the kind hosted by *Traveline*, but for the savvy traveller they provide something much more valuable: access to the timetable for every bus service that operates within the borders of their council.

LOCAL AUTHORITY WEBSITES

The manner in which local authorities in Britain discharge their duty to provide information about local bus services in their area varies greatly. Some host a 'bus timetables' section on their own websites. You may have to click through a few layers to get there, but it'll surely be worth the search. There are many fine examples of councils that do this very well and also regularly update their timetable listings. These are no-frills web services, may win no marks for slick design but they work well and provide access to essential timetable resources.

Good examples of the latter are Ceredigion (www.ceredigion.gov. uk), Argyll and Bute (www.argyll-bute.gov.uk), North Yorkshire (www. northyorks.gov.uk) and Cumbria (www.cumbria.gov.uk). Play with those four and you'll see it takes a bit of patience to navigate through from the council's home page to that part of the website dedicated to bus timetables. It is all too easy to be waylaid by the timetable for emptying dustbins or the procedures for reporting potholes.

Other councils have set up a dedicated website for supplying public transport information – but these are still websites that they maintain themselves. A great example of this approach is Suffolk (www.suffolkonboard.com). Some metropolitan areas have developed excellent websites covering all forms of public transport in their region. For example, Nexus (www.nexus.org.uk) covers Tyne and Wear, while Transport for London (www.tfl.gov.uk) gives the last word on public transport throughout the Greater London area.

GEOGRAPHIC INFORMATION SYSTEMS

The integration of timetable and map information is the ideal that dedicated bus users really need. And a flurry of entrepreneurial specialists in geographic information systems (GIS) court local authorities in the hope of securing contracts for the provision of local bus information. At their best, these public-private partnerships have produced systems that combine GIS intelligence with well-presented cartography. The leading player which has worked with local authorities in this area is a company called CHK Ltd. Their 'CartoGold' product underpins the best British bus timetable websites.

For some fine examples of this approach in action, just go to www.cartogold.co.uk, where you'll find links to public transport websites. Those for Devon, Essex and Powys are particularly good. It takes a while to really see how much information is available under these systems. But explore a little and you'll quickly be hooked.

GOOD OLD PRINT

We are great fans of printed timetables. And we are not the only ones. Marcel Proust loved timetables, using them to plot imaginary journeys linking Paris and the provinces. The fact that he spent long winter evenings poring over timetables may go some way to explaining why there was never a Mrs Proust.

Max Beerbohm's fictional hero Zuleika Dobson always kept a timetable to hand. And so do we. It always makes sense to have an escape route if one is needed.

Many local authorities in Britain produce printed bus timetables, usually aggregated into a series of booklets that each cover part of a county or region. In some areas, they are distributed free through public libraries and tourist information centres – elsewhere there is a modest charge to help defray the costs of production. The transport sections of council websites will usually tell you if printed timetable booklets are available and how to obtain them. Some authorities also produce good bus maps.

A printed timetable is great for taking with you on journeys, but they do date quickly. It's always wise to check online for service updates.

On the road

Many readers will long since have discovered that you can check upcoming departures for any bus stop in Britain. Every bus stop in England, Wales and Scotland has an eight-digit reference code. It is shown in timetables and usually on the bus stop. Just text that number to 84268 and within seconds you'll receive a message with the times of the next buses coming your way. This is a first-class service.

You can access similar information through www.nextbuses. mobi, but here the starting point is not the bus stop reference number, but rather your current location. So you can enter a postcode or, for example, 'Green Man, Ewell' and get a list of nearby bus stops. Click on your preferred bus stop from the list to reveal the next buses due to leave that stop. Technology has worked wonders in improving the lot of British bus travellers. ■

The Sceptical Bus Traveller

One man's tale of how he came to value the local bus services that stop at a rural bus shelter in Wiltshire

– by Simon Heptinstall –

Protestors angrily waved petitions as they gathered alongside the war memorial. Anyone arriving in my quiet Wiltshire village on that summer's day would have wondered what horrific new intrusion fired their passion. Who would have guessed that the unlikely source of their ire was that Atworth Parish Council had decided to build a bus shelter?

My village is a typical community of a few hundred souls clustered around the busy A365 road from Melksham to Bath. In this land of bespoke detached cottages and two-car families, buses are seen less as a public resource... more like something that holds up traffic.

Like most residents, I felt it was natural to rely on a private car, consoled by popular stereotypes that include: there are only about two buses a week, even they are unreliable, and no-one uses them so they are a waste of public subsidies. Surely buses are a noisy, polluting anachronism? To say I was a sceptical bus traveller was an understatement. Who would want to stand in the rain waiting for an expensive bus that never came?

THE ROAD TO DAMASCUS

Ah yes, standing in the rain. That's a sore point in Atworth. When the possibility of a new bus shelter was first raised, one parish councillor suggested the money would be better spent on umbrellas.

Nevertheless the idea was pushed through. A sum of £4,000 was to be spent on a new bus shelter. Behind the net curtains of smart detached houses, battle plans were drawn. Anti-shelterists were led by the editor of the village magazine and renowned amateur organist, Kenneth Spencer.

His campaign grievances were many: the insurgent shelter would detract from the adjacent Victorian clock tower/war memorial (Atworth's only significant monument, and the scene that appears on the village postcard); the village tax had to rise by 2.5 per cent to fund it; the decision was undemocratic because a village poll had found more people concerned with speeding traffic than public transport; and it would encourage gatherings of young people and create litter.

His magazine repeatedly thundered against the bus stop. A petition was raised. Meetings were held. Protesters gathered at the site to be photographed by the *Wiltshire Times's* photographer. Tempers began to fray. Magazine editor Spencer telephoned one councillor about the shelter and was told 'If you don't like it, call the cops.' The phone was slammed down. This was duly reported verbatim in his magazine.

As a journalist I found this unusual, as I knew the magazine was part-funded by the parish council. It was a little like the *Sun* leading a campaign against Rupert Murdoch. Perhaps unsurprisingly, the dispute was to lead to the hastening of the editor's departure from his post later in the year.

And the former editor to this day maintains that he and his wife's staunch anti-shelter stance had nothing to do with the fact that their house was right next to it. Sitting on their sofa, Mr and Mrs Spencer could stare right at the spot where the shelter would be erected.

ENDGAME IN ATWORTH

Despite everything, the authority of the council prevailed and the shelter appeared. Editor Spencer let his garden hedge grow to hide the sight of the hated construction.

Soon the innocuous shelter was accepted and forgotten, except by those who began to use it of course. And in one of the toughest recessions and wettest summers on record, it encouraged even the most hardened anti-bus car lover to rethink the case for public transport.

For me, the arrival of the new metal-and-perspex structure coincided with my son leaving the tiny village school for his new secondary school in Bradford-on-Avon. He had to catch the bus daily. He used the new shelter every morning.

In an idle moment, I checked the provision of services. I found that there were not just two empty buses a day – there were almost 30 buses each way daily. I started noting that almost every window seat was taken. I found myself musing about the vague possibility that the bus may be cheaper, more convenient and maybe even better for the world... possibly even something to be valued.

Then, after spending an hour in my car in a traffic jam of Christmas shoppers alongside an empty bus lane in nearby Bath, I decided to convert. I am now a willing bus passenger. Who needs the hassle of parking in Bath when a bus from my village will drop me right in the centre of the city?

Surprisingly, one day I found myself sharing Atworth's new bus stop with the former village magazine editor and anti-shelter campaign leader Kenneth Spencer. 'I was annoyed about the shelter at the time,' he confessed to me. 'But I've shut up about it now. The shelter was smaller than we expected. We now use the bus stop regularly. But my wife still won't stand under the shelter, even if it's raining.' ∎

Simon Heptinstall is a writer, editor and media consultant based in Wiltshire. Follow him on Twitter @sheptinstall.

MEET THE TEAM

Bus-Pass Britain Rides Again is the product of the second community-writing project that we have co-ordinated on behalf of Bradt Travel Guides. This book is very much a co-operative effort, with 50 different writers, including ourselves, contributing to this volume. At the end of each bus journey in this book, you will find a short note about the author of that text. Our hearty thanks go to all those writers. The majority of them would not describe themselves as being in any way professional weavers of words. Most are keen amateurs who rose magnificently to the challenge of writing with fluency and enthusiasm about bus journeys which were important to them. Without exception, they have been a delight to work with.

Our role has been as mediators of the enterprise. Susanne Kries was very much the driver of the bus. She kept the engine well-oiled and made sure the project stayed on schedule. Nicky Gardner was the conductor. She neither collected fares nor issued tickets but used her baton to keep our ensemble in order, setting the tempo and ensuring that the results of our collective efforts have a measure of harmony.

We owe a vote of thanks to many who kept us on the road. Were it not for Hilary Bradt, this project and its predecessor would never have taken place. It was Hilary's energetic support for local bus services that led to *Bus-Pass Britain* and now to this book. Hilary's colleagues at Bradt Travel Guides helped plan this community adventure and supported us along the way. In this context, we extend a special vote of thanks to Anna Moores, Rachel Fielding, Adrian Phillips, Janet Mears and Hugh Collins. We must also thank Ian West, Sales Director at Faber Factory Plus, for suggesting the book title.

Most texts are credited to their respective authors. All unattributed editorial material (such as the scene-setting texts for each region and the bus stop mini-features) was researched and written by the editors.

Nicky Gardner and Susanne Kries

INDEX OF BUS OPERATORS

Here you will find a complete list of all British bus operators featured in *Bus-Pass Britain Rides Again*. Some are companies which operate one or more of our 50 journeys. Others are interesting bus companies which have deserved a mention in the book. Where the reference is to an operator that runs one of the 50 journeys, we include here only the first page of the route – unless the operator has a further mention in the course of the route. The following list includes only currently operating bus companies.

INDEX OF PLACE NAMES

This index identifies places in Britain that feature in this book.

FEEDBACK REQUEST

The editors of *Bus-Pass Britain Rides Again* would **love to hear from you**. Are there things we could have described better? And we would in particular like to **hear of new journeys** which you judge might warrant inclusion in a new edition or follow-up volume. Don't forget to tell us a little about yourself and include your contact details (ideally an email address).

You can **reach us** by post as follows: The Editors, *Bus-Pass Britain Rides Again*, Bradt Travel Guides, IDC House, The Vale, Chalfont St Peter, Bucks SL9 9RZ. If you prefer to email us, please use info@bradtguides.com. You can also add a **review** of the book on www.bradtguides.com.

Please check www.bradtguides.com/guidebook-update-bus-pass-britain-rides-again for updates on this volume. This page is maintained by the publisher.